D0214430

Aliens Adored

Susan J. Palmer

Raël's UFO Religion

ALIENS ADORED

Rutgers University Press
New Brunswick,
New Jersey,
and London

Library of Congress Cataloging-in-Publication Data

Palmer, Susan J.

Aliens adored : Raël's UFO religion / Susan J. Palmer

p. cm.

Includes bibliographical references and index.

ISBN 0-8135-3475-5 (hardcover : alk. paper) — ISBN 0-8135-3476-3 (pbk. : alk. paper)

1. Raelian Movement. 2. Vorilhon, Claude. I. Title.

BP605.R338P35 2004

299—dc22

2004000305

A British Cataloging-in-Publication record for this book is available from the British Library.

Manufactured in the United States of America

I dedicate this book to all my intelligent, delightful students at Dawson College who have proved over the years to be such curious religionists and gifted researchers, and who have inspired me to keep on trying to understand new religions.

Contents

Acknowledgments

I thank the Social Science in the Humanities Research Council for the Standard Research Grant that enabled me to pursue this project. To Raël and the Raelians, I owe a special thanks for their openness and generosity toward a non-Raelian researcher. My friends have my gratitude—especially Steve Luxton, poet and publisher, for his patient encouragement, and Brian Sentes, a distinguished poet whose extensive knowledge of the UFO scene contributed exciting ideas to our first article. I am greatly indebted to John Saliba, J. Gordon Melton, and James R. Lewis for their wonderful studies on the UFO milieu. Finally, this book could never have been written without my students' interviews, field reports, and questionnaires—as we explored the amazing subculture of the Raelian religion together.

Aliens Adored

Introduction

How I Researched the Raelians

I first stumbled across the Raelians in 1987 at the Montreal Psychic Fair. I was with my friend James, who is a *shirag* (priest) in the Sufi order in the West, and we were strolling past the booths, checking out the pagan/New Age/Wiccan books. Most of the stalls were tended by black-robed witches reading the tarot or clients' palms. We watched an Ontario housewife in a coral polyester suit channel Catholic saints in a high, wispy, Toronto-inflected accent, as she lay in a coffin padded with turquoise satin. Then I spotted the Raelian guides—men whose long locks straggled down white turtleneck shirts, skinny chests weighted with heavy medallions. On drawing closer to peer at these, I saw the Star of David interlocked with—could that be a swastika? The booth displayed posters of UFOs flying through space.

"Hey, James! Look, here's a flying-saucer group!" We struck up a conversation with the two Francophone guides, who showed us Raël's books. The tall one invited us to participate in a raffle. We had to write answers to basic questions on astronomy and put our papers with our names in a glass bowl. "The winner will receive a visit from a guide, a free *Apocalypse* magazine, and a private viewing of the videocassette *They're Coming!*"

The next morning my phone rang. "Congratulations, Madame Palmer, you are the winner of the Raelian raffle." We set a time for the guide to come over, and I phoned James to invite him also.

"Hey, James, guess what? I won!"

"So did I," said James.

"What a coincidence! I thought there was only one winner."

"Susan . . . don't you get it?"

The Raelian guide who came to my house was named Gaston and had long dyed-blond hair. I couldn't tell if he was gay or straight. The *Apocalypse* had artful photographs of naked Raelians cavorting at their summer camp. Some photos were homoerotic. "Finally," I thought, "a gay NRM [New

Religious Movement]!"—but no, not necessarily, for there were other photos of the *Playboy* cheesecake variety. Others were quite abstract and artsy, including a close-up study of chest hair and skin pores with swirling galaxies in the background.

I was fascinated to discover that the Raelians were radical materialists. They were also free-love advocates, and I'd just finished writing a book on Bhagwan Shree Rajneesh, for whom "sex is the path to super-consciousness." I invited the Raelians to speak to my class on New Religious Movements at Dawson College. There, the students peppered them with questions, the Jewish kids challenging their use of the swastika and the word "Elohim" (the Raelians' name for the extraterrestrials who contacted Rael). I brought my class to the Raelians' initiation ritual, the Transmission of the Cellular Plan, at the Sheraton hotel. The guides let us distribute membership questionnaires at the meetings and conduct interviews. I had never encountered an NRM that was so cooperative, that actually liked being studied. It was part of their "we are the first scientific religion" stance, and an indirect way to "spread the message" among my students.

Some of my students were a bit taken aback by the Raelians' sexual effervescence. Xhua-xin, a conspicuously ornamental nineteen-year-old from Beijing, complained that while he was conducting field research, three different women had propositioned him outright or tried to arrange a date; he was shocked because "they were at least forty and old enough to be my mother!"

An eighteen-year-old Jewish girl from a strict Orthodox family interviewed an assistant guide who gave her a pep talk on the joys of sex, followed by a eulogy on her beauty. She confessed to me that the incident so disturbed her, she "kept worrying about it and couldn't sleep for a week."

On a field trip to the November 1989 monthly meeting, we observed how the Raelians celebrate their sexual adventurism. A pair of French guides stood up and announced they were looking for Canadian girls to marry so they could stay in the country. Then a local bishop took the mike and said: "Let us congratulate Philador. For one whole year she has been with the same man!" A pretty dark Quebecoise beamed while the Raelians applauded. Nikos, my chubby Greek student, was puzzled. "What's the big deal about that?" he whispered to me. "I've had the same girlfriend for three years, and no one ever congratulates me!"

I found the Raelian Movement fascinatingly original and undergoing unpredictable spurts of growth—a refreshing change from the meditation ashrams and Christian communes I had researched. Every time we dropped in on one of the meetings, held on the third Sunday of each month, there would be a subtle new twist to Raël's theology, a new project or missionary strategy, or an added ritual. I watched priests and bishops get promoted or demoted with dizzying speed. Raël himself would suddenly materialize in a cloud of charisma, like the devil leaping out of smoke in a miracle play, and take us on a journey. He would give us a guided-visualization tour of an alien planet or a utopian vision of a better future via cloning, or he would outline his new plan for demonstrations against nuclear testing and deforestation, or he would treat us to one of his stand-up comic routines that satirized the U.S. president, monogamous jealous husbands, and the pope.

I was about to embark on a fifteen-year adventure as a researcher, teacher, and writer. As P. C. Wren (a turn-of-the-century novelist whose French Foreign Legion books I devoured in my teens) often reiterated: "Truth is stranger than fiction." I was an avid reader of sci-fi at the time and had written a few short stories for the fanzines (they were always rejected). But soon my academic articles on the Raelians were in demand. UFO religions are even stranger than science fiction.

For years I enjoyed unlimited access to the Raelians' fascinating, rapidly evolving UFO movement. I attended many of the monthly meetings with my students in tow. We distributed membership questionnaires, wrote field reports, and conducted interviews. Every term I invited the guides to my classes at Dawson College and at Concordia University, where they gave well-organized, stimulating presentations and took questions from my curious students. I found the Raelians fun to be with, full of vitality, humorous and playful. As for Raël, his creativity seemed limitless. I wrote six articles and chapters and several encyclopedia entries on the Raelians, and it was my policy to show them to one of the bishops before they were published. While NRM scholars have noticed that new religions don't particularly appreciate our academic analyses of their passionate spirituality—and the Raelians are no exception—I was nevertheless impressed by the freedom they gave me to say whatever I wanted. I worked closely with the female bishop Nicole Bertrand, who on reading my chapter "Woman as Playmate" exclaimed: "Well, Suzanne, I find it so interesting reading an outsider's view of us that is objective, not negative, but somehow naive. I find it quite . . . amusing, . . . refreshing!"

Nicole corrected many small mistakes in spelling and dates and filled me in on the historical detail—but she never tried to edit my statements or control my opinions.

Then, in 2002, just as I was finishing the first draft of this book, I discovered I had been blacklisted by the Raelians. The tale of how this came about is, as Sherlock Holmes would say, "a singular one."

I blame it on the media. Journalists kept misquoting me or distorting my meaning. For a while I stopped calling journalists back, but then two journalists I had never even spoken to misquoted me.

At first I felt upset and angry at what I perceived to be an injustice, but in the process of trying to understand what had happened, I learned a great deal. The blacklisting forced me to think more deeply about my responsibilities as a researcher; I tried to empathize with Raël and to gauge his reactions (no easy task). In the end I decided my "excommunication" as a researcher said more about developmental phases in NRMs than it did about Raël or about me.

Around 1996 I first sensed changes afoot that impeded my access as a researcher. The venue for the monthly meeting used to be the Holiday Inn, where the Raelians rented a conference room—and essentially held a conference. In those early meetings I could watch the priests and bishops sitting in the front row, interacting with each other—joking, sparring, sitting on each other's laps. I could overhear them planning the meeting as it progressed. By 1997 the Raelians had rented a rather seedy old theater on St. Catherine East (the local red-light district). There they staged a carefully orchestrated show to train their ambitious young animators (level 3 in the Raelian six-step executive hierarchy) and to attract new members.

I sat passively in the dark stalls with the audience, watching video clips from Cirque du Soleil. Sexy young animators strutted across the stage in stiletto boots, breathing into handheld mikes. The trick of cultivating Raelian stage charisma was to appear entirely relaxed, to allow long, pregnant silences, and to share risqué jokes with the audience. The meetings had become a training ground where ambitious young leaders could hone their public-speaking skills to get promoted up the pyramid. Some of the bishops still led the sensual meditation, but the real leaders were now working behind the scenes, so the decision-making processes were now obscured by a slick, opaque patina of media savvy.

Meanwhile, the newsletter-magazine *Apocalypse* was revised—it was more polished, less "hokey." The customary photos of naked blissful Raelians cavorting at the summer seminars were now expunged. One day my favorite Raelian guest speaker, Michel Beluet, dropped in unexpectedly at my office at Dawson College bearing a gift of the latest Raelian promotional videos—but he wanted the old ones back in return. I explained that I'd left them at home, "and besides I am a church historian, I collect archival material." I saw this as a familiar trend in new religions—toward "slickness" and historical revisionism. (Roy Wallis notes this same development in his 1976 book on Scientology.)

After Raël set up his Clonaid company and began to promote its cloning services to attract investors, the Raelians adopted an even more proactive relationship with the media and held many press conferences. My pet NRM had gradually transformed itself from an informal, grassroots UFO-based social club to an efficient, streamlined public relations machine! I began to feel frustrated in my research efforts. In the good old days I could approach any Raelian who appeared interesting and request an interview. I had been turned down only twice, by two bishops: Daniel Chabot, who did not like what I wrote—"Il y'a beaucoup, beaucoup des fautes!" ("There are many, many mistakes")—and Rejean Proulx, who politely excused himself on the grounds that he was very shy and liked to keep his life private.

After 1998, however, my requests were often countered with, "You must first get permission from Sylvie Chabot" (Raël's public relations agent, also a Raelian bishop and the sister of Daniel Chabot).

By 1999, Raelian "cloning fever" had gripped the imagination of the press. I was besieged by journalists requesting interviews with me as the academic "expert" on the Raelians. I usually complied, since I enjoy holding forth on my favorite topic, NRMs. (When I go to dinner parties with my boyfriend, he often kicks me under the table and whispers, "Don't talk about *cults!*") I feel it is my duty as a religion teacher and a researcher to share my perspective on new religions with the public, to polish up my "sound bites" and hurl them like bowling balls, aiming to topple popular stereotypes of "cults."

But journalists are a slippery bunch, in my experience. They flatter you to your face, misquote you in their articles, and—once they have gotten their story—do not answer your e-mails.

"I heard you were told to 'get a life' in the *National Post,*" one of my Dawson colleagues quipped as we passed in the hall. I rushed out and bought the newspaper. The journalist who had grilled me for an hour for data on the Raelians (I could hear her computer keys clicking busily as we talked long distance) had presented all my research as if she'd gathered it herself (this, of course, is nothing new). Then she quoted a trivial off-the-cuff remark I had made on the Raelian women's dress code and commented: "This just goes to show that social scientists should get a life."

To be quoted in the *New York Times, Village Voice, Boston Globe, Los Angeles Times, Guardian,* or Canada's *National Post* or *Globe and Mail* enhanced my career as a scholar, but it handicapped me as a researcher. I received my first warning signal in the early 1990s when my bedside telephone shrilled at 1:30 A.M. It was a journalist in Japan wanting to ask a few questions about the Raelians. I listlessly complied—although our brief conversation was impeded by a crackling connection and the journalist's Nipponese consonants.

I felt the repercussions at the next Raelian gathering. Michel Beluet, director of UFOland and translator of Raël's first book into English, accosted me. "Well, Susan, Raël is not very 'appy with you. You have said bad things about us to a Tokyo newspaper."

"What?" I asked. "What bad things?" He did not know what the "bad things" were, only that they were very bad. I explained that I honestly had no recollection of what I had said in my semi-comatose long-distance conversation with the Japanese journalist. The Raelians forgave me. Michel promised to get me a copy of the offending article, but I never saw it.

I began to notice that some journalists were fishing for "bad things" when they interviewed me. "Now tell me honestly, Dr. Palmer," one journalist said. "What you've told me so far is only *good* news. Is there any *bad* news about the Raelians I should be aware of?"

I gave him my standard response (which I stole from Professor Eileen Barker at the London School of Economics): "We objective, value-free social scientists try to avoid judging the groups we're studying."

"Well, let me put it another way. In all your years of studying the Raelians, have you noticed coercive, manipulative behavior on the part of the leaders?"

"Well, sure, but no more so than in my women's Bulgarian choir or my PTA meetings. In any human organization you'll find people who try to control other people. Often they have to, just to get the job done."

I gathered that there was a groundswell of irate ex-members who'd been talking to the media.

By 2001, I was feeling a lot of pressure to get this book written. Journalists were just starting to find out all the interesting stuff I'd been hoarding for years—like Raël's angels. A free-lance journalist from *Penthouse* (whose participation in the summer seminar was so enthusiastic, they mistook him for a convert) spoke to me on the phone for an hour, begging me for the inside scoop on the angels. An outrageous conceptual artist/porno queen phoned and asked if she could interview me for a documentary film on her life. I wasn't sure how my appearance as a middle-aged, fully-clothed talking head in a film that extolled the radical feminist artistry of a porno star who made love to 250 men in rapid succession would further my scholarly career—so I declined.

I found myself in a ridiculous situation. The Raelians had hit the jackpot in their campaign to captivate the media. Here I was, the so-called expert, with journalists from the top newspapers fawning all over me—and yet my access was diminishing, while any two-bit journalist was granted interviews with Raël and Brigitte Boisselier, Clonaid's CEO. I would go to a Raelian press conference and be told to wait outside to see if there were any extra seats, because "this is for the journalists." And when the journalists kept asking me, "Are the Raelians *really* cloning a baby? Does this secret lab really exist?" I would have to respond honestly, "I haven't a clue."

One journalist excited my jealousy by claiming Boisselier had promised to consider his offer to be the Raelians' kept historian—to be flown to their secret lab to document their ongoing progress in an eventual story that would come out triumphantly with the first cloned baby. Now that Raël and Boisselier were being lionized as glamorous media stars, I was perceived as a plodding academic whose research could be relegated to the back burner.

I set up two interviews with Raël in 2001 that he (or Sylvie Chabot, I couldn't tell which) canceled at the last minute, just before he disappeared on one of his international speaking tours. This had never happened to me before. I approached Boisselier, who graciously made a date for an interview at my house—but didn't show up. I had given her a copy of my *Religion in the News* piece, "The Raël Deal," and now I wondered if perhaps she didn't like the rather flippant tone of my article, which examines Raelian strategies for manipulating the media.

I realized later that Boisselier must have been under considerable pressure at the time; the Food and Drug Administration was about to raid her secret cloning laboratory, the FBI was bugging her phone line, and she was under investigation by the grand jury in Syracuse. This was a time when discretion was advisable.

I made an appointment with Raël for an interview and was dismayed when Sylvie Chabot treated me like a journalist from some cow town in

Nebraska. "Raël only gives interviews Thursdays after 4:00 P.M.," she told me. I would have to drive out to his condo in UFOland, the Raelian estate near Valcourt, a small village two hours east of Montreal. I rented a car and phoned several times during the week to confirm the interview but received no reply. The evening before the appointment, Chabot e-mailed my office and requested a list of the questions I was planning to ask. When I did not respond within an hour, the interview was canceled, as I found out the next morning when I arrived at my desk computer. I was told: "Never mind. You can ask all your questions of Nicole Bertrand, and she can answer on behalf of Raël."

I was getting frustrated. In November, I attended a monthly meeting at Theatre Gésu where Raël appeared unexpectedly—his arrival is always unexpected, but extra security guards and a cadre of angels waiting outside to greet him are reliable signs. He spoke of cloning, of the "Elohimization" of the human race. After the meeting he passed me on the stairs. Always the gentleman, he said: "Suzanne! For a minute I mistook you for a teenager—you look so young!" (He knows how to please middle-aged women.) Then he congratulated me on an article that had appeared in the *Montreal Gazette* in which I criticized the French government's persecution of "*les sectes*."

"I am so glad now you realize what is happening in France," said Raël. I received the impression that he had been deeply affected by his unjust treatment in France, due to the antisect hysteria that erupted in the wake of the Solar Temple mass suicides, which had forced Raël and others to flee their homeland.

Seizing the opportunity, I again asked him for an interview. He graciously agreed but later canceled. I also approached Raël's beautiful companion, Sophie, at the December 6 gathering on Ile Ste Helene and gave her a letter for Raël that requested an interview and explained the scope of my book.

Meanwhile, I kept getting in trouble for what journalists said. A bishop phoned me at home: "Raël is not 'appy with what you said to the journalist from the *Village Voice*. She says you told her all Raelians are 'forced' to sleep with their own sex at the summer seminar." Way back in 1992 I had published a chapter in *The Gods Have Landed* that quoted a Raelian who described this as a recommended exercise at the summer camp, "for how do you know you have chosen your sexual orientation, if you haven't tried the opposite?" (Palmer 1995). I accommodated the Raelians by phoning the journalist and asking her not to print that quote. It is interesting to note the Raelians hadn't objected to the quote when I showed them my chapter in 1992. Ever since Raël had appeared before the U.S. Congress in March 2001, the Raelians seemed to be sweeping free love under the carpet.

I was so sick of journalists by December 2001 that I did not respond to a telephone message from a *New York Times* writer. When I saw how good her article on cloning was, I regretted my omission. But she went ahead and quoted me anyway, so it sounded as if she'd interviewed me. She had me contradicting the guides: "The Raelians claim 55,000 members internationally, but Susan Palmer, a sociologist who has studied them, puts the number closer to 35,000." Evidently she'd read my article published eight years earlier, when 35,000 was the correct figure. Since then the Raelians have expanded. They were not too 'appy about my implying in the *New York Times Magazine* that they were liars.

But it was the *Los Angeles Times* that finally got me blacklisted. I had a series of conversations with a journalist who, unlike the others I had dealt with, turned out to be an intrepid, energetic researcher. I was about to attend the Christmas-with-Raël weekend and had set up an interview, when Sylvie Chabot phoned to say I would not be permitted at the event unless I first spoke to Raël, who "was not 'appy with me," since the *LA Times* journalist said I had directed him to a French ex-member's Web site.

Since I had done no such thing, I phoned the journalist in a rage, and he was kind enough to e-mail Chabot and admit it was his error. But when I arrived at the snowbound camp, I was ushered to Raël's condo inside the fiberglass-covered straw building that was UFOland. We took off our shoes, knocked on Raël's door, and Raël himself greeted us and kissed us all on both cheeks. "So, Suzanne, how are you?" he asked in the mellifluous voice that always reminds me of French nightclub singers from the fifties—Yves Montand, Jacques Brel, Maurice Chevalier. His complexion was white and powdery, like a mime artist's or an eighteenth-century courtier's.

He beckoned us over to his study area, a large, high-ceilinged white room with patio windows overlooking the snowy forest that bordered the ice-covered artificial lake. Raël sat facing us, behind his enormous curved desk that with its setup of computers and gadgets reminded me of the spaceship's control panel in *Star Trek*. His samurai topknot was as black and shiny as an erect telephone—as if he were receiving continuous telepathic messages from outer space. Framed photographs of the model of the embassy the extraterrestrials wanted him to build and nude studies of Sophie, his young consort, adorned the walls.

I realized to my excitement that I was "on the bench"—on trial, so to speak. Could this be the tribunal that disciplined heretical Raelians, the Council of the Wise? I was flanked by three bishops—the two Daniels and Sylvie Chabot—and Raël was contemplating me sternly from behind his desk. He had before him a list of occasions on which I'd said something "*negatif*" about the movement: The Japanese journalist was brought up again, along with my presentation at a Center for Studies on New Religions conference in Rome, when a Raelian had stood up and angrily refuted my statement about the low birthrate among Raelians, and other occasions over the past fifteen years. Since Raël did not know what I'd actually said on these occasions, only that it was "something *negatif*," I couldn't defend myself.

I countered with, "Raël, you must have been interviewed by the media over a thousand times. Have you ever, in all your years of experience in dealing with media, known a journalist to lie, to misquote you, or twist your words?"

Raël laughed. "Yes, of course. Journalists lie all the time. I used to be a journalist myself, so I know what they are like."

I protested that I had always given the Raelians copies of my articles, and that I should be judged by what I wrote, not by what journalists said I said. I argued that I had always defended religious liberty and urged respect for religious minorities.

Raël leaned forward and suggested I might be secretly working for the Association de Défense des Familles et de l'Individu (ADFI), France's anticult organization. "It would be a perfect cover, to pretend to defend religious liberty but to spy for them on us."

I stared at him in amazement. My psychoanalyst father's jocular phrase came to mind: "Shades of paranoid schiz!" Raël turned to the bishops and asked for their opinion.

Both Daniels defended me as a sociologist who was "balanced" and "*objectif*." Suddenly Raël smiled and said: "You are right, Suzanne. Journalists always lie. So, you are free to continue studying us." He stood up, shook my hand, and briskly ushered us out the door.

I toddled out into the deep snow and made my way in the dark toward the lights of the hall where the Christmas party was in progress. I was overwhelmed by Raël's charisma. He is like a powerful, charming movie star or CEO. When I told my boyfriend how amazing Raël had been, he said, "Sounds like he gave you the slap-stroke technique."

The offending journalist later sent me his article in advance of publication, as promised; I wanted to be sure he did not misquote me. I could foresee that Raël would not be happy with the piece, which assaulted the credibility of Clonaid's enterprise and suggested that Raël was set up as the court clown at Congress to cast doubt on the respectability of cloning, and that Raël, in turn, had used Congress and the cloning furor to promote his UFO religion. But my quoted statements were standard neutral sociologese, nothing (I naively decided) that Raël could interpret as *negatif.*

I was wrong.

I received a peremptory e-mail from Sylvie Chabot ordering me to write a "droit de reponse" (right of reply) to the *Los Angeles Times* disclaiming its thesis and to send it directly to her, to be edited by her and sent on directly by her. Next I must contact the paper to make sure my letter got published. I was astonished. I could not tell if the Raelians seriously expected me to comply—if this were a test of loyalty—or if they were deliberately setting me up for dumping. I called my friend and mentor Eileen Barker (a sociology professor at the London School of Economics who specializes in new religions) in the middle of the night for advice.

"I think you need to explain to them that you are a sociologist," she said. "A sociologist's job is to collect data—everything is data—and to present them to the public in as accurate and in as value-free a fashion as possible." So I wrote Raël an "Excuse me, but I am a sociologist" letter, outlining what sociologists do and what they do not do.

I waited for several days; then the axe fell. Chabot wrote: "Since you refuse to send the letter, we have decided that you agree with the journalist's views. For this reason, you will not be admitted to any of the Raelian meetings in any country."

I was shocked, upset. "Who does Raël think he is—God?" I asked myself bitterly, then remembered that, well, he *does* claim that his immortal father is named Yahweh and that his half-brother is Jesus Christ. I was amused to see myself reacting like a disgruntled ex-member, wanting to denounce Raël and his censorship of dissidents—to expose Raelian injustice and vindicate myself.

"This is ridiculous," I told myself. So I resolved to write about the Raelian Movement as I had always seen it—as a harmless, delightful religious subculture bursting with vitality, whose values were far more responsive to contemporary dilemmas (overpopulation, sexism, racism, nuclear war) than were those of most of the great traditions—certainly than those of the Catholic Church.

But—one positive side effect of my blacklisting—I felt more comfortable about approaching ex-members, a process I had postponed until now. In the past, NRMs always reacted badly when I mentioned I needed to include the perspectives of former members in my study. Their reaction is understandable. After all, how would I feel if a researcher was writing my biography and asked for the phone numbers of my ex-boyfriends or, worst of all, my ex-husband?

But, as Eileen Barker had admonished me, "For the sociologist, everything is data."

By January 2003, I had made up with Raël. The Raelian guides were coming to my classes again. I have the journalists to thank, for they continued faithfully to misquote me.

"Is it all a hoax?" they kept asking. "Could this cloned baby be for real?" Over and over I explained I did not want to go on record pronouncing on the issue one way or the other and gave my reasons for suspending judgment. I said that the Raelians weren't stupid enough to paint themselves into a corner; that Dr. Boisselier was a serious scientist; that it was true Raelians liked to court the media, but they had never told an outright lie. Then I went on to extrapolate on what it would all mean if the cloned baby were indeed a hoax.

I was trying to deconstruct the "cult" stereotype and to point out the logical fallacies in the journalists' argument, which went like this: Raël and his Raelians have weird beliefs—in extraterrestrials who play God. But we rational, secular humanists know this ain't true. So if the Elohim (these extraterrestrials) are fake, Raelianism must be a fake religion. Thus, Clonaid's cloned baby must be a fake.

Journalists like to simplify statements and contrast points of view, so they portrayed me as "believing in" the cloned baby and used my sound bites to set up the skeptics. In some TV interviews I came across as a gullible cult apologist. But at least the Raelian bishops were coming to my class again.

I am still waiting to see if the "real" cloned baby will please stand up—and be tested. Until then, the story of what Raël and his followers have been up to is far more complex and interesting than what the journalists have reported. This is why I invite you, Dear Reader (as P. C. Wren would say), to read my book.

And what can we learn by studying the Raelians? First, I must confess, there are things about them I found paradoxical and that still puzzle me. The Raelians are a strange hybrid of futuristic and retro elements, of liberal and conservative attitudes. For one thing, they combine liberal social values with an optimistic faith in the march of scientific progress. For another, their environmentalist demonstrations are rooted in brash anthropocentrism.

Raelians espouse positive values appropriate for our overcrowded, planetary culture. Their values address the sources of human suffering unique to the twenty-first century. Raelians insist we embrace differences and stand up for ethnic, religious, and philosophical minorities. They deplore violence and march in demonstrations against nuclear testing. They are feminists, advocate strict birth control and the right to opt for abortion, and are outspoken in their demand that gays be respected. And yet, within the dissenting cultural tradition of the intelligentsia, they are a distinct minority due to their conservative, almost nostalgic, faith in science.

"Science is our religion!" is a Raelian motto. Raelians are true children of the Enlightenment. They verbally assault the Catholic Church, applying the familiar critiques of Rousseau, Marx, and Voltaire. Deploring mysticism, *obscurantisme,* and otherworldly spirituality, they turn to hard science to lead humanity to salvation.

But, oddly enough, they reject Darwin. They are Creationists, quite as militant as Christian fundamentalists in the Deep South, and have organized public debates in universities to prove that Darwin's theory of evolution is erroneous, and that alien scientists created all life from scratch through the manipulation of the genetic code.

The Raelians are like a throwback to the golden age of science fiction, when technology was benign and seemingly under control—and we all saw scientific advancement as our ticket to freedom. Science was understood as a procedural manipulation of the material world guaranteed to produce positive results and novel gadgets that would ensure human happiness—like penicillin and the next Chrysler model. But that was before the psychotic breakdown of HAL, the ship's computer in *2001: A Space Odyssey.* HAL's nervous breakdown dramatized a new fear of science and a distrust of bandit technology.

It is not that the Raelians are oblivious to the destructive power of technology. Indeed, Raël owes his very existence to the Elohim's emergency response to the devastation at Hiroshima, and his urgent mission is to stop war and ban the bomb. It is rather that the Raelians are uncompromisingly anthropocentric in their approach to nature. In the worldview of a Raelian, the human scientist stands at the center of the universe, dabbling on an artist's palette of DNA. Humans created all life on this barren planet with the broad brush strokes of nanotechnology. They created, then obliterated, the dinosaurs and the Neanderthals in a mood of artful experimentation. The extinction of various species is not a problem, so long as we preserve their DNA. Raël expresses the Elohim's environmental concerns: All Raelians must stop buying newspapers to protest the deforestation in Brazil; Raelians should limit their families to two children or, better still, stop breeding and wait to be cloned; genetically modified food will end world hunger and is less carcinogenic than organically cultivated crops. Any problem that science causes, science can solve.

Today, fifteen years since my first close encounter with Raël, I am writing this book because I find myself in the peculiar role of being the academic "expert" on the Raelians, who have become international media stars. Journalists still regularly quote and misquote me, and since the cloning claim, television crews from Europe invade my apartment and editors invite me to write encyclopedia entries and chapters in textbooks. And yet . . . I still haven't "figured out" Raël, and I am still puzzled by Baby Eve, the still covert clone.

It is all too easy to render a new religion in caricature and then dismiss it as absurd or pathological. After all, today's "cult" might grow up to become the Mormon Church, the Bahá'í faith, or the Jehovah's Witnesses of tomorrow. The Raelian Church might in a hundred years become one of those Bible-based Christian minority churches that are well known and accepted in society but branded by fundamentalist theologians as "heresies" because of their deviant interpretations of Creation, the Fall, and the nature of Christ. Just as we read news reports about Jehovah's Witnesses refusing blood transfusions, or Christian Scientists rejecting medicine, or fringe Mormons marrying underage girls, in a hundred years our grandchildren might read about Raelian nudist protest marches or Raelian transgression of cloning laws.

John Saliba, one of the preeminent scholars in the field of new religions and ufology, notes that one of the main difficulties encountered in the study of UFO reports is that they are not open to the process of investigation that has become the "normal procedure in the scientific world." He explains that UFO phenomena cannot be easily categorized, because ufology "does not fall into one of the established areas of academic study and there are no acknowledged experts who can be trusted with the task of verification" (Saliba 1995a, 207). In a similar vein, a new religion based upon "UFO phenomena" cannot be easily categorized. Is it a "real" religion, or just a pop-culture "cult"? Are its ontological assumptions concerning extraterrestrial intelligent life in the universe based on scientific facts—or must we relegate them to the realm of myth?

What "really" happened that brilliant winter morning when the man who would become Raël went walking in the volcanic mountain range of the Clermont-Ferrand? The hermeneutical problem this question poses is neatly analyzed by Saliba (1995a, 212): "Since a UFO report originates with the perception of an anomalous event, which is then interpreted, it is not easy to distinguish between what actually caused the UFO contactees' experiences and the interpretations given to the experiences themselves."

Did Raël encounter a genuine extraterrestrial vehicle and its pilot? Or did he experience a psychotic episode with hallucinations? Could it have been a calculated hoax, a deliberate decision to exploit the current UFO-sighting craze and write a popular book? Or was Raël swept up in a William Jamesian spontaneous, involuntary mystical experience that, because of its "ineffable" nature, needed to be clothed in contemporary religious language, and so he opted to reinterpret Bible myths in the contemporary languages of space exploration and technology?

We will probably never know what "really happened," and there will always be a difference of opinion between Raelians and non-Raelians, just as there is between Mormons and "gentiles" over Joseph Smith's sighting of the angel Moroni and discovery of the golden plates. Angel sightings have the same enigmatic quality as UFO sightings, and as Saliba (1995a, 208) observes: "There is a mysterious quality about UFOs which leaves the door wide open for all kinds of interpretations, both plausible and far-fetched."

Contemporary prophets are not awarded the benefit of the doubt granted to the great prophets in history. We don't ask impertinent questions about Muhammad's experience in the caves of Hira, where the archangel Gabriel informed him he was a "messenger" of Allah. Whereas nineteenth-century historians attacked Muhammad as a charlatan, non-Muslims today would be reluctant to challenge the messenger Muslims call the Seal of the Prophets. His last sermon and his *hadiths* might even evoke a fleeting sense of awe and respect in the breasts of Western secular humanists who promote pluralism and tolerance. And yet Raël and his "little green men" are universally mocked. Why? Is it because a prophet's call must be shrouded in the mists of time before it can be awarded dignity? Is it because Muhammad has billions of followers who defend his name?

It is not the job of a sociologist to meddle in theology. I cannot answer the question often put to me: "Is Raël *really* a messenger for extraterrestrials who really created life on our planet from DNA?" All I can do is describe Raël and his movement and attempt to analyze its social forms. To do this, I will begin with the premise that UFO sightings—and the UFO religions that sometimes spring out of them—have to be located in some way within the social context of the contactee-prophet and his followers.

Chapter One

Contactee Prophets in the History of Ufology

UFO religions are engaged in a difficult enterprise. They are busy constructing nascent cultures that integrate science and spirituality into one seamless cosmology. With an acute sensitivity to our current existential crisis, where scientific facts are chipping away at traditional religious truths, UFO religions spin webs of belief, extrapolating on the future and engaging in folk-science experiments. With these tools they explore the mysteries of our human origin, define our place in the vastness of the universe, and "prove" the existence of alien gods. Their ingenious attempts to blend, by shaking up, the mutually repelling "oil and water" of science and religion are highly successful—as far as the tens of thousands of believers are concerned, who are provided with intellectually fascinating doctrines and emotionally satisfying convictions.

If success can be measured by the size of the congregation, the International Raelian Movement (IRM) is by far the most successful attempt to reconcile the scientific with the religious worldview (their latest claim is sixty-five thousand members). This movement is strikingly original and differs from other contemporary "flying-saucer" groups in several important respects. To appreciate its unique qualities, one must first locate its founder Raël's early career within the history of ufology.

Raël (1974) writes that he started out as an unwitting contactee before he went on to found a religion. Contactees come in two varieties, according to J. Gordon Melton (1995, 2–4)—the pre-Adamskis and the post-Adamskis. George Adamski was a Polish immigrant to the United States who became the prototype of the contemporary contactee prophet after his extraordinary encounters in the California mountains and Arizona desert were recorded in two best-selling books in the early 1950s.

Adamski, who lived in California on Mount Palomar, where he had built an observatory, claimed that in October 1946, while he and his friends were watching meteor showers, they beheld a gigantic spacecraft hovering in the sky. In 1952, Adamski and six associates followed up by driving out into the desert to hunt for UFOs. By noon they saw a huge silvery cigar-shaped craft approach and hover, then drift away. Adamski got out of the car with his telescope and asked his companions to drive off, leaving him alone. Soon a small craft alighted and a handsome male Venusian with long blond hair and an extremely high forehead approached him. They spoke through gestures and telepathy, and the Venusian told him he had been sent ahead on a peace mission, since the aliens were deeply concerned about humanity's penchant for war, and the recent use of nuclear weapons was upsetting the harmony of the universe. One month later, Adamski received an alien artifact. Then he wrote *Inside the Space Ships* (1953), which became one of the most popular flying-saucer books of all time. He describes how he cavorts with beautiful, playful aliens from Venus, Saturn, and Mars and recounts his long conversations with aliens, during which they impart their occult philosophy. In later writings he claims to have boarded an alien craft at a U.S. Air Force base for a voyage to Saturn to attend a conference (Clark 1998, 21).

Before Adamski arrived on the scene, European and American contactees were well versed in spiritualism and theosophy. They communicated with extraterrestrials through spiritualist séances or via solitary astral travel (now called "ascension"), during which their consciousness left the body to roam through astral realms and outer space. Telepathic conversations with aliens often transcended language barriers. Moreover, the extraterrestrials they encountered were invariably from our own solar system.

By the time Adamski's influence was felt in the 1960s, contactees had amassed an impressive body of ufological lore, and they integrated it with occult teachings that can be traced back to the early mystical mentors of the nineteenth century—Emanuel Swedenborg and Madame Helena Blavatsky—and later through the schismatic movements they inspired: Spiritualism, Theosophy, and Guy Ballard's the Great I AM (Melton 1995).

The post-Adamski contactees were swept up in the 1950s resurgence of interest in hard science, particularly the "magical" machines of advanced extraterrestrial (ET) technology.

Flying saucers first entered the picture in 1947, when Kenneth Arnold, a private pilot from Washington State, beheld an echelon formation of nine bright flashing UFOs over Mount Rainier. Next, Adamski's books, *Pioneers of Space* (1949) and *The Flying Saucers Have Landed* (1953), stimulated the public's interest in exotic alien hardware. In the 1950s, the UFO began to replace astral travel as the preferred vehicle for contactees.

The second characteristic of post-Adamski contactees is that their alien visitors come from remote planets, no longer from our solar system (Melton 1995). The third characteristic is that, whereas nineteenth-century contactees tended to predict amazing scientific developments and to extrapolate on technology in the future, by the 1950s, the contactees who emerged in the wake of Adamski were far more cautious about referring to popular scientific theories of the day, whether they commented on the nature of the physical universe or predicted cutting-edge scientific developments. Their aliens' "scientific" statements were prudently less specific. Soon they avoided the hard sciences altogether, and the fringes of science became fashionable. Contactees of the 1950s and 1960s evinced a fascination for paranormal phenomena such as levitation, telekinesis, automatic writing, and dematerialization, and for quantum physics (Melton 1995, 7).

By the 1960s, the leading contactees tended to confine their messages to theological, ethical, or environmental matters. Their primary task was to deliver alien messages and warnings about the interface between modern science and culture. The ETs' deepest preoccupations were with atomic war, pollution, and the fragmentation of the human family (Melton 1995, 8). These messages avoided scientifically precise statements with their potential for error, and focused rather on religious concerns. They relayed the aliens' metaphysical reflections on humanity's problematic use of science and technology. They channeled extraterrestrials' advice on how to cope with nuclear weapons and the daily chaos of overcrowded urban life.

Raël fits the mold of the post-Adamski contactee, at least during his early career. He evinces a deep fascination with alien machines and hardware—not surprising in a race-car test driver. But Raël's aliens derive not from our solar system but from a far-off planet in our galaxy. And Raël's aliens have a great to deal to say about our penchant for war, our abuse of scientific knowledge, and the imperative to dissolve national and cultural boundaries so we can unite in one global community.

In many ways Raël's story of his contact experiences of the third kind (CEIII) follows the narrative contours laid out by Adamski. First, he sights a flying saucer during a solitary walk in the wilderness, and a beautiful, gentle alien alights with warnings about humanity's abuse of nuclear weapons. Second, he is invited aboard the spaceship, where he receives philosophical instruction. Third, the aliens promise the advent of extraterrestrials in the future. Fourth, the aliens award him an alien artifact. Fifth, he writes a best-selling book and embarks on a series of lecture tours. Sixth, he is made a willing "abductee" and taken on a flight to a far-off planet.

But there are striking differences between Adamski's career and Raël's. Adamski had a background in occult philosophy. He founded an occult society called the Royal Order of Tibet long before he saw a UFO. Raël has never dabbled in Oriental religion or Western occultism (to my knowledge), and his intellectual mentors are the philosophers of the Enlightenment, such as Voltaire, Rousseau, and Fourier; the French romantic poets; and the French popular songwriter Jacques Brel. The two men's views on race diverge. Adamski was accused of Nazi leanings because his aliens were always blond. Raël, however, speaks of seven races of Elohim who provided the DNA for the four races of humankind (the purple, blue, and green races died out).

Finally, Adamski never established a viable religious organization during his lifetime, only the informal Get Acquainted Club he started in 1957. He was elevated to prophet posthumously by his followers, who set up UFO cults based upon his teachings. Raël, on the other hand, claims religious authority over a large, international, highly organized congregation whose sixty-five thousand members participate in monthly meetings, initiations, and meditation rituals. But the messages of these two contactees are quite compatible. The Adamski Foundation's Web site promotes a philosophy "pertinent to understanding that Human Life is the rule, not the exception, throughout the universe, and that humanity has the capacity to choose peace." The message Raël received from the Elohim is based on those two premises.

Raël's philosophy is strikingly original compared to those of the other leading contactee prophets of our time. Raël completely ignores the teachings of Swedenborg and Blavatsky. These two were mystics, but Raël, by self-definition, is emphatically not a mystic. He adamantly rejects *obscurantisme, occultisme,* and *mysticisme.* His declared mission, according to his statement at the time of the founding of the Raelian Movement in 1975, is to demystify the world's religions. "Ils devront s'ácharner a démystifier les religions et a spiritualiser la science, sans tomber dans les piéges de l'ésotérisme et des sciences occultes et autres charlataneries" (Terrusse and Richard 1994, 32). (One must strive to demystify religions and spiritualize science, without falling into the trap of esotericism, the occult, or other types of charlatanism.)[1]

The other contactees who went on to become prophets and spiritual masters relied heavily on the ideas of Blavatsky and Swedenborg—ideas that filter through the schismatic and fissiparous New Age groups that sprouted from the rich compost of the 1960s and 1970s "cultic milieu" (Campbell 1972). During the 1970s these ideas spread like spores as UFO religions began to poke their mushroomlike saucer-shaped heads out of the undergrowth of forgotten knowledge.

First, there was the Unarius Academy of Science, cofounded in 1954 by a husband-wife team, Ernest and Ruth Norman (Tumminia and Kirkpatrick 1995). Ernest channeled "Space Brothers," and Ruth, a stenographer, recorded the messages. When Ernest died in 1971, Ruth assumed the leadership as "Uriel." Uriel continued to channel alien communications that spoke of her exalted past incarnations and invited the human race to join the Galactic Federation of thirty-one planets, whose ambassadors were scheduled to perform a mass landing near San Diego in 2001. The Space Brothers' spiritual teachings are obviously based on the wisdom of Swedenborg, Blavatsky, and Buddha. The appeal of Unarius to its members appears to lie in its corrective therapy and healing process based on revelations of past lives, which require theatrical reenactments of traumas experienced in previous reincarnations. Unarians believe this process will enable adepts to ascend to higher planes and planets.

Heaven's Gate was also influenced by Theosophy. Bonnie Nettles, who teamed up with Herff Applewhite to form a charismatic duo (later notorious as Ti and Do), was a former member of the Houston Theosophical Society. This celibate couple shared a disgust for mammalian existence, a fascination for extraterrestrial beings, and a sense of divine mission. They united into one entity called "The Two," wore identical windbreakers and beige slacks, ate off the same plate, and finished each other's sentences (see Balch 1982a). Although as individuals each fits the profile of "loser" (Herff was a maladjusted homosexual prone to schizophrenic episodes, and Bonnie was an unhappily married nurse), what began as a folie à deux blossomed into a thriving gnostic school. To convey the notion that spiritual knowledge is ineffable and defies linguistic definition, The Two playfully redubbed themselves "Guinea and Pig," "Bo and Peep," and "Ti and Do" (Balch 1982a) as their enigmatic charisma was gradually unveiled. They were alien walk-ins, the two witnesses of Revelations, and finally the two-personed god: He was the Second Coming and she, God the Father.

Bonnie had attended many New Age channeling circles and soon convinced Herff that his habit of hearing voices inside his head was not a symptom of psychosis but rather a sign that he was being contacted by spiritually enlightened astronauts who offered an original syncretism of Christian Bible prophecy, gnostic truths, and Star Trek lore (Balch 1982a).

The famous 1956 study of a UFO group's hushed moment of apocalyptic expectation, *When Prophecy Fails* by Leon Festinger, Henry Reiken, and Stanley Schacter, adopts the ethically dubious method of covert research: Festinger sent his students to infiltrate the group. "Mrs. Keech's" anonymous "UFO cult" was in real life Dorothy Martin's group, now called by the Blavatsky-sounding name Association of Sananda and Sanat Kumara. Dorothy Martin received warnings via automatic writing that a cataclysmic flood would occur in 1954, sent by an alien, Sananda, a thinly disguised ascended master.

The Aquarian Concepts in Sedona, Arizona, is a spiritual commune formed around the teachings of Gabriel, an Italian American musician, whose "point of origin is another planet." Gabriel channels messages from the Bright and Morning Star, as well as from other ascended master–like entities from "celestial overcontrol" who reveal the past lives of members. Aquarians see their community as the reunited "cosmic family" who lived with Gabriel in a previous existence.

The Aetherius Society, founded in 1955 by George King, an English yoga adept and trance medium, is also strongly influenced by Hindu mysticism (Wallis 1974). Its teachings include concepts like chakras, samadhi, karma, and kundalini; its symbol is the Sanskrit "OM"; and its rituals include the chanting of mantras. According to Robert S. Ellwood (1993), the Aetherians can be classified as belonging to the Theosophical tradition.

Ashtar Command, one of the best-known UFO religions, emerged out of the published messages received by contactee Thelma B. Terrill ("Tuella") in the 1970s. Ashtar Command was believed to be a fleet of alien spaceships circling the earth. Again, this NRM relies heavily on the occult traditions established by Blavatsky and Guy Ballard. Indeed, Christopher Helland has suggested that the Ashtar Command is basically Theosophy recast to include ufology almost incidentally: "The recognition of Ashtar . . . situates the belief system within a mythic framework that has developed the traditional I AM teachings into an accommodation of the UFO phenomenon" (Helland 2000, 38).

This brief survey of six of the more visible UFO religions indicates how closely intertwined Theosophy and extraterrestrial philosophy have become. Mikhail Rothstein tracks the disappearance of the tangible flying saucer within the New Age milieu and the emergence of a more spiritualized, hence versatile, image of extraterrestrial beings, so that "the emphasis is laid on the nonphysical realm where the awaited spiritual transformation will occur" (Rothstein 2001, 223). Raël might well be the only contactee prophet who steers away from the occult. So, one might ask, what does Raël preach, and what are his sources (aside from the Elohim)?

Raël's two main sources are the Bible and science. He renders a "scientific," "myth-as-fact" interpretation of the stories in the Bible. He also "spiritualizes" science and technology and evokes a feeling of awe and reverence around the power of science to manipulate, mutate, and create new life. The primary source of evil in the Raelian religion is found in humanity's potential to destroy life through the abuse of science. Lesser evils arise from monotheism and from U.S. imperialism. Unlike other groups, this religion does not mention evil extraterrestrials.

Raël is a radical materialist with a reverence for scientists—particularly those quasi-immortal human scientists the Elohim, who he claims are material beings and our creators. Raël appears never to have heard of bodhisattvas, the "White Brotherhood," or subterranean "Elder Brothers." Not one of his "space brothers" is named El Morya or Samana. Oriental concepts and esoteric symbols—chakras, reincarnation, karma, enlightenment, violet rays, and so on—do not feature in Raël's books. Even Raël's Elohim display little interest in spiritual matters and seem to spend most of their time, when they are not busy creating life on new planets, indulging in hedonistic, sensual pleasures reminiscent of ancient Rome. Raël's Elohim are "wholly man," 100 percent homo sapiens (albeit effeminate). They are pragmatic, atheistic superscientists whose technology appears miraculous to us only because it is twenty-five thousand years ahead of our own.

And Raël is fascinated by alien technology. A former race-car driver, he seems to approach UFOs rather like new test models for Formula One. He boards his first UFO for a Bible lesson, then two years later embarks on a trip to another planet in our galaxy. Swedenborgian soul travel is out of the question for Raël, since he is what William James (1964) would term an "epiphenomenalist." In a similar vein, Raël rejects "walk-ins"—Ruth Montgomery's notion in *Aliens among Us* that souls from other planets have come to earth to take over human bodies, an idea later adopted by Heaven's Gate and in some New Age circles (see Lewis 2000b, 224).

But the ethical content of Raël's relayed messages is consistent with that of other pre-Adamski contactees—warnings concerning the nuclear threat and our warmongering and the need to unite all races and cultures into one global humanity, among others. Raël's extraterrestrials also offer advice on how to establish harmonious human relationships between the sexes—but their advice is quite distinctive.

Ernest Norman's Venusians advocate monogamy and an orderly family life. Gabriel's "overcontrol" reminds Aquarians of their past lives in polygamy, and Ti and Do's aliens insisted on total celibacy for Heaven's Gate members (Herff Applewhite went so far as to arrange for castration surgery for himself and several male followers). But Raël's Elohim advocate non-procreative free sexual expression—hetero, homo, bi, masturbatory—and Raël even enjoyed an amorous night with biological robots.

Raël's Elohim do not confine themselves to ethical and theological matters. They have a great deal to say about the use of science to solve the world's problems. Science poses the ultimate threat to our well-being and survival, but it also offers the solution to this threat, and the key to immortality and a materialistic salvation. Thus Raël expounds a well-articulated philosophy that extrapolates on the cutting edge of our sciences and promises a legacy of advanced extraterrestrial science that will result in a technological utopia for all humanity.

But Raël avoids the trap nineteenth-century contactees fell into when their naive forays into the popular science of their time later proved to be full of awkward errors—just as old science-fiction novels and films feature flying saucers and computers that appear clunky to the next generation. Perhaps Raël is aware of the pre-Adamski dilemma of "clunkiness." He never describes the control panel inside the UFO, for example. At Raël's headquarters in Quebec, there is a model of the UFO Raël encountered, but as one climbs inside, all one sees is a circular cabin of seamless, light-penetrating fisberglass with no control panels or gadgets. In a similar vein, Raelians are forbidden to paint or sketch the Elohim. Perhaps this is one reason Clonaid's cloning labs are secret. (One journalist who phoned me for an interview joked about the Brita water purifier found in the FDA raid on the Raelians' secret cloning lab.) But errors in "clunkiness" loom on the horizon. The Raelians exhibited a cloning machine in the British Museum and are now selling it on the Web. Dr. Brigitte Boisselier, Clonaid's director, has recently been assigned by Raël to construct a "babytron"—the machine in which cloned babies will be placed to undergo accelerated growth.

By 1974, when Raël made his debut on the ufology scene, a schism had already developed among the leading international ufologists. There were two opposing schools of thought concerning the interpretation of UFO sightings and CEIIIs. Due to the sporadic, unpredictable nature of UFO appearances, very little theoretical or hermaneutical progress had been made since the 1950s. What existed was merely an accumulation of reports of anomalous experiences that could be neither totally dismissed nor further investigated. Perhaps out of a sense of frustration, many ufologists began to move away from the scientific "fundamentalist" position (the assumption that extraterrestrials are real persons in real flying machines) toward a more "liberal" and intellectual position that treated UFO phenomena as a new expression in the realm of myth, symbol, and folklore. They launched the "new ufology" school, which sought psychological, parapsychological, and even blatantly unscientific and occult explanations for CEIIIs (Clark 1998, xii). Aliens were suddenly demoted to the level of Virgin apparitions, fairies, ghosts, and the monsters of ancient legend. Even a few of the most rigorous scientific investigators in ufological studies (notably Jacques Vallée) defected in midcareer and opted for the new folkloric or occult interpretations that had become fashionable. The popular writer Whitley Strieber, author of *Communion* (1987), followed the same trajectory in his next book. It began to look as if ufology were entering a second wave of occultism of a more academic, intellectual variety than the first.

In 1973 came a resurgence of interest in the scientific approach toward UFOs. In October, a series of dramatic CEIIIs occurred in the United States (Clark 1998). The same year, J. Allen Hynek, a famous astrophysicist responsible for formulating the typology of encounters of the first, second, and third kinds, founded the Center for UFO Studies (CUFOS). CUFOS became an important forum for collecting and reviewing data and publishing reports. (Parallel to these developments, skeptics organized a new movement to debunk UFO studies.)

CUFOS was a second effort in the scientific investigation of UFOs. The first effort, the Condon Committee, had failed miserably. In 1948, the U.S. Air Force launched Project Sign to investigate UFO sightings. It was located at the Wright-Patterson Air Force Base and classified as secret. By the late 1950s the air force wished to drop the project, so it handed over its Project Blue Book (a compilation of data) to what became the Condon Committee at the University of Colorado. The Condon Committee, fraught with internal strife, issued a report in 1969 concluding that UFO phenomena could be attributed to natural causes, and that no further investigation of UFOs was warranted. This left many anomalies unexplained in a way that was most unsatisfactory for ufologists—a situation that fed the popular conspiracy theory about a military cover-up.

Raël's career as a new contactee unfurled amidst the widening rift between the "fundamentalists" and the "liberals" in ufology. Raël appears to side with the scientific investigators by rejecting psychological and occult interpretations of CEIIIs, and by embracing the notion of intelligent life in space with superior technologies. (Whether scientists welcomed him to their side is, of course, another matter.) His first book, *Le livre qui dit la vérité* (The book which tells the truth), came out in 1974, just as the public's fascination with extraterrestrial exotic hardware was at its peak. And this fascination was particularly acute in France.

France has provided a favorable environment for the ufology "cultic milieu" in several ways. First, France was ahead of the United States in its scientific investigations of UFO phenomena. As Thomas E. Bullard (2000, ix) notes: "One of the few government-sponsored investigation projects, and perhaps the only such effort to study the subject on its scientific merits without overwhelming political pressure or intellectual prejudice originated in France during the late 1970s. . . . The great European wave of 1954 established UFOs as a mainstay of popular belief on that continent and some of the most sophisticated UFO research continues to come from there."

Second, France was in the throes of flying-saucer fever by the early 1970s. French citizens had been seeing flying saucers fairly regularly since 1954, but, according to journalist Jean-Claude Bourret, a veritable flurry of flying-saucer sightings hit France in the early to mid-1970s. Jerome Clark (1998, xii) confirms this: "UFO waves—periods of intense sighting activity—would erupt with alarming frequency between 1964 and 1973."

France has a history of dramatic UFO sightings, beginning in the nineteenth century. On January 12, 1836, in Cherbourg, a glowing, doughnut-shaped object two-thirds the size of the moon appeared to rotate on its axis as it flew through the sky. On August 1, 1871, in Marseilles, an astronomer observed the uncanny movements of what he first took to be a meteor that changed directions, slowed down, speeded up, and hung in the sky for around eighteen minutes (Lewis 2000b, 222–226). The next rash of sightings commenced in the 1950s.

In 1954, Edmond Campagnac was among a crowd in Tananarive who witnessed two UFOs crossing the sky. The same year, the Mozin couple encountered an alien on the highway who had just alighted from his cigar-shaped starship near Montournere. Anonymous witnesses in 1956 in Plaisance beheld a luminous "moon." In 1957, two campers near Saint-Etienne witnessed the descent of a flying saucer. In the 1960s, dozens of UFOs were reported by respectable Frenchmen: a doctor-veterinarian, a mayor, a high school teacher, a gendarme (police officer), and a farmer.

But UFO sightings in France climaxed during the 1970s. In 1975, seven witnesses alerted the police after seeing two demispherical objects alight in a field near Boulogne en Haute-Marne. Between 1974 and 1975, there were numerous flying-saucer sightings, especially in La Nievre region: six sightings in February 1974, two in September 1974, three in July 1975, and nine in August 1975. These experiences were carefully collected and recorded not only by ufologists, but also by distinguished scientists and astronomers such as Maurice Villon, and by journalists and gendarmes. This uncanny phenomenon was made much of in the media. Witnesses were interviewed on radio shows like "Pas de panique" (Don't panic), hosted by Claude Villers (Bourret 1997, 100–107).

The witnesses unanimously reported brilliant luminosities, uncanny silences, and erratic, unexpected trajectories. It is interesting that the overwhelming majority of witnesses who came forward and agreed to be interviewed were solid citizens whose integrity and respectability was unquestioned within their communities. And the sheer volume was impressive. Bourret in the course of six years of research collected around five thousand accounts of direct observation in Europe, and he states that "by pursuing a systematic study of the accounts of UFO sightings, using all the sources available: media, army, police, scientific enquiries, one finds oneself in the presence of a colossal mass of information—from magazine articles to letters" (1997, 242).

Then an incident occurred that seemed to offer irrefutable proof of the objective existence of UFOs. This was the famous affair of the Turin airport on November 30, 1973, at seven o'clock P.M. Two pilots and a technician spotted a flying saucer. The airport's radar had detected this anomaly. Moreover, dozens of witnesses at the airport had observed it. Three weeks later, a twenty-seven-year-old sports journalist and race-car driver, revered by his followers today as "Our Beloved Prophet, Raël," encountered a UFO and its alien pilot.

The Raelians espouse certain theories popular in ufological circles, notably the "ancient astronaut" theory. When Erich von Däniken's *Chariots of the Gods* came out in German in 1968 (it was translated into French and English by 1970), it gripped the imagination of a generation of authors interested in UFOs or enigmatic archaeology (Sitchin 1976; Graham Hancock 1995). Von Däniken's work led to the establishment of the Ancient Astronaut

Society in the United States in 1973 (the year of Raël's encounter). Advocates of the ancient astronaut theory explain ancient ruins as airstrips or dwellings built by extraterrestrials in earth's prehistory (Andersson 2000, 22). Anomalous or anachronistic artifacts ("xenotechnology") discovered at these ancient sites, as well as certain passages in the Bible, are referred to as evidence for long ago extraterrestrial visitations. Pia Andersson (2000, 23–24) sums up the "ancient astronaut" hypothesis: "Space aliens arrived on earth once upon a time in the distant past. They found the planet ideal for creation and through insemination and genetic manipulation created a hybrid of homo erectus and themselves that became us. According to some theories, these creatures lived on earth for a long time and are often associated with the lost continent Atlantis and Mu/Lemuria. Humans came to call them gods—gods who came from heaven and could work miracles—though in fact they were simply using an advanced technology that human beings could not understand."

The ancient astronaut theory was already very much in vogue in France by the time Raël's first book came out in 1974. Jean Sendy in 1968, Serge Hutin in 1970, and Jaques Bergier in 1970 all wrote books pursuing the notion that planet earth was an ancient colonial outpost of an extraterrestrial civilization. Sendy's book, *La lune: Clé de la Bible* (The moon: Key to the Bible), is perhaps the seminal influence, but Sendy himself (1972, 53) credits Voltaire as being the first to insist that the God of Genesis, who made heaven and earth, should be translated as "gods." Sendy (7–8) also points out that in Hebrew "Elohim" is the plural form of "Eloha" and suggests that the Elohim were not immaterial beings but "physical angels with sexes." With this premise in mind, he concludes that "Genesis becomes a perfectly consistent story of a colonization of Earth by astronauts who came from the sky" and became "angels in human memory." Yahweh, Sendy suggests, was not an immaterial principle but rather the leader of the Elohim (63). The fact that these ideas, so strongly argued in *Le livre qui dit la vérité,* were already "in the air," so to speak, may account for its enthusiastic reception in France.

Many of Raël's first followers were sci-fi aficionados or amateur ufologists—watchers of *Star Trek* and readers of von Däniken, Jules Verne, and Jacques Vallée. After becoming Raelians, however, they lost interest in generic UFOs, in other contactee reports, and in ufology clubs, and listened only to Raël and what his aliens, the Elohim, had to say.

One priest guide who spoke to my class at Dalton College declared it had always been obvious to him that there was intelligent life outside this planet, but only when he met Raël had he "found something and it fitted!" He summed up the Raelian position on UFO sightings: "We often encounter ufologists or UFO addicts similar to trekkies who are interested in nothing but UFOs, but we're not interested in UFOs per se, just the message and those people who might be *inside* the UFOs."

While Raelians are quick to point to UFO sightings in the media as corroborating Raël's story, they dismiss the claims of career contactees as erroneous or "crazy." When UFOs appear, the Elohim are making their presence known to manifest their support for Raël's mission. Although Raelians do commune telepathically with the Elohim in their group rituals to "feel their love," only Raël is permitted to receive messages or to view the alien visitors. But many Raelians are CEII—that is, they don't speak to aliens, but they have witnessed and still witness UFO phenomena of the second kind. Raelians, for example, periodically experience an unusual kind of CEII—the sighting of luminous flakes, also known as "angel hair."

Angel hair is a rare phenomenon associated with UFO sightings, and the most famous incidence occurred in France in 1952. People of the town of Oloron were watching a cigar-shaped UFO, when suddenly "a plume of white smoke" escaped from one end. The plumes "left an abundant trail behind them which slowly fell to the ground as if dispersed," reported a school principal. When witnesses tried to gather the material, it turned gelatinous and disappeared, so it was never tested. Jerome Clark (1998, 4) notes that "reports of Angel hair have been rare over the past three decades" and mentions only three examples besides the famous French case.

Yet angel hair is observed periodically at the Raelian summer seminars and interpreted as proof that the Elohim are watching over the Raelians. Raël himself describes the first sighting in his book *Let's Welcome Our Fathers from Space:*

> On October 7th, 1976, about fifty Raelians were at la Negrerie, near Roc Plat in the Dordogne . . . for the first anniversary commemorating the time when Raël had been taken to the Planet of the Eternals. . . . Suddenly someone cried, "What is that falling from the sky?" Great flakes were falling from a near cloudless sky. They seemed to be made of a cottony substance, which, when touched, melted in a few seconds. Then someone shouted: "Look! There is something very shiny in the sky!" Two luminous objects both very bright were just above us. The fall of the flakes lasted about ten minutes; then the objects suddenly disappeared.

> The meaning of this event was that the Elohim were offering a sign so that Raël would not be the only witness to the Elohim's activities. (Raël 1987, 9–10)

John Saliba has suggested that all UFO phenomena are intrinsically religious in nature, "a new type of religion that attempts to formulate a worldview that takes into account modern knowledge of the universe and technological advances that include space travel." UFO religions aim to instill "a cosmic dimension into an earthbound religious worldview, and to inject into spiritual experiences the element of scientific verifiability" (Saliba 1995a, 54, 55). The Raelian Movement would synthesize the scientific with the religious worldview in a new and original way that pits the UFO against the crucifix.

Raël is a Frenchman, and France has a long history of violent anticlericalism and a strong *laicité* (secular or lay movement), although paradoxically, the Catholic Church remains a respected repository of French tradition that is on excellent terms with the government. For French-speaking Raelians, the UFO enters this landscape as a new iconoclastic symbol in stark opposition to the crucifix.

Heaven's Gate tended to attract spiritual seekers from the "cultic milieu" who were already familiar with concepts such as enlightenment, reincarnation, and ascended masters (see Balch 1982b). But Raël would appeal to a whole new audience from the French *laicité*. Sanctimonious atheists, secular humanists, and anticlerical humanists would respond to his debunking of religious mythology and his insistence that all mysterious ambiguous events can be explained by science—if not by human science, then by extraterrestrial science. And since extraterrestrial science is light years away and twenty-five thousand years ahead, and since we must accept on faith what Raël says about it, the Elohim's science begins to look very much like magic. Thus Raël gradually leads his people deep into the core of their scientific cosmology and out the other side, where they find their view of reality transformed. They are now true believers in a new fundamentalist, apocalyptic Abrahamic religion!

Chapter Two

The Last and Fastest Prophet

Claude Vorilhon was a French journalist who wrote in the 1970s for a sports journal called *Auto Pop*. He appears in a 1972 photograph as a gangly youth wearing a polka-dot butterfly tie and wire-rimmed spectacles (*20 ans,* 15). The future race-car driver drove a Volkswagen with fancy headlights, its sides painted with fanciful designs. He was twenty-seven, a family man who lived with his wife and their two infants in the village of Ambert. Their house, facing rue des Augustins, was built of the same volcanic rock as the mountain range of Clermont-Ferrand, where Vorilhon beheld a UFO descending. As he watched, an extraterrestrial alighted, an "*Eloha*" (the singular of the Hebrew *elohim,* meaning "those who come from the light"), who revealed Vorilhon's true identity: He was Raël, the last prophet sent by a race of superior scientists from a planet in another galaxy to convey a message to the human race. "Raël" derives from "Is-rael" and means the "bearer of Light" (Raël [Vorilhon] 1974).

In 1974, the very next year, Vorilhon published what his followers reverently refer to as "the Book": *Le livre qui dit la vérité* (The book which tells the truth). The book led to lectures and to interviews on French radio and television that were tongue-in-cheek in tone but served to make Raël a famous contactee and helped sell his book. For those who read and believe *Le livre,* Raël makes it clear that he is more than a mere contactee: He is the ETs' chosen messenger, a prophet—and not just any prophet, but the last prophet. The message entrusted to him could save the human race, which has been living in the "Age of Apocalypse" ever since the catastrophe at Hiroshima.

In 1979, Raël revealed himself to be even more than the last prophet. In his fourth book, *Accueillir les extra-terrestres* (Let's welcome the extraterrestrials), published that year, he reveals that he is the son of an extraterrestrial named Yahweh and the half brother of Jesus, Buddha, and Moses—

hence he is a god-in-flesh. He is the messiah of the Age of Apocalypse. Today, as we enter the twenty-first century, Raël presides over the largest, most successful UFO religion in the world, which boasts sixty-five thousand baptized Raelians in eighty-four countries.[1]

Raël the Boy

Before analyzing Raël's projected image and modus operandi, it is useful to look at the boyhood and background of Claude Vorilhon, born on September 30, 1946, in a clinic in Ambert, a small village near Vichy, France. His mother was an unmarried fifteen-year-old farm girl, and he was raised in the home of his maternal grandmother, a fervent atheist. It seems his unknown father was "not so very unknown [but] . . . a Jewish refugee" (Raël 1975, 185).

According to Raël's eighty-seven-year-old aunt Therese Vorilhon (Chantepie 2003, 10), Raël's biological father, Marcel, was a Jew who fled Alsace during the Nazi regime in World War II to live with his Jewish relatives in Ambert. He returned to his wife and family in Alsace after the war ended, leaving his teenage lover, Colette Vorilhon, pregnant in Ambert. Marcel continued to visit Colette after "Claudy" was born, and when the clandestine couple went off on trips, they left the infant in the care of Colette's unmarried elder sister Therese. When Claude turned seven, his mother placed him in a boarding school in Puy-en-Velay. "Claudy en a extremement souffert" (Claudy suffered intensely from that), claimed his aunt Therese. When he returned home, he had violent altercations with his mother and often arrived at his aunt's house weeping (Chantepie 2003, 11). As a teenager, Claude had a passion for the songs of Jacques Brel, whose singing style he imitated, accompanying himself on the guitar. When Claude was fifteen, his absent father died "*brutalement*" (brutally)—we are not told how—and his mother forced Claude to quit his studies and get a job (which implies that Colette received child support from her lover).

When I interviewed Raël on December 18, 1994, he described how he was raised, like many of his generation, within the antireligious culture of *la laicité;* he was not baptized as a baby and received a secular upbringing from his maternal grandmother. At the age of nine, he was placed in a Catholic boarding school. Unthinkingly, he took communion with the rest of the boys, not realizing he was committing a blasphemous act: "I will never forget the priests when they discovered that I was not baptized, running around on the lawn in their long black cassocks! I was forbidden to go to communion again."

Raël claims he felt little interest in religion as a boy and never had a religious experience. Nevertheless, he describes a sort of initiatory experience at the age of seven, when an old bearded hermit, an object of ridicule in the village, "lay his hand upon my head and I felt a strange sensation; . . . he looked up and pronounced words that I didn't understand."

Later Raël (1975, 187–188) learned that "Father Dissard" was the last living Druid "pope" in France.

Raël as a child had "no idea I would be doing what I am doing now, but I did not expect to be ordinary. What I wanted was to be the first French [race-car] driver, to be world famous—world champion for Formula One." He discovered the joy of speed at the age of nine while rolling downhill on his "small almost brakeless" bicycle: "The speed and especially the balance, the sense of trajectories and the struggle against myself, against my own reflexes, . . . the perfect domination of the body by the mind." Then he went to the Tour de France automobile race, and "from that day on my life was centered only around automobile competition, nothing else interested me" (Raël 1978, 189, 190).

I asked Raël in our December 1994 interview if he had read science fiction as a boy. He replied he had not but had been interested rather in poetry and philosophy. "I won a poetry contest at my school when I was eight."

When I asked Raël about his relationship with his mother, he replied: "She is living in Ambert. I don't see her very often, but we have a good relationship. . . . She supports me and my philosophy."

At fifteen, Claude Vorilhon ran away from boarding school and hitchhiked to Paris, carrying his guitar and two thousand francs. He was picked up by a race-car driver, who drove him to Paris and, flattered by the teenager's familiarity with his racing career, treated Raël to dinner and a free hotel room. That night they met two dance hostesses, and "it was there that I was really initiated into love making" (Raël 1978, 194).

The young Claude spent three years playing music on the streets and in the cafés and cabarets of Paris. He then had a fateful meeting with Lucien Morisse, the director of a national radio program, who was scouting for young talent. Claude signed a record contract and became a rising teen pop star on the radio. He took on a new identity, assuming the name Claude Celler, put out many records, and wrote a hit song, "La miel et la cannelle"

(Honey and cinnamon). He was saving up his money to buy a racing car, a dream he'd had since he was a young boy, but his prospects as a singer came to an abrupt end. Lucien Morisse, his sponsor, committed suicide in September 1970.

Vorilhon decided to work as a sports journalist to gain access to the exclusive world of car racing. He fell in love with a nurse, "Christine," and they married to accommodate her parents, then moved to Clermont-Ferrand, "close to my mother so she would enjoy being a grandmother" (Raël 1975, 195).[2]

There Vorilhon founded a racing magazine, *Auto Pop,* as a strategy "to submerge myself in that exciting world where man tries to surpass himself by surpassing others. . . . Thanks to some connections I had made through my magazine, I was able to compete in automobile races with great success, winning about a dozen trophies" (Raël 1978, 201). He raced cars for the next three years.

Patrice Verges, a seasoned sports journalist who used to hang out with Claude, says one would see him very often on the race-car circuit, trying out the new models. His wife complained he was never at home, leaving her to bring up two infants single-handedly. "He was chasing girls, leading a double life," she told a journalist (Chantepie 2003, 11).

For Vorilhon, car racing was more than a mere sport or a profession. He approached it as an ascetic discipline, almost a religious vocation. He was determined "to push back my limitations and control my reflexes better and better." Once he mastered his neurophysiological impulses, he became impatient with the limitations of technology: "Neither the sound of the motor nor the odor of the burned gas interested me." He dreamed of a more sophisticated vehicle "to enjoy only the sensations of driving, that is to say, at its purest level" (Raël 1975, 202).

He was about to encounter the ultimate in racing technology, a flying saucer, piloted by the ultimate racing champion, an extraterrestrial.

It is perhaps significant that Claude Vorilhon's close encounter occurred less than a month after his second career screeched to a halt through no fault of his own. On November 30, 1973, French prime minister Pierre Messmer announced on TV a series of drastic measures to limit speed on French roads and to suspend all automobile races and rallies. Claude's sources of funding, for both his journal, *Auto Pop,* and his test driving, were cut off.

The journalist who interviewed Claude's ex-wife emphasized the notion that Raël is psychologically inclined to assume new and fake identities, her implication being that Raël's role as prophet/messiah is all an act. But it is not unusual for singers and rock stars to assume stage names. That Claude changed his name "Vorilhon" to the more catchy "Celler" tells us more about the profession than about the psychology of the artist.

Raël the Contactee

Vorilhon's first contact with an alien was on December 13, 1973 (the festival of St. Lucy, whose name means "light"). He drove up into the Clermont-Ferrand mountain range, climbed into the center of an extinct volcano, and beheld what he first took to be a helicopter descending through the fog. Its red light hovered twenty meters above the ground before the mysterious craft descended and a child-sized human climbed down its ladder. Vorilhon described the creature's black hair and beard, its greenish skin and almond eyes, and the shimmering bubble that surrounded its head. Vorilhon boarded the parked spaceship and for six consecutive days returned for instruction in the "true" (as in demythologized and demystified) meaning of the Bible and the secret of humankind's origins (Raël [Vorilhon] 1974).

The alien introduced himself as an Eloha from a far-off planet in our galaxy. He explained to Vorilhon that life is neither a divine creation nor the product of the evolutionary process, but the work of extraterrestrial scientists who concocted plants and animals in a laboratory called Eden set up on earth, using stores of their own DNA they had brought with them to enliven a barren planet. The first homo sapiens, Adam and Eve, were created from the aliens' own genetic material, thus "in their own image."

According to this extraterrestrial perspective, the Book of Genesis is a ship's log recounting a scientific research project that sparked a bioethical debate on the Elohim's home planet. The creation of humans and the science lessons taught to Adam and Eve were surreptitious and illegal acts, resulting in the expulsion from Eden and the Flood. Yahweh was the head scientist who created life on earth, and Lucifer was the name of the Elohim's political party that decided to give humans awareness of their artificial origins (hence the ability and responsibility of humans, in turn, to clone human beings in homo sapiens' image in the future). Satan was the leader of the faction back on the Elohim's planet who vetoed the plan to create artificial human life.

The reason the Elohim chose our barren planet for their experiment is that Satan and his cohorts feared the consequences of carrying out biotechnological experiments on their home turf. The implications of this creation "myth become fact" (to use C. S. Lewis's phrase) is that we have reached a level of technological development that brings with it ethical dilemmas. The extraterrestrials have important moral lessons to teach us—we who live in the wake of Hiroshima and at the dawn of cloning. They have been through it all on other planets, many times before (Raël [Vorilhon] 1974, 1–21).

From Contactee to Prophet: The Schism

Raël claims that after meeting his Eloha on December 13, 1973, inside the crater of the Puy de Lassolas volcano, he returned every day for six days and wrote notes during the hour-long Bible lessons he received from the alien inside the spaceship. Then he wrote his manuscript and sent it to a publishing house in Paris. The director, Marcel Julian, told him it was "sensational" but wanted changes that Vorilhon disagreed with; he demanded it be returned. He was contacted by a famous television host, Jacques Chancel, who had gotten wind of the manuscript and invited him to appear on his show, *Le Grand Echiquier* (The great chess master). Vorilhon's contactee tale and his notion that the aliens were the "Elohim" of the Bible made him famous overnight. He received thousand of letters (many, of course, disrespectful). Next, Vorilhon appeared on the *Samedi Soir* (Sunday evening) show hosted by Philippe Bouvard (and co-hosted by a journalist wearing a green suit with pink antennae). But the public's response was so warm that Vorilhon was invited back on the show. Anxious about his manuscript, Vorilhon sent a registered letter to the publisher demanding it be returned, and found they appeared to have mislaid it. Courrèges, the famous fashion designer, contacted Vorilhon after seeing him on television and offered to accompany him to the publisher's office. Julian told them that he had given it to a reader who had disappeared on holiday. Finally, Courrèges retrieved the manuscript, and Vorilhon, suspecting a conspiracy to repress the message, resolved to publish it himself (Raël 1978, 203–205).

The very last issue of *Auto Pop* came out in September 1964, and thenceforth Vorilhon became the Elohim's chosen prophet, Raël, and devoted himself entirely to their mission. He awards his wife credit for offering to leave her nursing job to assist him in the publication and distribution of "that extraordinary document," but she herself recently told a journalist that she had been unaware of his extraterrestrial encounters until the book came out. She also complained that once the family moved into a large medieval cottage in Perigord, people responding to Raël's message were constantly coming and going—or staying. "It was a big house with open hospitality. Whoever wanted could come, and I was the maid," she said (Chantepie 2003, 11).

Vorilhon gave his first Paris lecture at the Salle de Pleyel in September 1974, and in November he rented a bigger hall for an audience of one thousand. In Paris he attracted a local group of followers and founded MADECH (Mouvement pour l'accueil des Elohims créateurs de l'humanite [the movement to welcome the Elohim, creators of humanity]). On December 13, 1974, the first meeting of MADECH's 170 members took place at Puy de Lassolas. MADECH was set up as a voluntary association with a president, a treasurer, and a secretary, who each signed a check for ten thousand francs toward the publication of Raël's first book. Vorilhon adopted the title Raël, given to him by the Elohim as their chosen messenger. The first edition of the newsletter *Apocalypse* was published in October 1974 and distributed to three hundred members, who paid their annual dues of fifty francs and wore medallions of the swastika inside the Star of David (the symbol Raël beheld on the hull of the Eloha's spaceship). By 1975, MADECH had set up headquarters in Paris. The group's stated mission was to demystify and demythologize the world's religions and to "spiritualize" science—without lapsing into occultism and the pseudosciences.

In April 1975, Raël called an emergency general meeting to restructure the organization, and the diverging aims of the leadership became apparent; a major schism was brewing. Charles Aymonier, MADECH's secretary, complained that the members of the executive were awarding themselves honorific titles like "secretary general" and "administrative director." At the same time, they were trying to lay down rules to rein in Raël's charismatic authority and "mettre au pas le prophete" (follow in the steps of the prophet). MADECH officials were becoming less interested in what Raël's extraterrestrials were saying and more involved in networking with other ufology groups and trekkies. To exploit the entertainment potential of the ET phenomenon, they were planning a moneymaking lecture series, with other contactees as the invited speakers.

Raël's reaction was characteristically decisive. By July, he had dismissed the top officials of MADECH and replaced them with a new seven-person bureaucracy. The bylaws of the voluntary association were modified, so that the second article now stated that the aim of MADECH was twofold: to spread the message received by Claude Vorilhon and to gather the funds necessary to build an embassy for the Elohim.

On August 6, 1974, Raël led a group into the Clermont-Ferrand mountains to meditate on the Roc Plat, a large flat slab of volcanic rock where he had met the Eloha. There, Raël showed them how to establish a telepathic link with the extraterrestrials—apparently with some success, for a message was received that MADECH was entering a turbulent period where harsh criticism would be directed against their prophet, to whom they must remain loyal.

At MADECH's next general assembly, in March 1975, held in a rented room at the Place de la République, Raël staged a purge of the leaders who wished to set up rules that hampered his creativity. Raël reminded them, "It is I who received the mission," announced he was leaving to hold his own meeting in the café next door, and walked out with a group of followers.[3]

On October 7, 1976, Raël experienced his second visitation from the Elohim, which took the form of a marvelous journey to their home planet, reminiscent of Muhammad's Night Journey or the shaman's ascent to the spirit world.[4] As Raël reports in his 1975 book, *Les extra-terrestres m'ont emmené sur leur planète* (Extraterrestrials took me to their planet), he woke up at night and suddenly felt the impulse to leave his bed and walk through the woods of the Perigorde region. As he stood in a clearing looking at the brilliant starlit night, the same Eloha appeared to him and invited him aboard his spaceship to spend twenty-four hours on the planet of the Elohim. There, Raël was introduced to Elohim society, whose political system he admired and later described in *La geniocratie* (1977b). Raël enjoyed the aliens' recreational facilities and describes his high-tech sensual experience, which consisted of making love to six female biological robots in a Roman bath all night. He was initiated into the secret of immortality, for he observed the cloning of his double in a vat. He was instructed in sensual meditation, a sensory awareness technique to activate psychic potential and grow new neural pathways, which he later laid out for his followers in his fifth book, *La meditation sensuelle* (Sensual meditation) (1980).

Jean Gary, today a Raelian bishop and one of Raël's earliest followers, told me in an interview in 1994 how he first read *Le livre* while working for Club Mediterranean in Israel, and decided to return to France and put himself at Raël's service. As he drove toward la Negrerie to call on Raël, he got lost trying to find the remote medieval farmhouse with "Embassy of the Elohim" written on the door. When he found it, he climbed to the first story and knocked. Raël's wife appeared and calmly announced, "Raël has just returned from their planet!" Gary describes her as "very beautiful, and seemingly reasonable and balanced." When Gary returned the next day, she sent him to the chicken coop, where he received his first impressions of Raël: "First all I saw of him was his bum, backing out on his knees, very muddy boots, . . . then Raël turned around, his hair and beard were full of straws. He greeted me warmly. I found him to be very natural, simple, down to earth. I felt here was a man full of sensitive feelings, a simple man. He was full of love, he reminded me of Jesus and his apostles."

Two years after its founding, MADECH was still giving Raël headaches, and in January 1976 he asked Jean Gary to move to Paris to help him resolve the mounting tensions within MADECH's executive. This was difficult for Gary, but he complied and discovered that the Paris directors were "comploter contre" (plotting against) Raël (*20 ans,* 39). Raël instructed Gary to read the "Prayer to the Elohim" from Raël's second book at the general assembly, and to order the dismantling of MADECH. Gary had difficulty gaining entrance to the meeting without a pass, but once inside, he showed the gathering Raël's letter and read the prayer from the stage. Total silence followed, then 90 percent of the members got up and walked out of MADECH (from "Ecoutons Jean Gary" in *20 ans,* 39).

The Raelian Movement, born out of the ashes of MADECH in February 1976, made important changes that laid the groundwork for a viable new religion based on messages received from on high by "the last of 40 prophets" (Raël 1987a, 104). All members of the new movement had to accept the authority of the "Guide of Guides" and those he appoints, and accept the authenticity of the message. The membership was divided into two levels: the more committed "Guides," who made up the "Structure" or hierarchy, and the more loosely affiliated "Raelians," who paid their annual dues and received the bulletin *Apocalypse.* A Council of Discipline was created, with the power to excommunicate errant members; an administrative body of three guides, the Council of the Wise, would handle troublemakers and heretics. New dietary guidelines banned recreational drugs and additives in food. Raël came up with a hymn for his new movement, "Elohim, Elohim," and sang it to his followers on several occasions, accompanying himself on the guitar.

The year 1979 saw the escalation of Raël's charismatic claims and the dramatic revelation of his messianic status. In *Accueillir les extra-terrestres,* published that year in France (and in English in 1987 as *Let's Welcome Our Fathers from Space*), Raël explains that he is the half brother of Jesus and Muhammad, and that their common father is an extraterrestrial named Yahweh who chose mortal women on the basis of their "virgin DNA" to bear his prophet-progeny. These women were beamed up to his spacecraft, inseminated, and then released with their memories erased.

Raël the Charismatic Leader

Raël has worked ceaselessly since 1973 to spread the message and claims in all his decisions to be merely following the orders of the Elohim. His typical strategy is to send guides ahead to a new country, where they set up his lectures with book sales and drum up local publicity with posters and radio and TV interviews. When I asked Raël in our December 1994 interview at the Holiday Inn in Montreal how he decided which country to visit next, he said: "I communicate with the Elohim once a year, on or around August 5. I hear a voice that tells me which country I have to go to that year. It is very difficult for me, all this traveling. Each year I hope to be able to stay home, but the voice comes again and gives me the plan."

I asked if he heard one voice or different voices. He hesitated, then replied, "It is one Eloha, the voice of my [extraterrestrial] father."

In that interview, Raël spoke of returning to the same spot in the Clermont-Ferrand mountains every August to commune with his extraterrestrial father and receive instructions for the new Raelian year, identified not as A.D. but as A.H., "After Hiroshima." Since 1993, Raël has found it advisable not to return to France, not only because he owes taxes on the sale of his books, but also because of the fierce persecution of "*sectes*" in the wake of the 1994 Solar Temple tragedy, the mass suicide/homicide of a Neo-Templar order in Quebec. Presumably, he still listens for the same voice at the advent of each new Raelian year, for, like prophets before him, Raël is driven by voices from the heavens. This became clear in his account of the first lecture he gave as a contactee: "Even though I had a dreadful case of stage fright, . . . everything went very well, the answers to the most difficult questions seemed to come by themselves to my lips. I felt some help coming from above, just as they had promised me. I had the impression of listening to myself answering things I could not know myself" (Raël 1978, 206).

Raël the Sportsman

After a break of twenty years, Raël resumed his hobby of competing in car races, one of the great passions in his life. The Elohim had asked Raël to give up racing and devote his energies to spreading the message, but in 1994, some of his wealthy Japanese followers took him to a racetrack in Japan and showed him a race car they had rented for him so he could compete. They argued that his racing could garner publicity for the movement. Raël accepted their offer, but only after insisting that none of the money used to further his racing career could come from the embassy fund or members' tithes. Thus, Raël's racing hobby is mainly supported by donations from a few wealthy Raelians in Japan and Europe who were already involved in the racing scene. Raël's race-car hobby has been touted as a missionary strategy to spread the message among the international jet setters who hang out at the racetracks.

During Raël's early racing career, he competed in the Slalom de Marmande in 1968, in the Cote de Gervovie in 1971, and in the Rally de l'Ouest and the Slalom de St-Nectaire in 1972. Raël, who specializes in ice racing, resumed his career by competing in ice races in 1994 in Japan, and in 1995 in Quebec City. He raced in the 1995 Canada Grand Prix, where he drove a silver Mazda, crossing the finish line twenty-sixth out of twenty-seven contestants. In 1996, he competed against Paul Newman; Newman finished third and Raël, fourth. They exchanged gifts, Raël awarding Newman a copy of *Let's Welcome Our Fathers from Space,* and the movie star reciprocating with a bottle of his famous salad dressing.

In 1998, Raël was dubbed "the world's fastest prophet" by his racing team, a committee devoted to raising funds to support Raël's hobby. He raced intensely throughout 1998, competing in Miami for the Motorola Cup; in Montreal; in Misano, Italy; in Trois-Rivières, Quebec; at Mosport in Ontario; and in Lime Rock, Connecticut, finishing as high as sixth and as low as twentieth. In 1999 he won third place in the West Palm Beach Moroso twenty-hour race and finished twenty-sixth out of thirty-six at Monza, Switzerland, and eighteenth at Mosport. He also competed in Quebec races held in Sainte-Croix and Trois Rivières. When Raël competes, like other car racers, he is surrounded by loyal fans—but Raël's fans are his followers, notably many charming, scantily clad Raelian women.

In November 2001, Raël announced his intention to retire from racing. But he continues to work out daily on his virtual car-racing video game in the privacy of the condominium he shares with his companion at Valcourt, two hours from Montreal, Quebec. Michel Beluet, the director of UFOland, the Raelian estate, told me in our 1992 interview there: "Raël exercises his muscles to keep in shape for the races. Racing is a terrible stress on the body, you have to keep very strong. It weighs up to two Gs when you go around corners, so Raël has to keep in very good shape."

Raël's Women

Raël is opposed to the marriage contract, echoing the arguments of the French eighteenth-century socialist philosopher Charles Fourier, who equated the marriage contract with social injustice that arises from private ownership. Journalists, familiar with the views expressed in Raël's *La meditation sensuelle,* often portray Raël as the stereotypical "cult leader" who sexually exploits his female followers. My impression, however, is that, while Raël is an enthusiastic practitioner of his philosophy regarding the existential pursuit of sexual pleasure, he is a serial monogamist.

Like many powerful CEOs, he changes his consort every seven years or so and over a twenty-year period has had three stable relationships. Raël's guides are discreetly incommunicative when I ask them about Raël's private life, but the rank-and-file Raelians impart gossip freely. The general word going around is that Christine was a loyal wife who supported Raël's mission and never challenged his claims—but the problem was, she was very low-key and matter-of-fact about it all. She lacked fervor and evinced little utopian enthusiasm. This put a damper on Raël's charisma.

For ten years after the founding of his movement, Raël continued to travel to different countries with his wife. The Raelians' official history, *20 ans,* by Marcel Terrusse and Michèle Richard, features a 1982 photograph of Christine in Africa carrying a baby in a shawl. In 1985, Christine left Raël and his movement. She claims she was tired of being humiliated by her husband's numerous mistresses and describes a family dinner with herself and their two children when Raël "let the axe fall by telling us that we were nothing to him. From then on, only the movement would count" (Chantepie 2003, 12).

Since the early 1980s, Raël had focused on spreading the message in Japan, and he soon had a Japanese consort. Japan possesses symbolic value for Raël, since Hiroshima is the birthplace of the Age of Apocalypse. In 1983, he paid a commemorative visit to the spot where the first atomic bomb was dropped on August 6, 1945 (*20 ans,* 83). At the Japanese seminar the following summer, Raël announced a new revelation to his followers: The Elohim had once established a base on Nohga Heights near Hiroshima. "That news had a very strong impact on us and plunged us into a state of intense emotion," write the authors of *20 ans,* Terrusse and Richard (83).

In 1987, Raël's new consort, a strikingly beautiful Japanese girl, Lisa Sunagawa, beheld shining filaments descending from heaven, the same phenomenon observed on October 7, 1976. This was interpreted as a sign from the Elohim, who chose to "deposer leur paragraph au seminaire" (put their stamp on the seminar) (*20 ans,* 118). Lisa then began to accompany Raël on his travels—to Lima and Miami, Brazil and Martinique. Raël spent his Christmas 1988 holiday in Switzerland with "sa douce compagnon" (his sweet companion). In 1989, Raël is photographed with his arm around Lisa in front of a mountainous background; the caption in *20 ans* (131) reads: "La prophete et Lisa, sa delicieuese compagnon japonaise." In a 1990 Radio Canada television documentary, *They're Coming!* filmed at Eden, the Raelians' camp in France, a slow-motion shot shows Lisa in a pink tutu, walking and holding hands with Raël.

Sometime between 1990 and 1992, Raël separated from Lisa and found a new consort, a fifteen-year-old Quebecois ballet student, Sophie. Her mother and sister are both Raelians. On the basis of meeting Lisa and Sophie, and of photographs of Raël's first wife, it is clear to me that Raël is a connoisseur of feminine beauty. From a woman's aesthetic perspective, it is interesting to note that all three women are "pure" specimens of distinct racial types: Christine was a voluptuous Mediterranean beauty; Lisa looks like a princess in a samurai film; and Sophie is a Nordic beauty, a fair-skinned, red-haired ballerina who resembles Leslie Caron.

Lisa today is a priest guide and a six-feathered angel, the highest rank in the all-female secret Order of Raël's Angels. Shortly after her break with Raël, she moved to Toronto, where she works as a dancer and is involved in running the local movement. From Toronto, she travels all over the world. She discreetly refuses to discuss her former relationship with Raël and remains on excellent terms with him. He holds her up as an ideal of femininity for the angels to strive toward, praising her as "the most feminine woman on earth" and the woman who most resembles the Elohim, who are "more feminine than the most feminine woman on earth."

Photographs of Sophie as Raël's "*compagnon*" first appear in issues of *Apocalypse* in 1993. As soon as she turned sixteen, he married her with her mother's permission in a low-key wedding at Montreal's city hall, witnessed by Michel Beluet. The marriage, which violated Raël's views on sexual ethics, was for convenience only, to avoid legal hassles when he transported Sophie across borders. He continued to refer to her in public as his "*compagnon*" (although she called him "my husband" when she spoke to journalists). In 2000, they were legally divorced but continued to live together by choice.

Raël spoke to me of his relationship with Sophie in our 1994 interview:

> She was at the right time and the right place with me, but what I see in her is her intelligence. People see her beauty, but there is so much more inside! What I love in life is to play—any kind of play—and she is so good to play any kind of game. When I met her, we played chess. We spend our days when I have nothing to do playing games. I love that. When you are with beautiful women, when you [start] to be old, it becomes boring, but growing old with an intelligent woman is much more interesting! We laugh together—if you are intelligent you have a good sense of humor—and for me it is very important to laugh. And she is so feminine, and I love femininity in woman. Ah, Sophie! I could talk about her all day!

In December 2001 at the transmission of the cellular plan, held at a restaurant on Ile Ste Helene in the St. Lawrence River, I found Sophie sitting beside the bishops in the front row, facing the stage where the baptism had just been performed. She was wearing tight slacks like leggings and a fuzzy sweater, her red hair in a ponytail. Now in her midtwenties, Sophie still looks like a teenager. When I asked for an interview, she agreed graciously and spoke with passion but diplomacy about her life with Raël.

"How did you become a Raelian?" I asked her.

"My mother explained the message to me when I was ten. It made sense. I immediately got it. I was initiated at the age of fifteen on April 1. Then, soon after, I met Raël at the airport."

When I asked her how she saw her role in the movement as Raël's consort, her reply took me by surprise.

"I think of it as a pleasure," she said; "it is not work. I love to think of Raël as a racehorse. He's always on the go, always rushing, he loves to race, to travel. So, I am like his little rabbit. The racehorse owners have found that the horse is happier if he has the same rabbit in his stable, so when the horse travels to different races, he always has his little rabbit waiting for him in his stall at the end of the day. So, I am like that little rabbit for Raël, waiting for him in his stall so he is happy."

While I realize hard-line feminists might balk at this statement, I was charmed by Sophie's unpretentious simplicity. I asked how she spent her days. She replied: "I cook, I clean the house, I just be with Raël. I like to live at Valcourt. It is so beautiful."

When I asked Sophie how she first met Raël, she revealed the esoteric spiritual nature of their romance, reminiscent to me of the medieval courtly love tradition.

> I first saw him at the airport; I was fifteen going on sixteen. A whole group was going to Dorval airport to welcome Raël, and they invited me. We made eye contact. We went out to a restaurant—the whole group. Then he called me on the phone. He kept calling me. We met at cafés, restaurants. We have been together ever since. He told me that when he was sick in 1984 and he thought he was about to die, the Elohim spoke to him. They told him that they had chosen a special woman for him, that this woman would be waiting for him. Then he felt better, and everywhere he traveled he was looking for her. As soon as he saw me, he recognized me as the woman he had been waiting for all those years.

I asked her what she had felt when she first saw him, and she replied, "I felt this was the moment I had been waiting for my whole life."

When I asked why they got married (thereby violating the Raelian antimarriage policy), she told me: "We had to get married; it was difficult for him to travel with me across borders, so we were married when I was sixteen, with my mother's consent. She is a Raelian and she was happy to see me happy. But we divorced a year ago. I never wanted to be married. For me, love has nothing to do with making a contract."

I asked Sophie if she were still pursuing her ballet career. "You know how it is in ballet," she answered. "You must practice three hours a day at least. I never had a career exactly. I was a student at le Grand Ballet Canadien. I went there for three hours every day for three years. But I quit when I met Raël. Now I dance for pleasure, and for others' pleasure. I do my own dancing."

Raël's Public Image

Raël's public persona is a complex blend of several images. He is a sportsman, a race-car driver, "the world's fastest prophet," and a hunter and fisherman. But he is also a philosopher, following in the footsteps of the freethinking skeptics of the Enlightenment—Voltaire, Descartes, and Rousseau—the heroes of the burgeoning *laicité* movement in the eighteenth century who exposed the hypocrisy of a decadent, oppressive, state-sponsored Church through virtuoso essays of pure logic, pithy humor, and ruthless wit.

And Raël is a scintillating performer. He tells jokes, he mimes, he dances and sings to his audience. His presence on stage is comparable to a rock star's or a comedian's. A European researcher who attended the 1991 summer seminar in Eden described to me how *Carmina Burana* was played to set the mood for Raël's grand entrance, how he leaped up onto the stage and paraded around with arms raised to a storm of ecstatic applause.

I have often observed how Raël's charisma is stage managed. For example, I was once lying with all the Raelians on a hotel floor during the November 1992 meeting at the Holiday Inn in Montreal. For this oxygenation exercise, the lights were dim and all the Raelians had their eyes shut while they focused on a sensory awareness meditation. A guide's mellifluous tones urged participants to feel the telepathic, loving presence of the Elohim. Suddenly a deep voice butted in over the microphone: "And they are with us here now, our fathers." It was Raël. He had crept in and taken over the microphone. The lights flared up and the prone Raelians sat up, rubbing their eyes and cheering. One guide leaped to his feet, grabbed the microphone, and proclaimed: "As I was lying here, relaxed, concentrating on the meditation, suddenly I felt a storm of peace! Then I knew Raël must be in the room!"

Raël's semi-expected sudden appearances were usually announced by one of the pretty young animators who served as mistresses of ceremony at the meetings. ("Who is coming? Could it be the greatest prophet of our time . . . the messiah himself?") I recall a particularly dramatic entrance at the February 2002 meeting, held at Theatre Gésu, when Raël bounded onto the stage wearing his customary white padded suit and samurai topknot and stood beaming while his Raelians gave him a standing ovation. He stood there smiling while the clapping went on and on and on. I thought it would be rude to stop and sit down, so I kept clapping along with the others, although my hands tingled and my legs were tired. I wondered if Raël was playing a trick on us or testing us, or if he simply needed this much applause to refuel his charisma. The moment became quite ambiguous as we waited for his signal. Then he began to bump his hips in rhythm, so the clapping became a beat, and the Raelians swayed their hips in sympathy. This too went on and on, until finally, he motioned us to sit down.

His followers perceive Raël as a pioneer of science. Despite his lack of formal earthly academic training, he is credited with a prodigious knowledge of scientific theory and future technology due to his instantaneous "chemical education" on the planet of the Elohim. As he has explained, "when an earth man is admitted to the world of the eternals, he undergoes a chemical education" (Raël 1978, 245). The Raelians regard him as a pioneer hero, even a martyr, of scientific progress, who will be recognized in the future on a par with Galileo and Copernicus, once persecuted because their discoveries also threatened prevailing primitive superstitions.

But Raël is, above all, a writer. Responding to the aliens' call to be their messenger, Raël wrote books broadcasting the message. He is not unlike L. Ron Hubbard, a successful science-fiction writer (envied by his peers for his ability to type ninety words a minute) long before he wrote *Dianetics,* the sacred text of Scientology. Raël too wrote his way up the ladder of fame. *Le livre qui dit la vérité* established him as a prophet. *Accueillir les extra-terrestres* established him as a messiah. But the book he published in between, *Space Aliens Took Me to Their Planet,* suggests that Raël has assumed the role and function of a modern high-tech shaman.

Raël's relationship with technology is shamanistic. As a boy he longed to be a race-car driver when he grew up. Initially, he achieved this goal with contacts he made when he reported on the racing world. Then, like every other race-car driver who risks his life in a race, he cultivated a fiery concentration that sharpened his faculties—a state of altered consciousness that resembles the "alert mindfulness" of a Zen archer, kung fu artist, or samurai swordsman. In the midst of a race, Raël must have experienced both moments of sheer terror and sensations of triumphant power. Squealing around the cantilevered corners of the racetrack, zooming past his rivals, a driver melts into his machine and becomes one with the engine.

The young Claude Vorilhon must have sensed what it might be like to be superhuman. Centimeters, milliseconds, away from death, through the driver's trained, intuitive mastery of a beautiful, sophisticated machine, he must have known what it felt like to be a demigod. Before he dreamed of founding "the world's first scientific religion," Vorilhon had already melded religion and science through driving race cars at death-defying speeds in a state of what Buddhists term "alert mindfulness."

During his twenty-seventh year, Vorilhon recounts, he boarded a vehicle whose silent, seamless technology left his race cars in the dust beside his boyhood brakeless bicycle. Unlike Raël, the primitive shamans in Stone Age tribal societies, who were part animal or bird, our modern shamans prefer to be part machine, for only machines possess refined senses and capabilities beyond the primate's. Where ancient shamans' mythic ancestors possessed the superior senses of creatures with scales, fur, or feathers who spoke animal languages before the Fall (Eliade 1950), the contemporary urban shaman does not bother with the animal kingdom, whose species humankind has conquered and debased. Raël 's "mythic ancestor" was not a beaver or a raven, but a superscientist from another planet who arrived in a spaceship, wearing a bubble.

The early shaman's powers were magical flight and the ability to speak the language of animals and spirits (Eliade 1950). Raël flies to the planet of the Elohim (Raël 1978) and communes telepathically with aliens through his topknot. Like the primitive shaman who often has a sexual encounter with an animal spirit, reenacting the primordial unity of human and animal before the Fall, Raël spends his first night on the alien planet making love to machines, the six alluring biological robots who conveniently appear and disappear at the press of a button, like genies conjured out of a bottle.

A shaman's apprentice must undergo an initiatory ordeal, a symbolic death and rebirth. Eliade (1950) gives an account of the Australian aboriginal shaman's apprentice who is dismembered and boiled until his bones are clean. The master shaman then lays the bones out in correct formation in the moonlight, the flesh grows back, and the apprentice jumps up, invincible. Raël claims he witnessed his own body being re-created from scratch in a vat, from organs to skeleton to skin. All Raël's "apprentices" must undergo postmortem dismemberment of their frontal bones (around the pineal gland or "third eye") in the hope of re-creation.

Raël describes his instant technological education as equivalent to that of the aboriginal sorcerer's apprentice whose brain is replaced with rock crystals. In his second book he tells us how, on the Elohim's planet, he sat on a padded armchair inside a machine, his head encased in a shell. Yahweh, his extraterrestrial father, told him: "This machine will awaken in you faculties. . . . From now on your brain will exploit all its potential . . . [and] you will . . . be able to heal with your hands." The same machine also turned him into a sort of remote-control robot through which the Elohim could see, hear, and speak (Raël 1978, 254). Like the shaman who is a throwback to the mythic ancestor, and who recaptures the power and mobility of the original man, Raël is on a quest for physical immortality. He seems certain he will live forever. He told the German newspaper *Frankfurter Allemagne,* in an interview that appeared in *Ananova* magazine on January 3, 2002, that he had written to a German doctor, Von Hagen, who preserves bodies through plastination. Raël, who in his will requests plastination, explained: "I admire this doctor who carries out plastination. . . . Then I will be able to see my old body in a museum and live on in another body as a clone."

Von Hagen welcomed Raël's request, the article reports. "The donation of his body is very welcome—it makes the use of the body after death more popular."

I asked Raël about immortality in our 1994 interview. "Raël, you know that you are immortal. Since you saw your body being cloned in a vat, does this mean you have no fear of death?" Raël replied: "I am not at all worried about dying but I am afraid—not 'afraid,' 'conscious' is better—of the possibility of becoming disabled, paralyzed. So I am careful—I do not want to be in a wheelchair! So I am slower than I was in my youth. I drive very fast on the safe circuits and in a straight line, but when I take the curve, I go a little bit slower. I am conscious of risk, of danger, which I was not in my youth—perhaps too conscious!"

As these different facets of Raël suggest, he is a complex, unique individual, a Renaissance man who defies facile categorization. He is highly intelligent, bursting with vitality, socially adept, and sensitive—and he enjoys life immensely. Anticultists and journalists armed with a few superficial facts try to stuff him into the pop-psychological profile of "evil cult leader," comparing him to David Koresh and Jim Jones. I find this ludicrous. Having observed Raël over the course of fifteen years, and having spoken to him many times, my impression is that he believes in what he says, he is not prone to violence, and he is not crazy. As a non-Raelian who does not "believe" in the message, I have to admit that sometimes what he says *sounds* crazy, but what is truth, after all? What is reality? I approach Raël rather as a creative artist, a kind of religious genius.

Most scholars would agree with Max Weber's premise (1947) that charisma is in essence a relationship between the leader and the disciples. Roy Wallis (1984) observes that charisma is "generated from the bottom up." Lorne Dawson (2002, 82) also sees charisma is an interactive process, for charisma is essentially a relationship, and one of "great emotional intensity; . . . followers typically place an extraordinary measure of trust and faith in their leaders." The leader's core group provides a task force that educates the outer rings of followers in the mysteries of the leader's attributes, often creating a kind of spiritual etiquette that serves to bolster the authority structure, not only of the leader, but also of the members of the core group.

The initial claim of charisma made at the outset of a prophet's career is not sufficient unto itself. Weber (1947) emphasizes the need for the *maintenance* of charismatic authority—the ongoing tasks a charismatic leader and his or her core group must perform to bolster the fragile authority that is unsupported by objective facts or by the surrounding social institutions. Charisma needs continuous legitimation. The success of a messianic/prophetic leader not only requires inborn qualities, but also demands consistent, overt actions—perspiration as well as inspiration.

The peculiar gifts and personal qualities that are associated with inspiration Raël owns in abundance. He is visionary, emotionally expressive, energetic. He is willing to take risks, to be unconventional. He exudes self-confidence; he is equipped with superior rhetorical and impressive management skills.

As for the actions required to maintain the charismatic identity, Lorne Dawson (2002) sheds new light on some of the problems that charisma confronts—problems that if badly handled could lead to serious conflict, even tragedy. He identifies four tasks in bolstering the leader's legitimacy.

The first task is "maintaining the leader's persona." This can be done through periodic bouts of "charismatic display" (Weber 1947). Raël's dramatic revelations that either invite a deeper level of commitment from his followers (the Order of Raël's Angels) or escalate his charismatic identity (from prophet to messiah) and his assumption of new titles like "the Last and Fastest Prophet" and "His Holiness"—all appear to be examples of this pattern.

Unlike many contemporary prophets who practice a measure of segregation from their flock and become mysterious and inaccessible (for too much exposure can undermine their aura of transcendence), Raël is fairly accessible. He appears frequently at the monthly meetings in Montreal (if always by "surprise") and his absences are due to his world travels. Raelians gather at the airport to greet him when he returns home, and they congregate at the racetrack to cheer him on. Raël appears surrounded by his entourage of beautiful women and muscular male bodyguards (whose hair and dress styles echo Raël's). Their presence pushes followers away to an appropriate distance. They provide cues concerning the etiquette required when one approaches the Elohim's Last Prophet.

Thus, the right proportions of formal distance and personal closeness that stimulate the charismatic relationship are maintained.

The second task Dawson (2002, 87) identifies is "moderating the effects of the psychological identification with the leader." He argues that if the followers become utterly dependent upon their leader for their salvation, their sense of reality or connection to the outside world is threatened. Moreover, a leader who is surrounded by sycophants can no longer receive the negative feedback, the healthy dissent, necessary for making informed, realistic decisions that will affect the group's future. Close advisors can find themselves in a position where they must use deceit to preserve their status and get the job done. This can lead to a breakdown in communication between the leader and his outer ring of followers, as the core group huddles around the leader to defend him from criticism.

There is a zero-tolerance policy concerning criticism of Raël and of his guides in the IRM. Dissenters must go before the Council of the Wise and are often stripped of their offices or ejected from the movement, a sure sign that the structure has become "an organizational milieu in which obedience is disproportionately esteemed" (Dawson 2002, 87). The danger is that obedience, rather than intelligence or management skills, will become a route to promotion in the inner ranks.

It is evident that Raël's guides do identify passionately with their prophet, even to the extent of renaming themselves in his image (Lear, Azael, Amidrael, and the like). Raël calls on the loyalty of his followers to defend him from verbal attacks and persecution, as he does in "The Beauty of Sacrifice," published in *Apocalypse* magazine in 1996.[5] This letter of Raël's caused ripples of apprehension in the French-speaking anticult movement, where it was interpreted as an invitation to mass suicide. It is clear this is not what Raël is actually saying, but he does ask Raelians if they are willing to die for their faith as Jews, Buddhists, and Christians martyrs have done, and he argues that it is better to die for who you are than to live a false existence.

To explain the passionate bond between the disciple and the charismatic leader, Dawson (2002, 87) asserts that "followers attribute charismatic qualities and power to a leader as a way of resolving the unconscious conflict they are experiencing between their ego and their ego ideal. Projecting the ego ideal—the internalized sense of what society ideally expects of them—on the leader, and then entering into a condition of deep personal identification with the leader allows the followers to satisfy vicariously the demands of the ego ideal, thereby relieving themselves of the profound psychological tension created by their actual failure to live up to the ego ideal." This analysis seems to fit the Raelian summer-camp experience, where participants engage in group confessions of sexual ambiguity or inadequacy, and join in the ritual casting off of sexual inhibitions. Raël's daily sermons on sensuality, our alien origins, and the need to cast off social conditioning provide the rationale for these exercises and make him the focus as the paradigm of the original self-motivated, sensual man.

The psychosocial dynamic resulting from this psychological shift is that the followers, released from their pangs of conscience, feel a close bond with the other members who are undergoing the same process. Thus, a "comforting group ego emerges, with the charismatic leader as its focal point" (Dawson 2002, 87).

The third task a prophet confronts is how to negotiate the routinization of charisma. Roy Wallis (1984) has argued that, while it is necessary to create institutions and delegate authority in an expanding new religious empire, the process of routinization will inevitably cramp the creativity of the prophet and dull the shining mantle of charisma. Raël deals with this problem, as others have, by firing his top aides (notably Legendre and Lear, as we will see) and by rotating the important tasks of national guide, continental guide, and personal assistant. Over the years, Raël has gradually replaced his inner circle of men with women, which now seems to represent a more spontaneous, emotional, less competitive (and certainly more decorative) executive through which charisma can be routinized.

The fourth task Dawson points to is that the leader must be perceived as constantly achieving new successes. Raël deals with this one simply by announcing new triumphs, whether they occur or not. "His Holiness the Dalai Lama has requested to meet with His Holiness Raël," one such announcement reads. Another reports mass fasting on the borders of North and South Korea to bring about the union of these torn countries. And Raël's charismatic image seems to change its shape. During the phase that included the announcement of the cloning of Baby Eve, his persona was that of the pioneer scientist. Today his image is transforming into the "great humanitarian" mold: The Korean borders fast evokes Gandhi, and Raël's forthcoming book, *The Maitreya* (as well as his anticipated meeting with the Dalai Lama) conveys the impression that Raël is an enlightened, compassionate Buddha. The result of these developments is that Raelians will more closely associate their leader with the great compassionate humanitarian saints of our era. That the

Dalai Lama has yet to meet Raël, or that the mass fasting has been postponed, does not undermine the message.[6]

Within this framework, Raël's blatant courtship of the media is not necessarily a symptom of a narcissistic personality, but rather a strategy to bolster his charismatic persona by broadcasting new successes. Unlike many great prophet-founders of NRMs, Raël nurtures secular ambitions. He wants to be a player on the international political and religious stage. He would like to engage in ecumenical dialogue with the Dalai Lama and with Israel's head rabbis. He has asked to address the United Nations. And he has achieved a measure of success. He spoke before the subcommittee on human cloning at the U.S. Senate in March 2000. He hobnobbed with famous scientists during Clonaid's heyday. He was officially received in December 2001 by the president of the Congo, Sassou Nguesso.[7]

All prophets confront daunting impediments in their effort to achieve social legitimacy. Raël seeks social recognition and respect as a spiritual master and as a social critic and philosopher of science, but he seems less concerned about impressing the world than impressing his followers through capturing the attention of the media. And when the media (predictably) assaults or mocks the prophet and his message, Raël exhorts his followers to rise up in defense of their religion and demand respect. Lawsuits are launched, letters of protest flood TV stations, press conferences and marches ensue that quell the media, and the resulting more respectful news coverage convinces the Raelians that their beloved prophet is indeed making a difference—and preparing the world for the Elohim's return.

Unsolved Mysteries in the Life of Raël

Three enigmatic episodes in Raël's life have yet to be satisfactorily explained. They are reminiscent of the conspiracy theories that abound in the UFO "cultic milieu."

The first is his period of temporary flight or retirement from running his movement. The second is the singular case of the Teesdale inheritance, a purported hoax. The third is, of course, Raël's role in the cloning of Baby Eve.

Raël's Retreat

In 1984 Raël took a year off from running his movement and went into retreat. The official report was that he needed to rest, and it was time the infant movement "learned to walk alone." *20 ans: La génération des pionniers* gives the official reason for Raël's absence from the 1984 July summer camp: "Raël in Retreat: Raël has decided, after 10 years of spreading the message, to go on a 'spiritual retreat' in a place held secret for an indeterminate period of time where he will continue to watch over the well-being of the movement that must function well without him" (90).

But there are other versions of this event.

According to his companion, Sophie, he was very sick and thought he would die, but then he heard extraterrestrial voices promising him his perfect woman, and this gave him courage.

A different explanation was provided by an ex-member who claims Raël had told her he had been arrested in France and held in prison, where he became very ill and had to have an operation. When he returned, she was shocked at his appearance. His long dark locks—"antennae" through which he received telepathic communications from the Elohim—were chopped off, he was very thin, and his personality had undergone a drastic change. She said he used to be informal, friendly, and unpretentious, but he suddenly began to behave in a dictatorial fashion and to demand adulation (see chapter 7).

An alternative, if preposterous, explanation came from a Raelian who has a taste for esoteric books and conspiracy theories. He told me that Raël had been kidnapped by evil extraterrestrials disguised as terrorists and held at gunpoint, blindfolded, and tied to a chair for a whole year.

When I interviewed Raël in 1994, I asked him about this rumor. He looked astonished. "Who told you this?" (I received the impression he was genuinely surprised and had never heard this tale. I could not disclose my source, due to standard research ethics, so I said, "Oh, some of the members.")

Raël demystified the story at once. "No, I took a year off because I was tired. The mission was so important for me, I was overdoing it and realized I was not practicing what I preached—to relax, avoid stress, lead a healthy life. After I went to the planet where I saw my body re-created and realized I was eternal, I felt I could push myself, ignore my health right now because I knew I had eternity to enjoy myself. But I lost ten kilos; I was not enjoying life anymore. I realized I was burnt out and needed a rest. So I stayed in France and visited Quebec for one year."

Raël's ex-wife Christine claims he experienced a similar episode in 1987 when he showed up at her door, burnt out as a guru ("ultime sursaut du gourou"), and rested for a while with her and the children in Frejus. She, a nurse, diagnosed him as clinically depressed ("his mental health was in doubt"); he suffered from insomnia and took sleeping pills. After spending a holiday with his family in Spain, he returned to lead the Raelian Movement. "Finally, the social recognition tied to the name 'Raël' made more sense than the anonymous 'Claude Vorilhon,'" she said. She complained that he left her "without a sou, and took away the children—not to take care of them, but to toss them out into the world—like him, at the same age!" (Chantepie 2003, 11).

That missing year is still a mystery. However, the history of religions shows us there is often a phase in the lives of great mystics and prophets called the "dark night of the soul." The fasting of Buddha, the despair of St. John of the Cross, and Jesus' temptation in the desert are the best-known examples of this phase of uncertainty, doubt, and passivity, during which the prophet awaits the helping hand of the Holy Spirit. Da Free John, who is revered as Adidam, a god-in-flesh, spent a year in retreat and wasted away to a skeleton, then returned with increased charisma. Bhagwan Shree Rajneesh took a three-year vow of silence, was tormented by back pain, asthma, and allergies, then emerged with renewed force. John Humphrey Noyes, founder of the Oneida Perfectionists, spent a year on the streets of New York ingesting laudanum and experiencing hallucinations before he received his revelation that he was the Third Coming of Christ.

Thus it appears that prophets often have doubts about their own charismatic claims, or reservations about the social role they must assume. Great saints and mystics must wrestle with demons. Like Dante in his inferno, they must descend into the pit of hell; witness sin, chaos, and madness; and even tiptoe past the devil, before they reach the steps of Mount Purgatory and can climb toward the light and music of God's majesty.

The Teesdale Inheritance

The only source of information concerning the second mystery, the Teesdale inheritance, is Jacques Vallée's book *Revelations: Alien Contact and Human Deception* (1991, 212–215). Vallée, a famous ufologist and astrophysicist who was a student of J. Allen Hynek, draws our attention to this enigma in the history of ufology. Vallée claims that in March 1988, an advertisement in *Nouvel Observateur,* a Parisian newspaper, announced that a British millionaire, recently deceased, had left his fortune to "serious organizations that have as their goal the establishment or the maintenance of relationships with extraterrestrial beings." Ufologists were invited to send their résumés to the trustees' office of Theard, Theard, Smith, and Theard in London. Jacques Vallée was intrigued and asked his friend, or "*correspondant,*" to respond to the ad. A year later, the correspondant received an invitation to an expensive restaurant near Notre Dame in Paris, where six representatives from the firm, in the presence of a group of lawyers, scientists, and a priest, interviewed three candidates for the inheritance. These candidates were Raël; Professor Raulin, a distinguished chemist from the University of Paris; and Vallée's correspondant. Vallée dismisses Raël as "a notorious sect leader who has claimed contact with an extraterrestrial being [and] has gone on to organize a worldwide movement."

Before dinner, a trustee read aloud a passage from Teesdale's diary in which he recounts two near-death experiences during World War I and a later uncanny event at Dunkirk, where he felt a "white and gold" presence and heard a voice identifying itself as "a sentinel for those who set life on the planet." On both occasions the alien presence gave him a strange object and made him promise that he would pass it on to scientists to analyze. Teesdale confessed he had never fulfilled this promise.

Then the company sat down to a magnificent meal, and after dinner, the commission withdrew to deliberate in private. They returned to announce that Raël had been chosen as the recipient of the Teesdale inheritance, since "he presents the profile that is closest to the spirit of the Testament." Raël was awarded a large laboratory cryogenic container that presumably held the alien artifact, and everyone left the restaurant. Vallée's correspondant was soon contacted by a Raelian guide, Dominique Renaudin. He also spoke to Raulin, the chemist. Vallée made some inquiries and discovered that there was no such firm as Theard, Theard; the address on the stationery was erroneous. Moreover, his efforts to trace the late Mr. A. P. Teesdale, born in 1916, suggested that such a man had never existed. To this day, the motives behind what appears to be a hoax remain a mystery.

Baby Eve

The third unexplained mystery in Raël's life concerns the covert clone. Does Baby Eve exist? If so, what was Raël's role in her creation? I discuss these issues in chapter 8; at the time of this writing, January 2003, many questions remain unanswered. The world's media have dismissed the cloning as a publicity stunt, a hoax. But, as I said to many journalists during this media blitz, "If it *is* a hoax, it's much more than a hoax."

Chapter Three

How to Construct a New Religion

Raël's first organization, MADECH, was not exactly a religion, although there were religious elements present. MADECH was rather a "platform society" (Schutz 1980), a loose organization composed of UFO dilettantes and spiritual seekers. Saliba (1995a, 22) describes typical UFO platform societies as "function[ing], not as cults that require membership and commitment, but rather as open places where views on UFOs are exchanged and UFO contactees relate their experiences. They include among their speakers experts in various fields of the occult sciences, like astrology, reincarnation, and the human aura. They tend to attract people who are interested in religious experience and do not hesitate to bestow a religious or spiritual meaning to sightings of . . . UFOs."

MADECH, as far as Raël was concerned, had gone off track and was heading in a direction that impeded his mission and trammeled his control and creativity. It took him two years to quell his misbegotten progeny, and once he had accomplished MADECH's demise, he set about constructing the framework for a religion.

Over the next few years, Raël added to his movement, piece by piece, the basic components of a church. *Le livre qui dit la vérité* had established a creation myth and eschatology. But there were still no rituals, no priesthood, no experiential dimension, and no coherent system of ethics. As a nouveau contactee, Raël had hobnobbed with fellow contactees and ufologists such as Jean Miguères, founder of CEIRUS (Centre européen d'initiation à la recherche ufologique à caractère scientifique [European center for the first scientific research on UFOs]), and Richard Glenn, the Quebec-based contactee and TV host. But as his identity as a prophet-messiah became established among his flock and the religious agenda was clarified, Raël distanced himself from his old contacts in the French ufology milieu.

The Raelian Religion

Raël gathered his followers together for an Assemblée Generale Extraordinaire on February 14, 1976, to modify the old bylaws of MADECH and proceeded to build his church.

The Social Organization

Raël dissolved MADECH's administration and appointed twelve guides "un peu comme les apôtres" (a little like the apostles) (*20 ans,* 40). The first block he set in place was a priesthood and executive to be called "the Structure." He simultaneously established the Council of the Wise, a disciplinary council to handle errant members and to control heretics. In the Raelian organizational pyramid, the broad base is composed of the loosely affiliated Raelians, those who have acknowledged the Elohim as their creators through the transmission (a kind of baptism) and who make up the overwhelming majority of members. They are the semi-active or associate members, who may or may not attend the monthly meetings, tithe, perform their daily meditation, and abide by the rules that govern diet, drugs, and sexual activity. All that is required for membership is the payment of an annual membership fee ($100, in Canada); all members receive the magazine *Apocalypse.*

More committed members join the structure, which comprises the peak of the organizational pyramid. They may be promoted up the structure's levels through voluntary work that furthers the two goals of the movement: spreading the message and building the embassy. The six levels are, from the base upward: assistant animator, animator, assistant guide, priest guide, bishop guide, and finally, the planetary guide or "Guide of Guides," Raël himself. The priest and bishop guides are empowered to transmit the cellular codes, that is, to "baptize" new members. The guides are empowered to reelect Raël every seven years (a procedure explained to me as a "vote of confidence"), and thus far Raël rules as the Guide of Guides. In 1998 there were 1,483 members of the international structure.

Ritual

The second block Raël added was initiation rituals and a meditation practice. In April 1976, Raël performed the first transmission on the Roc Plat with forty initiates. He claimed that Jesus had performed transmissions in his time, but that they had been applied erroneously to infant baptisms in the Catholic Church.

The transmission ceremony occurs four times a year, during the significant dates in the Raelian calendar. New members are called to the stage one by one, to stand before Raël or a guide, who then dips his or her hands in a bowl of water and holds the initiate's head. Both parties close their eyes and concentrate on establishing telepathic communication with the Elohim. Sometimes these baptisms are performed in a chain of transmissions, where Raël holds the head of a bishop, who holds the head of a priest, who baptizes a new initiate.

For the initiate, the "baptism" denotes formal recognition of the Elohim as "Our Creators" and promises (but does not guarantee) the chance of physical resurrection and the ultimate reward of eternal life, based on the individual's service to humanity during his or her lifetime. This symbolic/scientific action is based on the Elohim's teaching that individuals have a unique frequency pattern determined by their chromosomes, the genetic blueprint of their cells. The Elohim record every person's emissions, from conception on, to judge whether it is worth re-creating that person on their own planet. The guide, through his or her connection to Raël, acts as a carrier for the transmission by picking up the initiate's frequency and transmitting it to the Elohim.[1]

One bishop, Nicole Bertrand, told me in an interview in July 2003 that the science of the transmission is "more an act of recognition than anything else. Basically, what occurs is the vibrations of your genetic code of the cellular plan are transmitted to the Elohim. Our cellular plan is nothing else but an organization of matter with its own vibration. The reason this is done in a ceremonious fashion is because it constitutes an act of recognition of the Elohim as our Creators."

For Raelians, the transmission is not an empty ritual, or lip service paid to their "gods." On the basis of my and my students' interviews, they seem convinced that this is the key to immortality. As one priest guide put it: "I certainly hope I will be [cloned]. I have no way of knowing at this point in time. I certainly hope that the people who decide will judge me worthy of being re-created" (Unger 1990).

Because the extraterrestrials require a sample of the initiate's bone for the cloning process, initiates are encouraged to sign a contract with a local mortician. In Quebec, the Alfred Dallaire funeral-parlor chain sets up a booth at every transmission ceremony so that initiates can pay $500 and sign a form that gives the mortician permission, upon their death, to remove one square centimeter of the "frontal bone." I was told that the sections removed—these "third eyes"—were packed in ice inside a box and sent to a bank in

Geneva, where they were stored in an underground vault, awaiting collection by the Elohim. This funeral ritual is called the "lifting of the frontal bone." The purpose of the bones was explained to me by a bishop as "an act of recognition of the science of the Elohim, a statement of our faith in their power to give us eternal life through the genetic code."[2]

Raël writes that "the conservation of the frontal bone is a recognition of the Elohim as being our Creators, even after death. The cellular plan . . . of each individual is registered in an enormous computer which records all our actions, . . . and at the end of his life the computer will know if he has the right to eternal life on the planet where the Elohim accept into their midst only the most worthy of men and women" (Raël 1987a, 27–28).

In 1979, Raël added the "Act of Apostasy" as an obligatory step in preparation for the transmission. The act requires aspiring initiates to fill out a form letter renouncing their infant baptism and demanding that their names be struck off their former church's membership list. They must sign the letter before the transmission of the cellular plan. Since the overwhelming majority of the five thousand or so Raelians in Quebec were born into Catholic families, such letters almost invariably go to the Catholic Church.

Initiates are also advised (but not obliged) to draw up a will leaving their assets to the Raelian Movement (RM).

The next ritual Raël introduced to followers was an ecstatic technique, the sensual meditation, which he claimed was taught to him by the Elohim during his visit to their planet. Twelve Raelians were led through the first sensual meditation at the first Stage d'Eveil (Course of awakening), held in France on August 5, 1976 (*20 ans,* 41).

The meditation was a vital ingredient, especially for a religion that rejects the concept of God and the notion of an immortal soul, as it opened up an experiential dimension to Raël's congregation. The sensual meditation induces altered states of consciousness and encourages a sensitive connection between the body and nature—the ultimate aim being to achieve a "cosmic orgasm," explained to me by Gabriel Blutot, a Realian priest, in our interview at Dawson College in October 1999 as "the sensual experience of the unity between the self and the universe."

During the monthly meetings, members sit or lie on the floor in dim light, as one of the guides speaks gently through a microphone and leads everyone through a relaxation exercise called *harmonization avec l'infini* (harmonization with the infinite), the first stage of sensual meditation. This begins with deep breathing and a kind of mental anatomical travel through parts of the body, arriving eventually at the brain. Then, through guided visualization, all imagine they are on the planet of the Elohim and in telepathic rapport with them. Many Raelians perform the sensual meditation daily with a half-hour cassette tape that involves sensual awareness techniques and a guided meditation into the infinity of space and time, envisioned as a kind of macrocosm within microcosm—deep inside the "central nerve cell" of the brain.

Congregation

The third block on which Raël built his religion was a schedule of congregational gatherings, which added a social dimension to his sect. The first kind is the monthly meeting, which always takes place on the third Sunday of the month in every city where there is a Raelian presence. The second kind is the intensive training sessions over the summer, Stages of Awakening seminars held for one week in a rural setting. They feature Raël's daily lectures, sensual meditation, fasting, nonmandatory nudity, group confessions and testimonials, avant-garde therapy, and cross-dressing games in which gender roles are deconstructed.

In the early 1980s, a campground, Eden, was purchased in the south of France, near Alby, and in 1992 the RM bought 115 hectares in Valcourt, Quebec, for the summer seminars. Raël dubbed this land Le Jardin du Prophète (the garden of the prophet).

The summer seminar serves a major function in a movement that is not communal and has a loosely affiliated and diverse membership. It provides a recruiting arena and a space for members to encounter Raël, who inspires a fresh commitment to the message and the two goals of the movement. It is a place where Raelians form close interpersonal bonds and find new friends and lovers.

A second, more advanced Stage of Awakening offered the week after the seminar is an intensive training workshop for those already in the structure, or for those just entering it. Many Raelians who have participated in the first stage feel a stronger commitment to the cause and sign up for that second week.

This is also an occasion on which Raël reviews the annual contributions of each of the guides and reallocates their responsibilities in order to prune and strengthen the executive.

On the basis of their statements in interviews conducted by my students at Dawson College and Concordia University, participants in the summer seminars went home inspired by Raël's utopian vision of what the planet will be like after the extraterrestrials arrive. The camps' names—Eden and

Le Jardin du Prophète—convey a utopian sense of sacred gardens where Raelians can enjoy a temporary respite from social roles and responsibilities. Naked—like Adam, Eve, and the Elohim—Raelians report undergoing a kind of spiritual rebirth. The sensory stimulation exercises, the international, multiethnic quality of the nightly cabaret performances, all make the Raelian seminars a microcosm of the Raelian religion and provide a vision of the harmonious society that Raël saw during his visit to the planet of the Elohim. The summer-seminar experience gives Raelians hope for a new peaceful world in the future.

The third kind of gathering takes place around the transmission of the cellular plan, during the annual festivals held on dates that mark significant events in humanity's relationship with the extraterrestrials. August 6 commemorates the first day of the Age of Apocalypse (the day after the bombing of Hiroshima, August 5, 1945). December 13 commemorates Raël's 1973 first encounter, and October 7, his 1975 second encounter and visit to another planet. The first Sunday in April commemorates the creation of the first homo sapiens (Adam and Eve) by the Elohim in their laboratory.

Ethics

Although Raelians have been portrayed in the media as free-love advocates, taboo breakers, and anarchists, paradoxically, they adhere to a strict code of ethics. Raelian values are outlined in the videocassette *Values in the Millennium* as follows:

1. Take responsibility for one's own actions, and never obey orders that go against one's own conscience.
2. Respect differences; racial, sexual, religious, cultural.
3. Strive for world peace, and promote non-violence.
4. Put an end to the masochistic use of drugs that mutate the genetic code.
5. Share wealth and resources.
6. Uphold democracy, that will allow a democratic vote to usher in the geniocracy.
7. Promote non-violence.

Raelians are uncompromising in their stand against violence. Raël says, "The one holding the weapon is as responsible as the one giving the orders." Raelians believe that this precept would have prevented the Nazi atrocities, since Nazi officers could not have justified their actions as "just following orders." Raël preaches in *Values in the Millennium* that "the life of only one person is more precious than that of the whole of humanity" and that "even if the Elohim (God) asked them to kill someone, they should refuse."

Although Raelian sexual ethics certainly promote promiscuity and experimentation, Raelians do have ethical guidelines regarding sexual activity. The first rule emphasizes respect and mutual consent in sexual behavior. The individual's right to choose and sexual diversity are upheld. Guides who attempt to force their ideas or unwelcome sexual attentions on others are excommunicated from the movement for seven years (the time it takes to replace all their body cells). At one of the first meetings I attended, I was surprised to hear it announced that two guides in Europe had just been expelled for their persistent sexual advances toward two new female members.

The second rule is to practice safe sex. In July 1978 at the Course of Awakening camp near Montreal, a survey of participants to determine how to avoid the spread of sexually transmitted diseases led to the recommendation that henceforth participants should produce a medical certificate that attests to their freedom from contagious disease. The use of condoms was made obligatory, and campers were given bleach and sponges to scrub the shower stalls before and after use. AIDS patients, however, are not excluded from the monthly gatherings and the RM has on occasion held healing meditations for those afflicted with HIV.

More recently, the RM has articulated a strong taboo against incest and sex with minors (see *www.nopedo.com*). This move is partly the result of a recent trend in the French media and anticult literature to label all "*gourous*" (gurus) of "*sectes*" as pedophiles, part of the government's strategy via the Mission Interministérielle de Lutte contre les sectes (Interministerial mission to fight against cults) to *lutter* (fight) new spiritual, therapeutic, and philosophical minorities (see Palmer 2002).

The Raelians' public declaration of this system of values, which in many respects may be more in tune with the modern world than are Catholic ethics, indicates the Raelians' emerging pride and self-consciousness as a viable culture.

Finance

The International Raelian Movement's (IRM) main sources of funds are the income from Raël's books, membership fees, and tithes. Members sell Raël's books on street corners to recoup their investment, having paid for the books themselves. Raelians are encouraged to tithe 11 percent of their net income: 3 percent to their own national movement, 7 percent to the international movement, and 1 percent to Raël. But, by their own admission, less than half the members pay their dues; no pressure is exerted on them if they fail to contribute. The Raelian information pack notes that "members will never be told that they have contributed too little or too much." Raël claimed in an interview that more than 60 percent of Raelians do not tithe.[3]

The annual revenue of the IRM in 1995 was around $1.8 million Canadian (less than $1 million U.S.). The Canadian Raelian revenue was approximately $130,000, or 7 percent of the total. The declared purpose of members' donations is to build the embassy and to fund the translations of Raël's books, as well as to make videos, print flyers, and manufacture medallions. The RM's activities—the rental of halls and local publicity and parties—are supported by the 3 percent national fund. I learned in conversation with a bishop at the November 2000 meeting in Montreal that by 2001 the IRM had a budget of around $1 million a year, and more than $9 million saved toward the building of the embassy.

Missionary Outreach

Since Raël's first mandate is to "spread the message," the Raelians put considerable effort and ingenuity into missionary work. In a July 14, 2000, interview published in *Apocalypse* magazine, Raël describes his followers as the "army of the Elohim on Earth" involved in a "gigantic mission which will see the arrival . . . of our beloved fathers."

Members of the structure are committed to making the message available to those who are "already Raelian but haven't realized it yet," but they are instructed to avoid pressure tactics. While they believe it is their duty to "inform the public," Raël was told by the extraterrestrials that only 4 percent of humanity is sufficiently intelligent to understand the message, so Raelians are not disappointed by the skepticism and derision they often encounter.

Raelian missionaries invent whimsical ways to spread the message. In France there has been a recent lecture series with slides on crop circles; the lectures end with a subtle suggestion that this unexplained phenomenon could be a sign that the Elohim are supporting Raël's mission.

The Raelians' own church-history publication, *20 ans,* by Terrusse and Richard (1994), presents a year-by-year account of the global spread of Raelianism, the high points being the Japan mission in 1980, the Africa mission in 1982, and the Australian mission in 1990. But Quebec is still the headquarters of the movement. The early dynamic leaders are bishops and priests in Quebec, and it is in Quebec that campaigns are launched and creative ideas are tried out.

The first missionary outpost was Quebec, where Raël lectured on November 9, 1976, at Le Plateau to an enthusiastic audience of thirteen hundred, among whom, according to Mme. Morel (first president of the Council of the Wise), "irony and sarcasm were almost nonexistent!" She notes approvingly that abortion is legal in Quebec and one sees enormous placards advertising the clinics, and that prostitutes post their cards in public places, the result being a "spectacular decline in sexual crimes." She marvels that Quebec is three times the size of France but has less than eight million inhabitants, and that its birthrate is declining. "One finds that the people are free and happy," she observes. "That is all" (*20 ans,* 45). Adopting the slogan used by Quebec's pro-choice movement—"Le plaisir oui, la procreation, non!" (Pleasure yes, procreation no)—Raelians were successful in spreading the message through five radio broadcasts, television interviews, all local newspapers, and half a page in *La Presse.*

Sacred Architecture

All "cults," like churches, need a sacred center, a shrine, or a holy ground, notes R. S. Ellwood (1976). Christianity and Judaism have Jerusalem, Islam has Mecca, and the Raelians expect to build the embassy to welcome the Elohim and meanwhile have UFOland. UFOland opened in August 1997 in Valcourt, Quebec, on the Raelian estate, Le Jardin du Prophète, where the summer seminars are held.[4] The building was constructed entirely by Raelian volunteers and is the largest building in North America built from bales of hay and fiberglass. UFOland is a museum of ufological lore that functions both as a fund-raising enterprise to support the eventual building of the embassy and as a shrine to showcase Raelian beliefs and myths. Its director, Michel Beluet, explained to touring visitors in October 2000 that UFOland is "an interpretation center on the UFO phenomenon and particularly the message of Raël. . . . Its purpose is not to recruit but to inform."

The museum's first room displays a model of the UFO that Raël describes in his first book, *Le livre qui dit la vérité,* and the largest replica of DNA structure in the world, as well as a small model of the embassy, a doughnut-shaped white building complete with a vestibule, a conference room, decontamination chambers, a hotel for the extraterrestrials, and even a dining room for the extraterrestrial visitors. The displays in the other six rooms include audiovisual presentations of the Raelian message, UFO sightings, and conspiracy theories regarding military cover-ups. The crop circles in England, the science of robotics, and the human DNA structure are displayed through models and photographs. Room 4, designed to evoke the interior of a pyramid, enshrines the theories of von Däniken by presenting "evidence" that the Elohim visited ancient Egypt and many tribal cultures. Room 5 represents the interior of a cell multiplied 200,000 times. The solar system is displayed in room 6, where a video explains the concept of infinity; photos and text attacking Darwin's theory of evolution and lauding the rapid advances in cloning line the walls.

UFOland was closed to the public in 2001. On the basis of my conversation with its director, my understanding is that the revenues did not justify the cost. Moreover, it was difficult to muster voluntary labor, since Valcourt is almost two hours from Montreal, where most of the Canadian Raelians live.

The Quest for Social Legitimacy

By the early 1980s, the Raelian Movement had blossomed into a full-fledged NRM with its own sacred text, rituals, and community-building activities. Despite its antireligion stance and radical materialist philosophy, the IRM began to resemble a church, for the Raelian philosophy offered the individual a path to moral amelioration, unity with the sacred cosmos, eventual proximity to humanity's revered creators, and a means to overcome death. Raelians began to express pride in their new identity and demand recognition and respect as an authentic religion.

The IRM's first success in gaining legal recognition as an authentic religion came in Quebec, where Raël and thirty Raelians set up a Canadian branch in 1977 and appointed Rejean Proulx (a chartered accountant) as the first national guide of Canada. Canada was the first country after France where the message was "implanted," and the Canadian movement, the first to have a legal structure with a charter, became incorporated in March 1977.

By March 1995, the RM had acquired religious-corporation status in Quebec. This meant the new Raelian Church could apply for tax-exempt status from the federal government. Raël explained in a press interview that although Raelians are atheists, "it's a question of discrimination. 90 percent of our members were Catholic and they paid a dime [a 10 percent tithe] which was tax deductible, and now when they give a donation to the RM they have the right to benefit from that deduction. It is an administrative question."[5]

The Raelian Church's application was refused by the *loi d'impot* (tax department), on the grounds that it did not conform to the tax officials' notion of what a "religion" should be. Although the Raelian bishop handling the case provided ample evidence that Raelians have religious beliefs, rituals, and an organization devoted to worshiping higher beings, it was the higher beings themselves who were disqualified. The tax officials argued that the Elohim were not "real gods," because they were material beings with physical bodies. God or gods must be spiritual immaterial creatures to qualify as divinities. This decision has been appealed. Meanwhile, the Raelians had achieved tax-exempt status in the United States as the Raelian Religion.[6]

Manipulating the Media

The Raelians' strategy for gaining social acceptance and free publicity might be compared to that of the Church of Satan, which rose rapidly to prominence by the early 1970s, as its founder, Anton Szandor LaVey, "seized opportunities for publicity" that relied on his theatrical use of satanic/devil-worshipping imagery to entertain and shock the public (Lewis 2002, 214).

Paradoxically, it is through concocting, then carefully monitoring, a mild level of cultural conflict that the IRM has won a measure of public tolerance and acceptance. Just as LaVey became an American icon, a pop-culture hero who even appeared in the film *Rosemary's Baby,* Raël, with his samurai topknot and white padded suit, has become something of an international celebrity due to his controversial stance on cloning.

Raël's charismatic career can be charted by his periodic press conferences, where he dramatizes his stance on public issues: deforestation, votes for minors, condom machines in Catholic high schools, the pope as a "mass murderer," genetically modified foods, nuclear testing, and so on. After the controversy stirred up by his statements dies down, spin-off articles appear that describe Raël's dress and Raelian fashion, Raël's theme park, and the beliefs and practices of his "UFO cult."

As a new religion, the IRM is mocked and censored for its "deviant" beliefs, which are, of course, no more or less irrational than the religious tenets of mainstream religions. The Raelian PR team tries to get over this hump by inoculating the public against an intolerant reaction. It feeds the media selective doses of entertaining weirdness and mild controversy in order to promote a familiarity with, and tolerance of, Raelian beliefs. In this way, the Raelians are also working to forestall the kind of massive allergic reaction to unconventional religions that is currently sweeping France, China, and eastern Europe.

The Raelians are provocative. They deliberately concoct controversies to attract the attention of the world's media. Their press kit is a veritable pageant of colorful controversies, such as the masturbation conference, the funeral practice of "lifting the frontal bone," anti-Catholic marches with crucifix-burning invitations, and Operation Condom for high schools. In 2003 they staged nudist demonstrations, such as one in which they proclaimed, "Yes to GM Foods!"

In retrospect, these controversies might be viewed as testing grounds in the Raelians' twenty-five-year apprenticeship in riding the media. They have succeeded to a remarkable degree in baiting and reeling in journalists to their press conferences, in shaping the substance of news reports, and in harnessing the power of the international media to indirectly spread the message of their own covert religious agenda.

For Raël's quest for media coverage is no mere narcissistic indulgence. It is simply the most efficient way to "spread the message" given to him by the Elohim, to let every human on earth know the "Truth" about humanity's origins and the existence of "Our Creators."

But the level of controversy is carefully controlled, and the IRM's conflict with society has remained at a low level. Raël responds in a prudent fashion to signs of escalating hostility and hastily backpedals or drops a project if secular authorities react adversely to it.

During the early 1990s, for example, the Raelians organized Planetary Week for the first week in April and planned a global action calculated both to attract media attention and to demonstrate to the public what Raelians believe and stand for. The most outrageous—hence successful—actions, eliciting the most media support, were Operation Condom and the "Oui au Masturbation!" campaign.

Operation Condom was a project launched in 1992 as a well-publicized protest against the Montreal Catholic School Commission (MCSC) decision to veto the proposal to install condom machines in its high schools. A "condom-mobile" financed and staffed by the Raelians toured the provinces of Quebec and Ontario and parked outside Catholic high schools, where they distributed ten thousand condoms to the students during recess, as well as large pink buttons that read "Oui aux Condoms à l'Ecole" (Yes to condoms in school). The driving force and spokesperson for this campaign was the guide Marie Marcelle Godbout, a transsexual and long-term volunteer counselor for women with AIDS. She explained to the press that she was protesting the "ostrich-like stance" of the MCSC and quoted daunting statistics on teenage pregnancies and sexually transmitted disease in Quebec. Another guide claimed that it was a goal of the movement to teach people to live by pleasure for pleasure's sake, and that being handed a condom conveys to teenagers a positive attitude to sex.

Buttons bearing the slogan "Oui à la Masturbation" were handed out at the Montreal Jazz Festival, around the time of the Raelians' July 7, 1993, Masturbation Conference. This appears to have been the brainchild of Daniel Chabot, bishop guide and former national guide of Canada. The conference was called "Yes to Self-Love" and presented three speakers: Betty Dodson, who wrote *Sex for One;* Raël, who wrote *Sensual Meditation;* and Daniel Chabot, author of *La sagesse du plaisir* (The wisdom of pleasure). Betty Dodson, a "sex therapist and specialist in the use of masturbation," is quoted in a conference flyer as making a near-apocalyptic statement about ushering in the millennium through mass masturbation: "My futuristic fantasy for sexual liberation goes like this. It is New Year's Eve 1999. . . . At the stroke of midnight the entire population of the world will be masturbating to orgasm for world peace." One of my friends who attended the conference reported watching Betty Dodson's film about middle-aged ladies masturbating therapeutically in a circle. Raël gave a speech on how self-love links us to the cosmos, and Daniel Chabot spoke of the psychological benefits of masturbation, which are in turn linked to the higher process of spiritual self-fulfillment. For Raelians, sexual pleasure results in the growth of new brain cells, creates new links between neurons, and thus leads to increased intelligence and the eventual re-creation of the individual by the Elohim. Enjoyment of sex, for Raelians, relates to the belief that the Elohim created humans with the capacity to experience pleasure and told Raël that they wanted their creations to enjoy their bodies free from guilt.

I remember feeling puzzled by the Masturbation Conference at the time and asked a guide how promoting masturbation could possibly further Raelian religious aims. He replied, "But Jesus himself recommends masturbation in the Bible."

"Where?" I asked. "Show me the passage."

"When Jesus says, 'Love thy neighbor as thyself.'"

Daniel Chabot soon became a controversial figure in the media. The Corporation professionnelle des psychologues du Quebec held a deontology inquiry during the first week of July to determine whether Chabot was using his professional status to attract converts to his sect, and whether his speech on the therapeutic benefits of masturbation and his involvement in an "*erotique-esoterique*" religion conflicted with the scientific principles generally recognized by members of his profession.[7] Chabot launched a legal suit against the corporation and sent a letter to all psychologists in Quebec protesting the statement the director made to the media: that Chabot was "contaminated" by his religious beliefs. Chabot lost his case but proceeded to charge the corporation with violation of his human rights.[8]

In a strategy to promote their idiosyncratic creationist beliefs, the Raelians organized a public debate on January 23, 1996, between Raël and Cyrille Barette, professor of biology at the University of Laval in Quebec City. The event, which attracted an audience of seven hundred, surprisingly became quite heated and evoked strong outrage, expressed in a flurry of news articles that raised the question of who invited Raël to the University of Laval in the first place, and why the students' association had spent money on him.[9]

Anticult Attacks and Self-defense Strategies

Like most successful NRMs that are radical but conspicuously successful, the Raelian Movement has become a target of anticult organizations in the Francophone countries where the Raelian presence is strong—France, Switzerland, Belgium, and Quebec. Anticult propaganda issuing from the Union of Associations for the Defense of the Family and Individual (ADFI) and Info-Sect (in English, Info-Cult) has had an impact on media coverage of the Raelians. Since journalists rely heavily on the anticult movement (ACM) as their source of information and opinion regarding unconventional religions, many stories on Raël betray an anticult bias. Some journalists have even gone out of their way to "expose" the Raelians. One Quebec journalist signed up for the 1991 summer camp and sneaked around the tents at night tape recording couples making love, sounds that were broadcast on a radio show that portrayed the Sensual Meditation Camp as an unbridled sex orgy where brainwashing was perpetrated and sexual perversions encouraged. Some parents reacted with alarm. One nineteen-year-old complained that her mother, on finding her listening to the sensual meditation tape, insisted that she see a psychiatrist.

Some journalists portray Raël as a sexual libertine who enjoys a luxurious life at the expense of his followers' pocketbooks. The IRM has adopted a litigious strategy of aggressive self-defense toward the more stigmatizing news reports written by irresponsible journalists. As a Raelian lawyer explained to me: "We are on our guard when we see journalists. . . . We sue them because we demand respect. . . . We are not con artists or nutcases."

The Raelians sued Paul Toutant, a Radio Canada journalist, for suggesting in his December 12, 1979, report that Raël was motivated by greed, and that donations toward the embassy were lining his pockets. Referring derisively to Raël's prediction of the aliens' arrival, Toutant hoped Raël would have enough time to "*dépenser son fric*" (spend his dough). When the case was tried in the superior court, Judge Jean Provost stated that although Toutant's report that Raelians contributed over a million dollars a year was accurate, that did not give him the right to conclude that Raël pocketed the proceeds.

Another libel suit was slapped on a publishing company, Spiromedia (associated with a Catholic countercult group), for publishing articles with titles like "Une escroquerie financière," "Une imagination folle alimentée par l'occasion," and "Un instinct de pouvoir et une sexualite debridée" (A financial swindle, A lunatic imagination fueled by opportunity, A feeling of power and uncontrolled sexuality).

Several fascinating lawsuits have been launched *against* the RM. A well-publicized ten-year legal dispute concerns the last will and testament of Madeleine Belzile, a former nun, who became a Raelian at the age of fifty-one and had her first sexual experience at the Sensual Meditation Camp. She died in 1985, leaving her estate (a $40,000 house, a $1,500 car, and assets of $50,000) to the Canadian RM. Her brother, Alphonse Belzile, a struggling farmer with fourteen children, claimed she had been the dupe of brainwashing techniques and the seductive attentions of a guide, Rejean Proulx, who was named six months before her death as the executor of her will. (As the president of the RM, he was the executor for all wills.) To the embarrassment of Proulx, a rough draft of an unsent love letter was discovered among the late nun's possessions, read out in court, and published in Quebec's *La Presse*. Proulx denies there was ever any sexual relationship between them, merely the usual hugging and kissing customary between Raelians, but Alphonse Belzile argues that Proulx's sexually seductive attentions were "des maneuvres frauduleuses pour lui soutirer ce testament" (fraudulent maneuvers to extract the will from her).[10]

The controversy of longest standing in the Raelian religion is the Dechavanne affair. Raël's decision to make Quebec his permanent home was mainly the result of an incidence of ambush journalism perpetrated by a television host, Christophe Dechavanne. This show branded Raël in the eyes of French viewers as a depraved cult leader who breaks up families, encourages single mothers to become nymphomaniacs, and endorses pedophilia.

In October 1992, Raël was invited to appear on *Ciel mon Mardi,* the television talk show hosted by journalist Dechavanne.[11] Raël was part of a panel, along with a priest and a psychologist who were egregiously critical and judgmental toward Raël's views on sexuality and child rearing. An embittered apostate, Jean Parraga, was unexpectedly introduced on the show, and he launched into a diatribe of excoriating accusations. He claimed that Raël was holding Parraga's wife and children prisoner in the sensual meditation campsite, that Raël had engineered his family's breakup, brainwashed his wife, and encouraged her infidelity. He brought up the issue of a child's tragic accidental death at the camp the previous year—the child was riding a bicycle and fell into the empty swimming pool that his father was working on. Parraga suggested that this was a case of murder or ritual sacrifice and implied that children were routinely sacrificed and sexually molested during the sensual meditation seminars.

It was clear whose side Dechavanne was on. Parraga, elegantly dressed, presented himself as a concerned father and heartbroken husband. What went unmentioned was his conviction as a smuggler and dealer in drugs and stolen cars. Later he spent several years in jail for *proxenetisme* (pimping, or running a prostitution ring).

The history of this apostate is an extraordinary tale.[12] Jean Parraga is a French citizen who owned a car repair shop and during the mid 1980s smuggled cars and drugs between France and Algiers to sell on the black market. Soon after he and his wife, Sylvie, became Raelians, he was arrested at the Algiers border for attempting to smuggle into the country a stolen Mercedes whose doors were stuffed with hashish. When Parraga complained how very unpleasant the conditions were in the Algiers jail, the Raelians raised funds in their community for bail and hired a lawyer to have him transferred to a more comfortable prison in France.

When Parraga was released, he was enraged to find that his wife and two children had lived with a Raelian guide for two years. He assaulted the guide during a Raelian conference but was restrained. In August 1992, he claimed that his wife and children were being held prisoners at the campsite of the Stages of Awakening seminar in the south of France. He left death threats on their answering machine, alerting the guards, who called the police. When Parraga attempted to enter the camp gate, carrying a gun to assassinate Raël, his way was barred by the camp security force and the local police. The Raelians were outraged that this man was presented as a respectable citizen and concerned father on the television show, and that his drug dealing, jail record, and murder threats were not mentioned.

Encouraged by the public's response to his TV appearance, Jean Parraga then formed an association called Action Plus to fight the Raelians, whom he accused of stealing his money, his wife, and his two daughters. Association members included Dechavanne's assistant, two lawyers, a journalist, and a police inspector. To fund his new project, Parraga set up a prostitution ring with three women, Katia, Maeva, and Lola, who offered "sexual relaxing massage." Parraga was arrested and charged with "*proxenetisme aggravé*" (running a prostitution ring across national boundaries), since he and the women were spending winters in Albertville, France, and the summer in Barcelona to take advantage of the market opportunities afforded by the Olympics. One woman, Cecile, left Barcelona, lodged a complaint against Parraga of brutal beatings and harsh treatment, and contacted the Raelians. In the autumn of 1992, in spite of four condemnations for contraband of cars and petty trafficking in hashish, Parraga was released from prison and launched an unsuccessful lawsuit for custody of his daughters, who continued to reside with their mother, a successful singer, in the south of France.

As a result of this defamatory broadcast, several Raelians lost their jobs or their children in custody battles, and Raël fled the country. Raelians were urged in a newsletter to write letters of protest to the television station, which was inundated with hundreds of letters from all over the world for several years. Dechavanne retaliated by suing Raël for "incitement to violence." The judge appointed to the case decided to order Raël to appear in court on these charges. Raël stayed in Canada but agreed to ask RM members to stop sending letters. He demanded a public apology in return, and the two parties agreed to drop the feud.

April 25, 1996, marked the end of the conflict. A missive, "Letter from Raël," sent on that date to all members of the RM with the heading "Freedom of Expression No Longer Exists in France," informed them that Dechavanne had withdrawn his complaint against Raël, and that the judge had committed himself to dismissing the charge: "I am thus asking all Raelians to stop writing to Christophe Dechavanne. After four years of continuous but futile protest to get a right to reply, which would have allowed us to reestablish our dignity and our respectability, it is time to turn over a new leaf! French justice refused us this right to reply. Instead . . . we will write to . . . international legal institutions to which our letters have a better chance of showing some effect to retrieve our dignity, which has been shaken by the French legal system."

The Dechavanne show precipitated a series of articles in the French media alleging that Raël "preached pedophilia." In "La curieuse leçon des petits hommes verts" (The strange lesson of the little green men), which appeared in the Montreal newspaper *Le Devoir* (July 12, 1993), journalist Stephane Baillargeon wrote that the Raelians "defended the opinions of pedophiles" and that "certain former Raelians have accused the guru of too much fondness for little girls" and recommended that the Quebec government set up an investigation into the RM along the lines of the Guyard Report of the inquest on *les sectes* in France.

When Raël wrote a letter of protest clarifying his position, *Le Devoir* refused to publish it. Raël then launched a legal action for defamation and publishing "propos mensonger, malicieux, injurieux et calamnieux" (false, malicious, injurious, and calumnious statements).[13] After some negotiation, on September 7, 1994, the newspaper published Raël's letter, which states that the rumor is an ignominious defamation, and that Raël and the RM "have always condemned pedophilia and promoted respect for laws that justly forbid the practices that are always the fault of unbalanced individuals."

Le Devoir then published Baillargeon's response to Raël's letter, in which Baillargeon pointed to a potentially controversial passage in Raël's 1977 book *La geniocratie* (Geniocracy) that could be construed as indicating a tolerance for pedophilia: "Adolescents must have the right to a sexual, political, and religious life" (115).[14] One priest guide explained this passage to mean that Raelians respected the eighteen-year age limit, but if teenagers wished to have sex among themselves, that was their right.

Some Raelian publications convey stern intolerance toward pedophiles. Daniel Chabot, a Raelian bishop, wrote: "When we speak of sexual freedom, we must respect the laws of the country in which we find ourselves. Here, in Canada, it is forbidden to have sex with minors. And the Canadian Raelian Movement respects that law. Therefore all members who violate that law will be susceptible to prosecution before the law. Is this not clear enough?"[15]

Another reassuring document is the contract all Raelians sign before starting the Stages of Awakening, which includes six rules; two of these are "not to have sexual activities with or in the presence of minors" and "to respect the provincial and federal laws."[16]

Today, in spite of only one Raelian out of sixty-five thousand members being convicted not of rape, but of inappropriate touching of a minor, the IRM in French-speaking Europe (and to a lesser extent in Quebec) has, through the "rumor effect," gathered infamy as a dangerous sect that preaches and promotes sex with minors.[17] The unsupported and stigmatizing allegations of pedophilia have had a devastating impact on the lives of many Raelians. Several have lost their children in custody battles. Two Raelian bishops who offer sales personnel training workshops in France had their contracts canceled when the companies found out they were Raelians.

Several Raelians in France have been fired from their jobs because of their association with a stigmatized "sect," including several distinguished professionals. Francois Pithon, an ophthalmologist at a hospital in Roanne, France, went on a three-week public fast in September 1992 to protest being fired and stripped of his title as *chef de service*. He was reinstated after attracting considerable publicity, with the help of fellow Raelians (*20 ans,* 160).

Raelian bishop Brigitte Boisselier, famous as Clonaid's CEO, was the director of a research project for a French chemical company, Air Liquide, until 1997, when she was fired after she "came out" in the media as a Raelian in support of human cloning. She also lost custody of her youngest child when her ex-husband sued successfully for sole custody and restricted visitation due to her involvement in a "dangerous sect."[18]

FIREPHIM: Fighting "Religious Racism"

In 1992, Raël and his guides responded to the mounting anticult pressure in France by pursuing a self-defensive course that includes lawsuits and public demonstrations and that culminated in the founding of FIREPHIM (Federation Internationale des Religions et Philosophies Minoritaires), an organization dedicated to protecting the rights of religious, philosophical, sexual, and racial minorities.

At the Raelians' November 1992 meeting in Montreal, Raël requested donations for the widow of Jean Miguères, a fellow French contactee and the author of esoteric books on extraterrestrials and near-death experiences. Miguères had been brutally gunned down in the street by his father-in-law, who had been in communication with the French anticult organization ADFI. Raël insisted that although he disagreed with Miguères's ideas, he nevertheless had the right to be heard—and to receive protection for his freedom of speech from France's Charter of Rights. Raël read out a long letter he had written to Miguères's widow and urged his followers to sign a form protesting the French government's granting of financial support to anticult agencies, who promote hatred toward religious minorities. Raël then published a book in 1992 denouncing the French government's support of anticult organizations, *Le racisme religieux financé par le gouvernement socialiste* (Religious racism financed by the socialist government), and simultaneously founded FIREPHIM.

When journalist Jean-Luc Mongrain attacked the Raelians on his program on Tele-Metropole in Montreal in early December 1993, FIREPHIM sent seventy Raelians to the station to stage a protest demonstration.

Raelians dramatize their moral imperative to "respect differences" by marching every year in the international gay parades. Many Swiss Raelians have served prison sentences for refusing to submit to military service, since Switzerland does not recognize conscientious-objector status. Raelians have organized demonstrations against nuclear testing and are encouraged by FIREPHIM to write letters of protest against various violations of human rights.

On March 29, 1992, FIREPHIM staged a weeklong demonstration against the Montreal anticult center Info-Sect, carrying placards proclaiming "No To [anticult] Racism!" and "Protect the Rights of Religious Minorities!" They stood outside the office of Info-Sect, referring to it in their interviews with journalists as "an anti-religious criminal organization."[19] They did this in response to Info-Sect's exposé, published in *Le Devoir* on December 4, 1992, of Raël's "fascist" ideas on government, which warned the public against Raël's *Geniocracy* as "a serious threat to democracy."

In France, the Raelians have sued more than a hundred newspapers that have called Raël a "racist," based on France's Centre de documentation, d'éducation et d'action Contre les Manipulations Mentales (Center of documentation, education, and action against mind control [CCMM]) report that quoted an isolated passage from one of Raël's books. In one paragraph, Raël undergoes a temptation offered by an evil extraterrestrial named Satan: to rule the world by subjugating blacks and Jews. But in the next paragraph, it becomes clear that Raël *rejects* this dubious offer and proceeds to preach tolerance, acceptance of diversity, and free choice (1979, 88–95). One could compare this anticult strategy to a deliberate misquoting of a Bible passage concerning the temptation of Christ to show that Jesus was a "Satanist."

None of these lawsuits were successful, however, because the journalists testified that they were quoting directly from the CCMM's official account of the "Raelian *secte*."

Besides defending their religion through lawsuits and letters to the press, the Raelians have fought discrimination through public demonstrations and street theater. In addition to picketing outside Montreal's Info-Sect, they marched in the nude in Switzerland and staged a demonstration in Paris on December 10, 1998, the fiftieth anniversary of France's Declaration of Human Rights. Eighty Raelians met at the Place du Tricadero, carrying banners that demanded rights for religious minorities and wearing yellow star stickers on their clothes inscribed, "Membre d'une secte!" They were herded into a parking lot by gendarmes and held there all day. Nearby restaurants were told to refuse service and bathroom facilities to Raelians.

Raelians have also protested their ostracism from public space in France. A guide I interviewed in Paris informed me that over the past three years, 70 percent of the RM's contracts for rented spaces to hold their meetings had been canceled at the last minute, after a phone call from ADFI warning the hotel of the "*secte.*" When in 2000 the mayor of Castre ordered their meeting canceled, Raelians who turned up for the meeting found a police barrier and a TV crew on hand to film the "violence." They pulled out yellow stars, pinned them to their arms, and faced the television cameras (*Apocalypse,* first trimester, 2000, 41).

Rodney Stark's Eight Conditions for Success

The survival and continued expansion of the IRM appears likely, according to the eight conditions for the success of an NRM proposed by Rodney Stark (1987). He bases his criteria on his study of the Mormons, a small persecuted minority in the nineteenth century that evolved into a large international congregation, still denounced as heretical but firmly established as a respectable minority church in most countries. The RM satisfies seven of Stark's conditions—and Stark claims that if an NRM exhibits five or more, its success is probably assured.

Stark's theory contains an interesting statement about the implications of a new religion's conflict with its host society. Stark notes that a high level of tension between an NRM and society invites repression and stigmatization, whereas a low level of tension may result in membership attrition or in the erosion of religious values and discipline through "creeping secularization." Thus, a new religion exhibiting medium tension fulfills one of Stark's conditions for success. The IRM deliberately maintains a medium level of tension with its surrounding host society.

Certain Raelian actions appear designed to shock the public, but others are designed to appease. A moderate level of controversy and conflict vis-à-vis society unites members in a self-defensive posture and highlights their identity as a separate society. Raël's guides are adept at planning provocative demonstrations that will titillate the media and capture the attention of the public. But the IRM is flexible and accommodating. Too much tension or any sign of escalating conflict is a signal for Raël and his guides to backpedal, to reduce tension. The history of the IRM's carefully cultivated controversial stances and its masterful manipulation of the media illustrates this point eloquently.

Stark's seven remaining conditions for the success of a new religion include cultural continuity, effective mobilization, normal age/sex distribution, a favorable religious ecology, close network ties, resistance to secularization, and the socialization of children. The Raelians do not socialize their children into Raelianism and maintain a low birthrate, and since theirs is a young religion that attracts youth, it does not yet have a "normal" age/sex distribution. However, six of Stark's eight conditions are fulfilled.

The Raelians have cultural continuity. Raelian beliefs refer directly to the Bible and retain the outward shape of the Judeo-Christian tradition, which is perhaps why so many disaffected Catholics and ex-priests are drawn to the movement. But the message also resonates with secular ideologies—with atheism, secular humanism, the sexual revolution, feminism, gay pride, and antinuclear peace movements. I would argue that a large part of the Raelian success story is related to its cultural continuity with both the Christian and the conflicting scientific worldviews, which the Raelian message attempts to reconcile.

As for a favorable ecology, the Raelians tend to flourish in countries that uphold principles of religious freedom and tolerance, as in Canada, Japan, and the United States. Countries inhospitable to religious pluralism, like China, Iran, Greece, and, more recently, France (since the Solar Temple disaster and the ensuing 1996 Guyard Report), respond to Raelian activity with heavy doses of persecution. Also, as Stark notes, the condition of primary competitors—the conventional faiths—is an important variable. Countries where the forces of secularization and industrial development have rapidly and recently eroded traditional religious, moral, and family values offer hospitable soil for "implanting" the message.

The rapid growth of the RM in Quebec in the wake of the decline of the province's ultramontane Catholic hegemony is an example of this pattern. The Catholic Church reigned supreme in Quebec until 1960. But when the bishops returned from the 1960 Second Vatican Council, where they had advocated reform, they found their flocks diminishing rapidly. Dramatic changes in Quebec culture ensued. Between 1961 and 1971, active membership in church-sponsored social movements like Catholic Action dropped from thirty thousand to three thousand. In the same decade, the number of priests in the Montreal region declined by 50 percent, and women's religious orders declined by 22 percent (Bibby 1987). Some of these former priests and nuns received the Raelian message and were instantly promoted to the rank of priest or bishop, due to their Bible training and teaching skills.

A delegation of Quebec bishops reported to Rome in 1974 that Quebec society had become, according to Bibby (1987), segmented, pluralistic, and secular, among other degeneracies. In view of this precipitous decline of the Catholic Church, the appeal of Raël's godlike aliens with their anti-Catholic, pro-science, body-conscious, and politically correct philosophy might be better understood.

It is not unusual for the prophet-founders of new religions to be surrounded by a congregation of tens of thousands, even hundreds of thousands of adoring followers—and yet find themselves demonized in the media and ostracized, even persecuted, by the larger society. L. Ron Hubbard, Reverend Sun Myung Moon, Moses David, and Bhagwan Shree Rajneesh are examples of this paradox. The media is responsible for the public's awareness of esoteric religions and their leaders, and is the public's almost exclusive source of information regarding them. The media is generally unsympathetic toward "cults" and churns out stigmatizing news reports and hostile deviance labeling, using words like "cult," "sect," "brainwashed," and "mind control"—terms that indicate the journalists' heavy reliance on the anticult movement.

Raël has managed to overcome this hurdle by bearding the lion in its den, so to speak. Instead of waiting until journalists noticed his burgeoning new religion and wrote the usual snide "cult" stories on its wealthy leader, its gullible brainwashed zombies, rumors of sexual and financial abuse, and its kinky, kooky beliefs, Raël invites them to press conferences that highlight an issue or a controversial stance. The news stories that emerge will then focus on the "weird cult" that is saying or doing something interesting and relevant, not just on the "cult" contemplating its own navel.

Chapter Four

Mutating the Millennium

The Raelian religion is intensely millenarian. Emerging from the Abrahamic tradition, this new religion takes up the strands of Jewish messianism and prophecy and reinterprets St. John's Revelations. But it also embraces our contemporary faith in scientific progress. Raël preaches a kind of technological utopianism that promises to provide ultimate meaning for humanity, and even godhood for worthy humans.

Raël's prophecies are understood as alien messages. The extraterrestrials have given humanity a deadline to prepare for—their landing in 2035. If we spread the message, unite the world in peace, and build an embassy to greet them, they will return on or before that date and award us the gift of their advanced technology. If we fail, they will turn their backs on us in disgust as we blow ourselves to smithereens in a final holocaust.

The Raelians' two overriding aims are explicitly millenarian: to spread the message and to build the embassy. Many of their subsidiary projects, such as installing the world government of the geniocracy, evangelizing the Jews, closing down the Vatican and dethroning the pope, and opening UFOland to the public, are oblique strategies to prepare the nations for the mass landing of starships that will bring the Elohim and the thirty-nine prophets to Jerusalem.

Raël announced a new chronology in 1977: Henceforth a new era had commenced with the day after the bombing of Hiroshima on August 6, 1945. Thus, 1977 became "year 31." This revision of the Western calendar highlights the millenarian aims of the group and reminds members of the emergency situation of living in the Age of Apocalypse.

The finer points of Raël's millenarian mission are addressed in this chapter. How do Raelians understand their prophet's millenarian goals and seek to fulfill them? How does Raël manage to stir up millenarian excitement and drum up commitment to the ongoing preparations for the aliens' advent? And how might he deal with the situation if the Elohim fail to show up on schedule?

Before we can answer these questions, we must explore Raelian theology.

The Theology

Two ideas stand out in Raël's theology. The first is that humans are very close to the "gods"; both are mere mortals and of the same species. The second idea is that salvation can be achieved only through free will and individual choice.

Raël's first book, *Le livre qui dit la vérité,* unveils the secret of humanity's etiology as an "eternal regress of artifice."[1] Not only we, but also our creators, were concocted in labs from DNA matter by other superior scientists from an alien planet, who in turn . . . , and so on. This belief implies a godlike potential latent in earth's human race—if humankind can come of age and resist the overwhelming temptation to use science as a destructive weapon and obliterate all planetary life in a nuclear holocaust, then our creators will return and reward us with their advanced scientific knowledge. Then we, in turn, will travel to distant planets and set up laboratories for genetic experiments to create beautiful life forms, and eventually new men and women "in our own image." If the "gods" are human, then we humans can become gods.

Raël's parables convey a radical faith in free will and the individual's power to choose. The Raelian version of the fall of humankind is not unlike the Mormon one: The struggle between good and evil turns into a debate concerning humankind's ability to make rational, independent choices. For Mormons, this means moral education; for Raelians, it means learning to handle scientific knowledge in a responsible fashion.

According to the Elohim's explanation of Genesis, "God" is a team of godlike extraterrestrial scientists who land on earth to create life. Their director happens to be called Yahweh, who is the president of the Council of the Eternals, governing their home planet (Raël 1987, 89). The devil splits into two warring parties: Satan and Lucifer. Satan heads a political party that is opposed to creating humans, regarding them as a potential threat and rival to their creators. Lucifer, the "Light bearer," was the head of the team on earth who created the first "Adams and Eves" in a laboratory. Since he loved his creations like his own children, Lucifer decided to teach them science and informed them that their creators were not "gods" but men like themselves (88–89).

For transgressing the rules, Lucifer's team was punished by being stranded on earth, and their spaceship was removed. They then commenced to breed with the daughters of men. Satan at that point amassed proof of humankind's aggressive tendencies and convinced Yahweh to destroy the humans on earth with a nuclear holocaust, which caused the biblical great flood. Lucifer and his team managed to save some specimens of humans and animals by storing them in a spaceship ("Noah's Ark"), which orbited earth until the radioactive atmosphere subsided.

At this juncture, the Elohim learned that their own origins were artificial (i.e., they were made by humans), so they resolved never again to destroy humanity (Raël 1987, 90) and decided to help Lucifer reimplant the life forms preserved in the "ark." "Yahweh understood . . . that if men are violent they will self-destroy when they discover energies enabling them to enter an interplanetary level of civilization" (Raël 90).

A recapitulation of this mythic struggle takes place in Raël's own life, according to his fourth book, *Let's Welcome Our Fathers from Space* (1987a, 96–106). This contains a new revelation concerning what transpired during Raël's visit to the planet of the Elohim in 1975. Raël tells us how he was caught up in a political struggle between two parties. One was led by "Yahweh," who sees humans as essentially good and capable of overcoming their tendency to self-destruct with nuclear weapons, and the other was led by Satan, who views the human race as inherently evil and bent on self-destruction. Satan tried to enlist Raël's aid in "accelerating the final cataclysm which will purge the universe of beings who are only the result of an unsuccessful experiment." In exchange, his party would make Raël "very powerful and rich," depositing ten billion francs in a Swiss bank account (96–97). But Raël in return must preach racism and stimulate a global nuclear holocaust, from which he would be rescued by a UFO and later would return to earth, where he would become a world dictator. Raël sanctimoniously declined this offer, opted for free will and the power of the individual to choose, and joined the party led by Yahweh. Yahweh's message for the human race, via Raël, is: "It's your move!" When Raël returned to earth, his message contained a warning and the promise of a reward: "Our inheritance is ready, let us hope that the child will not die at birth" (98).

THE ACTIONS

Before the Elohim can return to earth, the Raelians must realize two goals. They must spread the message and build the embassy. But Raël happens to be a highly creative and energetic institution builder. As his movement has matured and developed, so the means of reaching this double-pronged goal has expanded. Preparations for the arrival of the Elohim are now sevenfold.

Raelians are engaged in missionary work to "spread the message"; they raise funds; they check out sites for the embassy; they try to educate Jews concerning the presence of the Messiah; they lobby to establish a world government and a peacekeeping army based on the rule of geniuses; they strive to make the world a more peaceful, tolerant place through demonstrations and social activism; and they work to depose the pope and restore the Vatican land to the Italian people. More recently, Raël has launched two projects that have a millenarian purpose. Since 1998, a cadre of beautiful girls has been in training to serve as hostesses and companions to the aliens and, in 2002, the Raelian-inspired Clonaid company claimed to have produced the world's first human clone.

Spreading the Message

Raelians are constantly engaged in missionary work, but in a low-key, informal manner. They wear their swastika medallion in the workplace and hand out *Le livre* to interested colleagues, lovers, family, and friends and invite them to the meetings. The guides' missionary efforts are more formal: They hold public lectures on controversial topics like evolution, cloning, and crop circles. Then they invite discussion and obliquely inform their audiences of the message, presenting it as a personal belief rather than as a compelling dogma. Raelian missionaries tend to be casual and not insistent, for they are instructed by Raël to avoid pressure tactics. Members who attempt to force their missionary ideas (or unwelcome sexual attentions) on others are excommunicated from the movement for seven years (the time it takes to replace all the body's cells).

Building the Embassy

As the first step toward building the embassy, Raël announced, the nation of Israel must grant the Raelian Movement land for the purpose of this construction.

The cooperation of the Jews in the Raelians' millenarian activity was considered essential, because the ancient Israelites had a special covenant with our creators. According to Raël's racial theory, the Jews are descendants of the extraterrestrials who mated with the "daughters of men" to produce the "giants of old"—hence Jews are more intelligent (as indicated by all the Jewish winners of the Nobel Prize) than the other races, who were merely concocted in test tubes.

Once it became apparent that the swastika symbol on the Raelian medallion was deterring Jews from joining or cooperating with the Raelian Movement, Raël broadcast a new revelation. The swastika would henceforth be discarded and replaced with a daisylike symbol representing the "cycle of infinity in time."[2]

In 1996 the Raelians established a shrine or sacred center, UFOland, a UFO Disneyland whose purpose was to raise money that would go toward the eventual building of the embassy. This seemed to imply a postponement of the advent of the Elohim, but in 1998 another event occurred that promised to hasten their arrival. Raël announced a new revelation at the December 13, 1998, celebration of the Raelian church in Quebec City: "The Elohim have asked Raël not to limit his choice to Israel and the surrounding countries for the site of the construction of the Embassy. The time has come to address all nations. The country that will accept the Embassy on its territory will be the planetary center of spirituality and science for the next millennium."[3]

The Raelians understood this event as signaling the imminence of the Elohim's arrival, for all those I spoke to at the next Raelian meeting felt that things were happening faster than anticipated, and all were ecstatic at the idea of participating in this historic event. However, the Jews still had first choice: "The time is near, and the time allotted to Israel to accept the Embassy for the Elohim is almost over. Israel will have to make a decision that will commit its future dramatically, and the time is near."[4]

Transmissions and Cloning

The Raelians' baptism, the transmission of the cellular plan, has always promised (while not actually guaranteeing) a kind of physical immortality that was called "regeneration" or "re-creation" in the early days of the movement. This process is now understood to mean human cloning. In the November 2001 meeting, shortly after the publication of his book *Oui au clonage humain* (Yes to human cloning) (2001a), Raël promised everyone in the room under the age of fifty-six (his own age at the time) that, thanks to cloning procedures, they could all have the opportunity to live forever. This implied that we humans could take care of our own immortality needs without relying on extraterrestrial goodwill and scientific assistance. In the IRM, cloning holds a millenarian significance. As Raël explained on this occasion: "Creating life in a laboratory and traveling into space are important facts which support the concept that life was created by the Elohim."

Since the extraterrestrials demanded a sample of the individual's bone for their cloning process, the funeral ritual called the "lifting of the frontal bone" was instituted to facilitate a possible re-creation of the body after death for Raelians in good standing (see chapter 3).

My students were told by Raelian guest speakers in the late 1980s and early 1990s that the frontal bones (boxed and packed in ice) were residing in a bank vault in Geneva, Switzerland, awaiting eventual collection by a UFO. My initial understanding was that these relics were in storage for the Elohim, who would eventually need them for their regeneration procedures.

This notion was challenged by a Raelian bishop whom I interviewed in November 2000. He insisted that these boxes of bone had *always* been intended for the use of *human* scientists, once the cloning technique was worked out. He explained that the Elohim, with their advanced technology, did not actually need a piece of bone, but that the lifting of the frontal bone represented a symbolic pledge or hope for Raelians—that they would indeed be worthy of regeneration. I assumed I'd got the story wrong, but on returning home, I rooted out an old notebook from 1988 and turned to my notes on the guide Michel Beluet's guest lecture to my class at Dawson College. I found that, in response to a student's question, he stated that the boxes would be collected eventually by the Elohim. One explanation for this slight recasting or reinterpretation of prophecy (if, indeed, that is what it is) is that the Raelian Movement is undergoing the familiar process of secularization. Or it could mean a recasting of prophecy. Since Raelians regard the recent scientific breakthrough in cloning technology as a confirmation of prophecy and a validation of their creation story, recasting the purpose of the lifting of the frontal bone would emphasize this new triumph. Certainly, if it is to be human scientists who will effect the resurrection of the dead, the need for the Elohim's physical manifestation is not so pressing.

Human Rights Activism and FIREPHIM

The Elohim's concern over the well-being and sustainability of our planet has galvanized Raelians into activism, as we have seen, from marching against nuclear testing and writing letters of protest against various violations of human rights to handing out free condoms to Quebec high school students and protesting deforestation by boycotting newsprint and relying exclusively on electronic media. All these activities are part of a master plan to raise the awareness of humanity so that it will choose life over nuclear self-destruction.

Geniocracy and the Raelians' Political Aspirations

In 1977, Raël published *La geniocratie,* which describes the system of government he observed while touring the planet of the Elohim: a meritocracy and oligarchy of scientific geniuses and creative artists chosen on the basis of intelligence-test results to rule the planet. The utopian dream of the Raelian religion in the 1970s was to establish a "geniocracy," a perfect society based on the rule of geniuses.

This was more than a utopian fantasy; when Raël returned to earth, it became an urgent political movement. The millenarian purpose was to prepare the earth for the return of the extraterrestrials: "You will also participate in the creation of a worldwide political party advocating humanitarianism and geniocracy, as they are described in the first message of the Elohim, and you will support its candidates. Only via geniocracy can humanity move forward into the golden age. . . . There is no scientific or technical problem insurmountable for human genius as long as human genius is in command." If the Raelians could set up a world government of geniuses, then the danger of a nuclear holocaust would be averted: "The faster you place geniocracy in power the faster you will suppress the risk of cataclysm," for "a being with a deficient brain can threaten world-wide peace" (Raël 1977b, 223).

In 1978, the Raelians held a press conference to announce their intention of creating a new political party, or "le mouvement pour la Geniocratie Mondiale" (the movement for worldwide geniocracy). They presented three candidates for the local French legislature, and in March 1978 they managed to vote a Raelian, Marcel Terrusse, onto the city council in the town of Sarlat.

While Raël was away in December 1977, police searched his house and seized his files in front of his wife and two children. Some of the top guides were also targeted. Police broke into and searched Jean Thierry's apartment in Paris, and Jean Gary's apartment met a similar fate a week later. A number of guides were taken to police stations and held for questioning. It appears that the combination of a swastika symbol (which by error was printed backward on one of their posters) and a "fascist" political platform (as well as the usual concern regarding "*les sectes*") fueled the strong police control measures.

Raël's reaction to society's hostile reaction to his political aspirations was both rational and prudent. Raël ordered his followers to abandon the pursuit of geniocracy, explaining that "we must chose between spreading the message and the geniocracy. We are not ready to fight on two fronts. . . . [At any rate] thus far we lack a tool to measure the intelligence of an individual" (see *20 ans,* 56).

While the geniocracy was no longer a project that could be realized in the "real world," it had an enduring influence on the Raelian Movement itself, whose internal organizational structure is modeled on the two-class system that Raël said he observed during his alleged visit to the Elohim's planet. Raël describes a society comprised of 700 upper-class Elohim living on the Planet of the Immortals, and 8,400 terrians on a lower-class planet. These Elohim are periodically recloned immortals who cannot reproduce but "unite themselves freely as they wish [without] any form of jealousy" (Raël 1978, 243). On the lower-class planet, people are limited to two children per couple and must go before a review board to be judged for cloning privileges.

The Raelian organization is a mirror of this "sacred canopy," for it is also two-tiered, and the guides, like the immortals, tend to renounce marriage and children, whereas the rank-and-file Raelians live more conventional family lives, like the terrians.

Years after the geniocracy project was abandoned, Raël still, on occasion, made efforts to promote the aliens' political agenda for our planet. He has a mandate to establish a world government and peacekeeping force to defuse war and preserve peace between the nations, and ultimately to dissolve all national boundaries and institute a world currency. But as the prophet-founder of a small religious group branded a "cult" in North America and a "*secte*" in France, Raël encounters discouraging obstacles when he attempts to make his voice heard in the international political arena.

Raël therefore confronts a tension—a disjunction between what the extraterrestrials on their planet expect of him and how secular authorities on our planet respond to him.

To resolve this tension, his strategy has been to resort to a kind of symbolic politics. Periodically, the Raelians organize a ritual reenactment of a historical event in the public realm to dramatize their cause. Raël replicates a treaty signing or summit meeting within his own congregation. These events are staged in or near real historical sites or power sites, government offices, sacred shrines like Mount Fuji, Geneva's Palace of the United Nations, or Vatican City.

On April 7, 1985, about five hundred Raelians assembled in front of the UN Palace in Geneva. Raël's request for an audience with one of the UN leaders had just been turned down. So Raël spoke to his followers: "I came here to speak of Peace, Brotherhood and Love. But for them, for these hypocritical bureaucrats, to want to build a happy world for its inhabitants to live in is regarded as an insult. The doors of their palace are bolted, under the pretext that it is Sunday, and they don't want to be bothered. Symbolically, we turn our backs . . . because we Raelians are building the Palace of the Earth!" (*20 ans,* 96).

On Friday, December 11, 1998 (53 A.H.), the Raelians staged a similar demonstration in front of the UN Palace to commemorate the fiftieth anniversary of the Universal Declaration of Human Rights (inaugurated on December 10, 1948). The Raelian religion took the declaration one step further, introducing the Planetary Human Rights Charter. Its opening statement proclaimed: "A world government must be in place quickly and democratically. This government will mainly focus on Humanitarianism, so that the well-being of all humans will become its main concern as opposed to greed and power (as is currently the case)" (*Apocalypse* 113, 53 [1998]).

In this way, even though Raël is not often invited to the halls of power, the Raelians are assured that they are raising their voices and making a difference in the world.

Evangelizing the Jews

Raelians uphold the great Abrahamic tradition that accords the ancient Israelites a special covenant with the Creator. Raël's first book, *Le livre,* says the Elohim need the nation of Israel to provide land on which the Raelians can build the embassy for the extraterrestrial landing. Persistent efforts were made to gain Israel's cooperation in this endeavor. According to the Raelian "timeline," in December 1979 the Elohim telepathically sent the same dream to five rabbis and to Israel's president Menachem Begin, and guided Raël's hand in a letter he wrote to each recipient.[5] In 1989, the Canadian Jewish Congress received many complaints from Montreal Jews concerning two billboard advertisements, erected at a cost of $25,000 near the expressway and the Jacques Cartier bridge. The ads showed a UFO bearing a swastika inside the Star of David approaching earth, with the slogan, "Welcome our ancestors."

Michael Crelinsten, executive director of the Quebec region of the Montreal Jewish Congress, referred to the Raelians as "a benign, if somewhat loony group" and declared: "We wrote [saying] we have no intention of infringing on their freedom of expression, but that we find their logo offensive and find it inappropriate of them to proselytize in front of synagogues on the Sabbath." The priest guide Léon Mellul, a Moroccan Jew and hotel manager, telephoned Crelinsten and responded that "he didn't want to be insensitive, but it was critically important that the Jewish people in particular receive this message."[6] In October and November 1991 (during the Jewish New Year), the Raelian Movement sent letters to the Israeli government and its embassies demanding a plot of land in Jerusalem for the embassy—and warning them that if they refused, the Elohim might withdraw their protection of the Jewish people. The letter had a distinctly apocalyptic ring to it: "Les temps de l'Apocalypse sont effectivement arrivés. Le Messie attendu est tout près de vous. . . . L'avenir d'Israel est entre vos mains" (The time of the Apocalypse has arrived. The awaited Messiah is among you. . . . The future of Israel is in your hands).

The Raelians then redoubled their efforts to spread the message among the Jewish people and to enlist their support in lobbying Israel to grant the land. The priest guide in charge of this project was Léon Mellul, one of the rare Jewish converts to Raelianism. Mellul set up a mass baptism in Israel at the very spot where John the Baptist baptized Jesus, as the triumphant conclusion to the Raelians' whirlwind missionary tour of Israel. Unfortunately, only two prospective converts showed up, because, as Mellul explained to me, a bus broke down and journalists had been told to boycott Raël's press conferences in Jerusalem.

In eager anticipation of the Israel mission, Raelians had renewed their efforts to drum up local Jewish support in Quebec. On April 6, 1991, a team of Raelians stood outside twelve Montreal synagogues on the Sabbath, distributing pamphlets that proclaimed Raël the messiah. During the week of June 16, 1991, Raelians distributed nine thousand pamphlets to Jewish homes in Montreal. In an interview at the Raelian meeting at the Holiday Inn in the spring of 1992, Léon Mellul told me: "If Jews accept Raël as the Messiah, the embassy will be built in Israel and the Elohim will come back. If they don't, the Elohim will take away their protection of the Jewish people." Local rabbis interviewed on the radio were not amused by Raël's theory that Jews are descendants of the extraterrestrials who mated with the "daughters of men." Nor did they appreciate the evangelistic efforts around their synagogues.

In December 1991 another request was sent to Chief Rabbi Morechai Eliyahou, who acknowledged the request in January. In November 1993, the Raelian bishop Leon Mellul handed another letter directly to Prime Minister Yitzhak Rabin, but Rabin responded in December that he could not accede to the Raelians' request for land.

Finally, Raël decided to resolve the situation in a rational way and defuse the conflict. The Raelian Information Pack (February 1992) announced that, "out of respect for the victims of the nazi holocaust and in order to make the building of the Embassy in Israel easier, Raël decided . . . to change the symbol of the Raelian Movement replacing the Swastika with a galaxy look-alike symbol which represents the cycle of infinity in time."

The Raelians planned a new festival for December 1993 called "Peace for Israel and the Whole of the Middle East." This was scheduled to begin on the twentieth anniversary of Raël's meeting with the Eloha, but it had to be postponed due to Israel's failure to respond to Raël's request for an endowment of land for the embassy.

By 1998 Raël had announced the new revelation he had just received from the Elohim that the embassy did not have to be built in Jerusalem. Recently, I have been told that the guides are looking into a site on one of the Hawaiian islands.

Bringing down the Vatican, Dethroning the Pope

One still-puzzling feature of the Raelian Movement is its recurring anti-Catholic campaigns. These would appear on the surface to contradict Raël's message of universal tolerance and "respecting differences" of race, religion, culture, and so on. But the Raelians' anticlerical, pope-bashing, Vatican-closing crusades are in fact a necessary step toward realizing the Raelians' millenarian goal. Just as the conversion of the Jews and their return to Israel is a necessary precondition to the Second Coming for Protestant evangelicals, so the demise of the Catholic Church is necessary before the Raelians' message can be established on a global scale and the embassy can be made ready for the advent of aliens.

Raël's second book, *Space Aliens Took Me to Their Planet* (1978, 336–337), states: "The Church has no reason to exist any longer, for it was entrusted with the spreading of Jesus' message in the expectation of the age of the apocalypse. This age has come and the church has used means of diffusion which are shameful; . . . the heralded signs are there! The unidentified flying objects. . . . 'There will be signs in the skies!' that has been written long ago." In a Dantesque passage, clerics who wear the "bloody clothes" of the Catholic Church are told they will be "reproached with all [their] crimes." The pope has been sternly warned by the extraterrestrials: "If the Pope does not sell all the properties of the Vatican to help unfortunates he will not be admitted among the righteous to the planet of the eternals." These passages explain why the Raelians persist with their anti-Catholic campaigns.

A Raelian invited to speak to my class at Dawson College startled my students by bursting out, "The pope is a criminal, a mass murderer!" This was actually a misquote of Raël's press release, "The Pope's Apologies Are Not Enough!" (March 20, 2000), in which he accuses the pope of "2000 years of crimes against Mankind," and "the support of slavery, torture and . . . hundreds of thousands of victims burned at the stake." Raël suggests that the Vatican should be sued and forced to compensate the descendants of Huguenots and of Muslims in Jerusalem whose property was "illegally seized" and that the Vatican land be given back to the Italian people.

In 1986, Raël and his followers sat in a restaurant across from the Villa Pamphili park, a few hundred meters from the Vatican. Raël began the evening by announcing that he was the true "pope" and "not that usurper in the Vatican!" The evening revels lasted until 2 A.M. and ended with Raël's singing the hymn to the Elohim, accompanying himself on the guitar (*20 ans,* 10).

The Catholic Church in Quebec has thus far received more than five thousand letters proclaiming the act of apostasy, by which former Catholics renounce their baptism and proclaim their new allegiance to Raël and the extraterrestrials.

Anticlerical jokes abound wherever Raelians congregate. During one *soirée theatricale,* Raelians performed a skit starring Pope John Paul II. The pope arrives in paradise to find he is surrounded by a bevy of voluptuous naked biological robots and encounters Yahweh sniffing the flowers created by Satan and strolling arm in arm with him, admiring Satan's creations.

On October 7, 1994, Raelians entered St. Peter's Basilica in Rome and a guide began to perform the transmission of the cellular plan in front of a baptismal font (they brought their own water). Catholics complained to the Vatican guards, who politely escorted the group to the gates of Vatican City. The same week, Raelians presented the pope with a copy of Raël's book, *Le livre.* When newspapers later reported that the pope had fallen in the bath and broken his ankle, the guides credited the accident to his shock at recognizing the truth of the Raelian message (personal communication).

In July 2001, Raelians attracted attention in northern Italy and Switzerland by distributing flyers on the streets that warned parents not to send their children to Catholic confession, because, they claimed, more than a hundred priests had been convicted of child molestation in France. The French Raelian Movement was subsequently sued for libel by the vicar at Episcopal de Geneva.[7] The judge dismissed the charges, since the Raelian attack had been aimed at convicted priests, not at the whole of the Catholic Church.

The purpose of this action was to point out the double standard that applies to new and old religions. Two Raelian guides I interviewed in Paris said they were "sick and tired of being branded as 'pedophiles' in the French media." This was in the wake of the highly publicized trial of one Raelian out of sixty-five thousand with a troubled history of pedophilia, as mentioned earlier. In a press release on August 25, 2000, "The Raelian Religion for the Prevention of Pedophilia through Sex Education," Raël had announced the founding of NOPEDO, an organization dedicated to educating the public about the dangers of pedophilia (www.nopedo.org).

In October 2002, the Raelians resumed their anti-Catholic campaign by walking in an anticlerical parade, carrying candles and handing out crosses to high school students and inviting them to assemble at the park beside Montreal's Mount Royal and toss them into the bonfire. The youth were also given letters of apostasy to sign and send in to the Catholic Church renouncing their baptisms. The Quebec Assembly of Bishops accused the Raelians of "incitement to hatred." Several school boards tried to prohibit them from "consorting with students."[8]

Raelian guides were dispatched to Rome to collect signatures on the street for their petitions to dissolve Vatican City and take back the land and the wealth of St. Peter's to be distributed among the Italian people. When I asked a Raelian why they were doing this, he replied, "Don't you know, Raël's mission is to overthrow the pope and give the Vatican lands, which the church stole—for there was never a vote—back to the Italian people."

Raël continues to pit himself against the pope: "Everything he is against, we are for . . . contraception, homosexuality, divorce. All the values we espouse, he opposes."[9] In January 2003, shortly after the cloned-baby announcement, journalists who wished to interview Raël were told by his PR agent, Sylvie Chabot, that they must bow in his presence and address him as "His Holiness."

From "Pre" to "Post"—Two Types of Millennialism

The advent of the Elohim clearly depends on human effort and cooperation, and thus the Raelians fall into the "postmillennialist" category of millenarian religions. This means that, instead of expecting a sudden, cataclysmic supernatural intervention to bring about the end of the world (as do premillennialists), the postmillenarian Raelians anticipate gradual progress toward the realization of heaven on earth. This will be achieved through their own work of reforming, improving, and educating humankind. Only when human society has succeeded in cleaning up its act will the "second coming" (of the extraterrestrials and the forty prophets, in this case) occur.

"Postmillenarian" is a term most often applied to describe the end-of-time expectations of mainstream Protestant denominations. The classic difference between a pre- and a postmillennialist is that the former believes Jesus will return *before* the thousand years of peace, whereas the latter expects him to show up after the millennium is pleasantly under way. But there is an alternative definition of the term by Hexham and Poewe (1986) that is more relevant to the new religious context.

A peculiar brand of the more charismatic type of postmillennialism is found in utopian communes formed around a *living* messianic figure. Commune members believe that, since the messiah has *already* arrived—but only they recognize him (or her)—they must be living in the millennium already (see Hexham and Poewe 1986). Since the surrounding world is evidently a fallen place, they argue that the millennium has arrived, but only inside their community; those outside are still experiencing a premillennial hell. Often this conviction is accompanied by a perfectionist belief that since their messiah and his "sons and daughters" are pure and sinless, they can expect to enjoy some kind of immortality.

Other new religions based on a living god-in-flesh have espoused this notion of overcoming death. Messianic religions such as the Unification Movement of Reverend Moon, the eighteenth- and nineteenth-century Shakers founded by Ann Lee, and the Oneida Perfectionists of J. H. Noyes all conform to this type. Unlike these other messianic movements, the Raelian Movement is not communal—but members do enjoy a two-week communitarian utopian experience during the summer Awakening seminar in Eden. There they cultivate sensory awareness in a nudist society and gather around Raël, their messiah, who speaks of the perfect society he visited on the planet of the Elohim. He advocates free love and cloning, and imparts to them an inspiring vision of the limitless potential of the individual human being.

Wessinger (2000) presents a more precise typology of millennialism, "catastrophic" versus "progressive." The catastrophic vision looks toward a sudden, soon, violent end to the world brought about by supernatural intervention, where only the righteous are saved ("raptured") in the nick of time and placed on a cloud from which they might enjoy a grandstand view of global destruction. After the dust has settled, they will descend to rule and restore the earth—under Jesus' thousand-year reign, if they are Christians. The progressive vision of the end is more gradual, gentle, and human centered. The onus is on humankind to improve society and human nature so as to transform our unjust, chaotic world to bring about a heaven on earth that is palpable, the product of human effort. Only then will God (or gods) descend to rule over a just world.

Raël's eschatology corresponds to the progressive type of millennialism.

But the early prophecies of Raël reveal a catastrophic strain that adds suspense and shading to his optimistic human-centered vision. The Elohim's first warning to humankind of impending potential self-destruction contains the threat of extraterrestrial intervention in human affairs, which will be nonviolent but nonetheless humiliating: "But if human beings remain aggressive and continue to progress in a manner which is dangerous for other worlds, then we will destroy this civilization and its repositories of scientific wealth, and there will be another Sodom and Gomorrah until such a time as humanity becomes morally worthy of its level of scientific understanding. If you do not, however, and if you become a threat to us, we will only have to destroy your stocks of bombs without sending offensive weapons against you" (Raël [Vorilhon] 1974, 91).

After Raël's second encounter, in 1975, these radical apocalyptic passages were deemed apocrypha and expunged from future printings of his first book, *Le livre qui dit la vérité,* in favor of a seamless "progressive" scenario. A later publication, *The Final Message,* tells us that the Elohim themselves reject this passage and explain it as a mistake in transcription:

> We must correct a passage in the first message we gave to you that you wrongly transcribed concerning an eventual intervention on our part to destroy humanity. It must be made clear that we will not intervene. Humanity is now arriving at a turning point in its history, and its future depends only on itself. If you can control your aggressiveness towards each other and your environment, then you will reach a golden age of interplanetary civilization. . . . If, on the other hand, your civilization gives way to violence, then it will destroy itself, either directly or indirectly, through all this. (Raël 1998a, 223)

But even after rejecting the possibility of supernatural intervention, an ominous undercurrent lingers in Raël's theology: the threat of nuclear apocalypse.

Raël also incorporates another catastrophic characteristic into his end-of-time vision—the doctrine of the "righteous remnant" (an interpretation of Revelation 21:3–4). This is a characteristic feature of the pretribulationist vision of Hal Lindsay and other writers in the Bible prophecy tradition who predict that a "righteous remnant" will be snatched up in "rapture" while the wicked must undergo the trials of the tribulation and Armageddon (Martin 1982).

The Elohim warn us in *Let's Welcome Our Fathers from Space* that if we do not reach "a level of wisdom equivalent to [the] level of our technology," a nuclear holocaust is "unfortunately what awaits humanity with a ninety-nine percent chance of occurring" (Raël 1987a, 125). Even so, Raelians who strove in vain to avert it will be rescued at the last minute and placed in safety on the planet of the eternals. According to Raël's "New Revelation," Raël the "Sixth Seal" of St. John (the black sun, earthquake, and sky that recedes like a scroll) refers to the "final . . . greatest danger of all—atomic war." Only Raël's followers will be saved. A huge computer in the sky "which follows all people from conception to their death" will select "those who have had their cellular plan transmitted after reading the messages." And the number of those who have been "sealed in the forehead" will be "close to" 144,000 (115).

Raël refers to Revelation 21:3–4 ("He shall wipe the tear from their eyes; and there shall be no more death, neither sorrow nor crying . . . for the former things are passed away") and explains that "this is a description of the planet of the eternals, where all people saved from the final cataclysm will live with us eternally, while waiting for the earth's atmosphere to settle down, so as to reimplant another civilization of peaceful men." Thus Raelians in good standing find themselves in the following win-win situation: "So all of you who recognize us as your Creators, and who recognize Raël, . . . do not despair if you see that the great majority of men remain violent, aggressive and stupid. Whichever way you look at it, your efforts will be rewarded. Either humanity will develop an interplanetary consciousness and . . . enter the Golden Age, or the planet will self-destroy, but we will then save you so that you can rebuild a new world" (Rael 1987a, 125).

Raelians appear confident in their privileged role in these forthcoming events. As one Raelian animator, "Madeleine," explained to my student Anna Pascal in an interview at the December 1992 meeting, there are several possibilities.

> They are waiting until we are 144,000 Raelians on earth. . . . Until we are that proportion, they will try to stop our auto-destruction. But, once there were [*sic*] 144,000, there will be a breaking point. Either we will destroy ourselves or we'll enter the Golden Age. Now we are 30 to 35,000, we will not destroy ourselves before we reach 144,000—or if we do, they will take the Raelians that are on our planet and re-create them on their planet. When "they" do come, there will be a big change on earth. Everyone will

> have to be taught who they are, there will be many conferences. Their coming will be like the reunion of parents and children after many years. I can't wait to see them, to see what they look like, to see how they live.

Thus, one can find a certain narrative suspense and flexibility in Raël's unfolding revelations. The end result is that he maintains a creative tension between the pessimism of the catastrophic and the optimism of the progressive view—"creative" in the sense that it generates commitment and action. Raël's more upbeat statements about averting nuclear war galvanize Raelians to spread the message more energetically. If, however, the statements were *too* hopeful—that is, if the Elohim revealed that through its good work, the human race was out of danger and had only to sit back and await the extraterrestrials' coming—it could lead to laxity and declining commitment to the cause. As one guide aptly expressed it: "If we were to find out for sure the Elohim were definitely coming three weeks from now, it would eliminate our power of choice. We would all drop our jobs. It is better we don't know exactly; then it is our choice whether we recognize the Elohim and help Rael." So, periodically, when the Raelians are becoming overly complacent, a note of fear or doom tends to color the Elohim's next message to humankind, relayed through their messenger, Raël.

The Oral Tradition

One of the great dilemmas of the prophet-founder of a new religious movement is that he or she must engage in a dual task that involves juggling paradoxical realities. On one hand, they must create a mythic, poetic alternative reality for their community that is insulated from the secular world and imbued with a sense of mystery and ultimate meaning. On the other hand, they must communicate that vision to potential recruits, business associates, and the media, disguising it in rational language to avoid appearing threatening and weird. They must unveil their ultimate truth in increments, saving the sacred core until last, so it won't be dismissed outright as absurd or pathological. A good example of this juggling act is found in the Children of God, who distinguish between "milk for babes" and "meat for disciples" (Millikan 1994, 182). One of the most vulnerable areas of an NRM is the prophecies of their leaders, and here a certain flexibility in the oral tradition proves useful. From an outsider's point of view, prophets who mention a specific date on which a divine advent or doomsday will occur are inviting disconfirmation and ridicule.

This is where the advantage of field research becomes evident. Having observed millenarian excitement on the spot, I have noticed how rumors and informal updates of Raël's prophecies keep expectation and commitment alive, as well as build a kind of buffer to withstand the impact of disconfirmation. Thus, a comparative study of written and oral teachings—and of the followers' response to them—gives us a better idea of how prophecy "works" in new religious subcultures. On occasion, Raël's public speeches give us news concerning the advent of the aliens that is more precise than the predictions in his books. Rumors sprout up among his followers, idiosyncratic interpretations of how soon "they" will return, of how the IRM is making rapid strides in setting up a world government or bringing down the Vatican, or getting nations to agree on nuclear disarmament, or cloning the first baby, or putting an end to third-world hunger. These rumors are like ripples in a cornfield. They are ephemeral, but they do indicate which way the wind is blowing.

Oral prophecy can alter empiricism and reinterpret past predictions. The Raelians appear to rely on their oral prophecy traditions as a kind of safety valve that responds sensitively to external pressures (persecution, responses to missionaries, or media ridicule), as well as to internal ones (defections, challenges to leadership).

Ellwood (1973) and Wallis (1984) have emphasized the importance of studying the oral tradition in NRMs. The living, ephemeral oral tradition is a characteristic that distinguishes these young "cults" from mainstream "churches." The prophet-founder of an NRM, these writers argue, has the creative advantage of potent charisma "untrammeled" by sacred texts accompanied by a subsidiary tradition of exegesis and interpretation. In this context, an oral tradition proves invaluable. Prophecies not yet written in stone can be recast and updated—or moved forward or back in time—in response to the administrative and social needs of the group. Often the chain of authority is weak ("I heard it from Pierre, who heard it from Suzie, who heard it from Raël"), so when an informal Raelian prophecy proves false or inconvenient, the guides can point to Raël's books and insist, "But Raël never said that!" Thus an interplay between the written and oral prophecies provides flexibility, so that Raelians can simultaneously work to promote their own careers, socialize within their satisfying subculture, and yet feel inspired and ready for the not-quite-imminent return of the Elohim.

This interplay of prophecy occurs around the issues of the advent date and the fate of the frontal bone.

Nowhere in Raël's books is a date cited for the return of the Elohim, and yet until the late 1980s, the date 2025 was often mentioned as the final possible date for the arrival of the Elohim and the thirty-nine prophets in Jerusalem. This date was later changed to 2035. One Raelian explained to me that Raël had mentioned that the Elohim would return *no later than* 2035. When I asked, "What happened to 2025?" the bishop said, "It was *always* 2035. You made a mistake!" But at the February 19, 2000, Raelian meeting when I spoke with another bishop, he noted, "I seem to remember it *was* 2025, then Raël said that between the years 2025 and 2035 the presence of the Elohim would become manifest—that things would happen so that humanity would become aware." He also contradicted my first informant: "It doesn't have to be *exactly* 2035, that's just a ballpark figure."[10]

Raël himself has often demonstrated a willingness to accommodate society by backpedaling on some of his projects that evoke negative responses from the public—like the swastika medallion, or the French Geniocratie party. He has even (as advised by the Elohim) moved the possible site of the embassy from Jerusalem to Hawaii.

One might argue that these adjustments suggest that the movement is becoming increasingly secularized. Alain Bouchard (1989), a Quebec researcher on the early Raelian Movement, observed during one of our conversations that the Raelians have increasingly tended to *deemphasize* the extraterrestrial component in favor of the psychological and emotional benefits they receive by working for the goals of the movement. He gave as an example his interviews with a guide in the 1980s who stressed the importance of feeling a sense of telepathic communication with the Elohim while performing the transmission of the cellular plan. Bouchard compared this to the recent statement of a guide who insisted he focused only on the individual's inner potential and tried to convey a feeling of love during the ritual.[11]

There were times when the Raelian Movement appeared to be turning into a "world-affirming" group (Wallis 1984) as opposed to a world-rejecting "flying-saucer sect." It might be described today as a psychotherapeutic social club (the Raelians at one time even dubbed their movement "Club Meditation"). At the meetings, techniques to promote individual success and well-being have replaced telepathic communication with Elohim as the original otherworldly goals have been increasingly downplayed. If one compares the Raelians of today with those of the 1970s and 1980s, they appear now to depend less on the extraterrestrials and more on the Raelian social institutions and networks to provide meaning in their lives. A rather startling confession from the lips of a Raelian angel interviewed by Thalia Vaillancourt (2000) confirms this notion: "Even if I were to find out there were no Elohim and they would never return, I wouldn't really care, because I have given my life to something I love!"

But Raël is still full of surprises. He is, after all, a prophet.

Confronting the Crunch of Disconfirmation

Today the Raelian Movement is around forty years old. The site for the embassy has not yet been located; the Raelian "Church," even after sixty thousand baptisms, is still branded a "cult" or a "sect" in the media and still occupies the social margins. The possibility of global nuclear war looms larger than ever on the post-9/11 horizon. Raël has become a media star because of his participation in the race to clone, but he is not yet awarded the respect due a pope or Dalai Lama. Ex-members complain of what they regard as Raël's deviation from his two initial goals. Is it possible that Raël's prophecy has been overly specific—heading toward that embarrassing crunch of disconfirmation if and when the embassy is completed and UFOs fail to hover over Jerusalem on the fateful eve of December 31, 2035?

Rodney Stark has an interesting observation concerning the perils of prophecy in his 1996 amplified version of his 1986 theory of how new religions succeed. To his original eight conditions, Stark adds two new ones that he deems necessary for NRMs' success and survival into the future. One of these deals with the problem of prophetic disconfirmation: "New religious movements are more likely to succeed if their doctrines are non-empirical" (1996, 136). The Raelian doctrine is uncompromisingly empirical: The aliens must descend in material bodies and metal machines by 2035 at the latest. If this prophecy is not fulfilled, either Raël or his successor(s) will have only one recourse, according to a theory proposed by J. Gordon Melton.

Melton's seminal article, "Spiritualization and Reaffirmation: What Really Happens When Prophecy Fails" (1985), offers many examples of groups that experience failure of prophecy and then opt for one of two routes to avoid doctrinal failure and public embarrassment. One route is simply to postpone the date of Christ's Second Coming (or its equivalent). The other is to "spiritualize" the event, insisting it *did* really happen but occurred invisibly on some ethereal plane or in the spirit realm. This latter route will not be an option for Raelians and their eighty-nine-year-old prophet in 2035. Since only the material world exists and any transcendental realm or reality is discarded, how would it be possible for the aliens' return to be "spiritualized"?

THE DILEMMA OF LITERAL PROPHECIES

Raël's revealed truth about humankind's origins might be categorized as belonging to the "ancient astronaut" school of Bible exegesis. In this ufological approach to studying the Bible, "God becomes an astronaut . . . living on a faraway galaxy. Divine revelations are . . . teachings from space creatures and miracles are awesome interventions by intelligences who are technologically superior to the human race" (Saliba 1995a, 34).

Raël's radical premise is that there is "neither God nor soul," and he rejects monotheism in favor of a materialistic polytheism—"gods" who are mere homo sapiens (albeit godlike in their extraordinary longevity and mastery over an advanced technology). "God is not impalpable and immaterial. He is in fact in heaven" (Raël [Vorilhon] 1974, 227). In Saliba's words (1995a, 34): "The supernatural in this view is reduced to the super-technological." What was once considered transcendent becomes immanent—wholly material, reduced to atoms and dust. The individual's only hope for immortality now resides in his or her genetic program—DNA—and in the ability of scientists to manipulate it.

From this basic premise, Raël extrapolates on Bible passages with inventive flair—and plodding consistency. Like Thomas Aquinas, "Divine Doctor" of the Catholic Church, Raël's mission is to reconcile God's revelations and miracles with human scientific facts and discoveries. But unlike the author of *Summa Theologica,* he speaks not as a theologian, but as a prophet.

The Raelian Movement has always placed strict emphasis on the *literal truth* of its first revealed text, *Le livre qui dit la vérité*. This and subsequent texts were presented (and accepted) as precise, literal, factual accounts of truth. The Raelians might be categorized as fundamentalists, in that they consider their sacred text to be literally true and to provide a blueprint for how humans should live their lives (see Lawrence 1989). Margot Morel, a founding member of MADECH, confirms this when she writes redundantly: "J'étais conforté dans l'idée que la vérité était vraiement écrit dans le livre qui dit la Vérité" (I am comforted by the idea that the truth is truly written in the book that tells the Truth) (*20 ans,* 45).

Raël himself adheres so strictly to the written prophecies that he once ordered an entire printing of his second edition of *Le livre* to be consigned to the flames because of one tiny error. Raël's texts, dictated via their messenger by extraterrestrials descending from the sky, tell us that the world was created exactly twenty-five thousand years ago; for example, Raël (1987a,

163) says, "Let us not forget the Elohim are 25.000 in advance of us." Raël is very precise about his dates.

Given this literal, fundamentalist stance and precise date prediction, it may appear to nonbelievers that Raël is setting his religion up for failure. But this is where an escape hatch appears—the Raelians' faith in the merely human, in the godlike potential of human scientists.

Secular Humanism—or Secularization?

It may be a sign of the institutionalization that comes with maturity (see Weber 1947) that the movement is beginning to place more emphasis on values and guidelines in dealing with everyday life, and less on telepathic communications with the Elohim. This becomes apparent in the videocassette *Values in the Millennium*.

Raël's charismatic image has altered accordingly over the years, from an eccentric young contactee to a prophet-founder to something resembling a New Age therapist or guru. Videotapes of Raël's lectures in the 1980s show an earnest, rather self-effacing young man intent on conveying objective facts and important information concerning humanity's destiny, as well as articulating a philosophy that reconciles religion with science. Today, his speeches tend to lack mythic and doctrinal content—perhaps because he's said it all before so many times—and his utterances are more inspirational than informative. In the videos shown at the monthly meetings, Raël walks in slow motion and exudes love, joy, and mystery. "Well, have you decided to be happy?" he asks, while the camera cuts to beautiful Raelians embracing each other in a pastoral setting. Members are no longer instructed in telepathic communication with the Elohim, but rather are urged to cultivate an inner "harmony with the infinite." The French word "*conscience*"—meaning awareness, thoughtfulness, consciousness—is frequently used. Thus Raelians appear to have moved into the "religion" of secular humanism, which holds the core of the individual to be sacred and invested with ultimate meaning.

The Raelian Movement appears to be undergoing the familiar process of the institutionalization of charisma. Raël's leadership is past its volatile growth spurt and is well into the "routinization of charisma" phase (Weber 1947). In the early days, Raël was more approachable, spontaneous, and informal. Anyone could talk to him. Today, members must book appointments in advance and often end up talking to a bishop as a substitute. As the movement expands internationally, Raël must delegate authority to his bishops and priests. For new initiates today, it is far less likely that it will be Raël himself who performs the transmission of the cellular plan. As Raël becomes more distant and inaccessible, his stature grows to the gigantic proportions of his image on the video screen at the monthly meetings. As an ex-member complained: "In *Le livre* Raël tells us *not* to worship him. He says 'Don't look at my finger, look to where it's pointing.' But today, we have to bow down before Raël—we are literally told we have to bow 'because this is a way leaders are shown respect in other traditions.' Since when have we tried to be like other religions?"

The "Elohimization" of Humanity

One could argue that Raël's literal, palpable, material vision of the end of time is courting disaster. But since the margin between humans and gods is so thin, if humankind can advance quickly enough, there will be no need for the gods to appear at all!

Thus, it is possible that in this new human-centered, more secular orientation, in turning humans into gods—what is called "Elohimization" in Raelianese—Raël has found the escape hatch to avoid prophetic failure. The extraterrestrials, who take center stage in Raël's early writings, are moving offstage to make room for humankind, which under Raël's tutelage is developing Elohim-like qualities.

This notion of humankind's close kinship to the "gods" is hardly original. The IRM is retracing the theological steps of some the most successful and enduring small sects and churches of the nineteenth and twentieth centuries: Theosophy, Mormonism, Christian Science, New Age, and Scientology.

Bednarowski (1980) has noted two consistent themes in the otherwise disparate theologies of these new religions. They all emphasize the proximity of humankind to God, and humans' potential to become gods. Her chapter "The Dead Learn Forever" shows us how the "old new religions" all claim that education and self-improvement continue in the afterlife, that learning is an eternal process.

Thus, while Theosophists aspire to become "ascended masters," Scientologists train to become "operating thetans," and New Agers strive to awaken the god within, Raelians hope to be re-created as virtually immortal space-traveling superscientists/artists.

Extrapolations on the Future

What are some possible scenarios for 2035? If I were a science-fiction writer, rather than a mere researcher, I would be tempted to extrapolate and come up with three possible scenarios:

1. The Elohim will arrive on schedule, Raël will be vindicated, and humanity will refocus its energies on space travel and genetic engineering, clone extinct species, and give up devastating the planet with war and indiscriminate procreation.
2. The aliens' advent will be postponed by Raël or his successor—either before the due date or immediately after the failed advent.
3. Raël will announce a new revelation that congratulates humankind on its good work, explaining that, since our scientists are busy cloning away, there is no need for our creators to put in an appearance, since we have graduated to becoming cocreators ourselves—and our next mission is to step up our space programs and venture out into space to meet them.

Of course, there are other depressing scenarios that we have witnessed frequently throughout the history of heresy. The IRM could fizzle out due to schisms and squabbling over the succession—or be stomped out by fierce persecution. An even more depressing denouement could result from the convergence of U.S. and Muslim "nuclear theology"—in which case the Elohim will turn their backs on humanity in disgust.

But at this point I think the third scenario is the most likely. Of course, skeptics might point out that by placing on his followers the burden of ushering in heaven on earth, by proclaiming that humanity is undergoing "Elohimization" (turning into Elohim) through scientific advancement, Raël avoids the uncomfortable challenge of a possible prophetic disconfirmation when the embassy is made ready and the Elohim fail to materialize.

Chapter Five

A Visit to the Court of Raël

How can I describe the atmosphere of a Raelian meeting—the scintillating, foppish glamour of the guides, their self-deprecating/self-promoting humor? Every time I attend the monthly meeting in Montreal, I think of the court at Versailles, where Louis XIV's pleasure-seeking courtiers mingled with pious cardinals, both dabbled in intrigue with beautiful ladies, and everyone orbited around the Sun King.

Raël's hierarchy of guides is no less a court—a court of elegant men with long curls cascading down their backs who gather to discuss philosophy, science, and politics. Raël's court is a charm school, an academy for developing skills in rhetoric, for refining the senses, and for cultivating courtly manners. The guides model their speech patterns and body language on Raël's—and copy his charisma. Some ambitious guides have actually gone so far as to change their names to be identified more closely identified with Raël. An ex–Catholic priest legally changed his name to Amidrael (friend of Raël); Quebec's youngest bishop changed his name to Lear ("Raël" backward). The Italian guide calls himself Ezraël, the Belgium guide, Uriël; the African bishop, Zadou, is now Azael. An ex-member on the warpath calls himself Exraël.

Raël's courtiers greet each other with elegance and warmth, with the Quebecois peck on both cheeks (left first for Francophones—only the clumsy Anglophones start on the right, and bump noses). Raelians show more physical affection and body language than one might see in most religious congregations. They embrace, kiss, massage each other's shoulders, pat each other's butts, and exchange sexy jokes.

Women guides are quite as active as the men. They sashay across the stage, breathe huskily through the microphone, and caress their boyfriends and each other during the meetings, reveling in their newfound, uncensored *sensualité*. Raël's court is studded with alluring young women artfully dressed so as to flaunt their breasts, midriffs, and legs. One teenager who is much sought after sits through the meetings, her tulle crinoline skirt hiked up, tossing her ponytail and licking lollipops. The few children present tend to keep a low profile. Women's dress styles range from *Paris-Match* elegance to leather décolletage to rock-star exhibitionism. Long flowing hair is fashionable, and some wear their hair bleached and tousled, reminiscent of Brigitte Bardot in her St. Tropez heyday. In the 1980s to early 1990s, all the male guides wore long tresses, but as Raël's hairline receded (it is now tied in a samurai-style topknot), most of the guides adopted short, blown-dry, blunt-cut hairstyles or slicked-back ponytails. Although Raël continues to wear white, the male guides, who used to wear white padded suits reminiscent of Star Trek, have reverted to mainstream clothing. One Raelian who isn't a guide or even a bodyguard shows up regularly to meetings in a padded astronaut-style suit that is an exact replica of Raël's—only black. When I asked a bishop about this, she replied, "It's not in very good taste, but we let him get away with it, for we believe in freedom."

My first impression of Raelian men—slender, soft-spoken, long-haired, earringed, touchy-feely Francophones—was that many of them were gay. As I got to know them and their girlfriends better, however, it became evident that very few of them preferred men to women, although many had experimented with making love to a man, usually in the context of a threesome involving a woman (personal communications). When I asked a guide to give me an estimate of the number of homosexuals in the movement, he replied rather coldly: "We don't think in such narrow categories. Some of us are unisexual, some are bisexual, some are trisexual—and a few of us are even quadrasexual." When I timidly asked what the last category might represent, he leaned forward and whispered, "With the Elohim!"

And Raël's court, like that of King Louis, is a hotbed of gossip and intrigue and sexual adventurism, with lackeys currying favor. All orbit around their beloved prophet, Raël, who is the "Ear of the Elohim," the key to the galaxy. While his blood is not as blue as Louis XIV's, his DNA is divinely alien.

My Students at the Monthly Meetings

Raelians do not own church buildings or establish centers; they hold their meetings in rented spaces on the third Sunday of every month. In Montreal these spaces have ranged from the Holiday Inn to a cabaret theater in the red-light district to an old Jesuit seminary's lecture hall.

I have attended Raelian meetings with my students intermittently since 1987. The Raelians are ideal for a class research trip for two reasons: They are entertaining and they love being researched. My students are always excited and intrigued at the prospect of visiting a UFO group and frequently bring along their friends, girlfriends, boyfriends, and siblings—and sometimes even their parents. They distribute questionnaires, set up interviews, or just chat with available Raelians. They lie back, relax, and close their eyes for the oxygenation exercise, and many have had their photos taken with Raël.

Before our excursions, I make a point of giving my students a pep talk to explain Raelian sexual ethics. I emphasize that Raelians respect the individual's power of choice, so if students find themselves "hit on," all they have to do is politely decline. "In Raelian culture it is good manners to express sexual attraction for others, so don't be overly flattered and take it personally," I warn them. "Even I, your teacher, have been propositioned at the meetings." (This usually convinces them not to take advances too seriously.)

The Raelians have been remarkably hospitable and receptive to our research efforts. Two young Raelians are stationed at the door to greet newcomers and explain the message to them. After the formal meeting, students who are standing around uncertainly with batches of questionnaires and lists of interview questions are pleased to find that many smiling Raelians come up to them and volunteer to be studied. I usually stand or sit off to the side with the students and try to keep a low profile, especially since we were invited to sit up on the stage and I was introduced erroneously and much to my chagrin as "Susan Palmer, the professor of sexology."

I learned a great deal from watching my students' reactions to the Raelians. As an academic steeped in the microsociology of NRMs, I couldn't just sit and watch Raelians "do their thing" with a fresh naïve eye. I was constantly mulling over theories in my mind—patterns of charisma, conversion, commitment, and so on—trying to apply them to what I observed. I was always comparing the Raelians to other groups I had researched. But my students brought an innocent, playful curiosity to the meetings. They noticed things I missed and came up with their own insights. I got a sense of how Quebecois youth in the larger society were responding to the Raelians, and what they might find appealing or off-putting.

My students' reactions to Raël were diverse. Some described him almost reverently, as "wise," "intelligent," "charismatic," "loving," while others (suspicious of "cults") dismissed him as "silly" or "phony." Raël's "style" fascinated them. For example: "Raël was dressed in an 80's style karate suit, indicating the difference between him and those who have not encountered the higher knowledge of the Elohim" (Lindy 1993); "Raël stood before me in a white space cadet suit, quite hilarious actually, and what was even funnier, he was wearing those little white seventies Reeboks. He spoke quite beautifully, . . . a beautiful articulate French with a soft and mellow tone [that] can get anyone to relax and let go and, by letting go, becom[e] more receptive" (Collins 1992).

My students also commented on his charisma. "I noticed him walk in with two young attractive women. . . . He was not very tall, and had long, curly brown hair. He wore a white cloth outfit that looked like an over-sized sweat suit. . . . He emphasized the importance of the individual to make the difference for himself, to overcome society's hatred and make the change . . . sudden and immediate, we must do it now [he said]. He compared this to an ejaculation, an 'orgasm of the mind.' I was surprised to see how the audience reacted; . . . I failed to see the mysticism, spirituality or charisma in Raël, although his followers certainly saw something I did not" (Friedman 1993).

Danielle Lindy, in her field report of the December 13, 1993, transmission of the cellular plan, reproduced a rousing fund-raising speech by a female priest guide. It provides a good example of how Raël's guides educate his followers in the recognition and support of charisma. "'Do we think about Raël enough? Are we faithful enough? Raël loves us and wants to be with us. To attain his goal, over the past 20 years he has been demystified, but now we must reflect, understand his reality, his importance. We must realize he is special and mysterious; he is a prophet. Raël is the messenger, the ambassador, and that is the reality of his existence. The movement exists, it is growing and they [the Elohim] will come. We must give to the prophet, respect him. He is very much like Jesus. He is also like us, but he is more.'" Lindy comments: "She said she was embarrassed to have to say this in front of him. Then, she asked the audience if they loved Raël. They replied, '*Yes!*' in full force. The priest guide concluded: 'If Raël lived a life of luxury, would we still love him? Yes we would. But Raël is humble. He gives everything to the Elohim. We must take care of him. The Raelian revolution will come, but Raël needs to exist physically, here on earth for the movement to exist. We should therefore spoil Raël. Don't forget, the movement doesn't pay *one cent*. Raël doesn't touch a penny. Money from the movement goes back *into* the movement. The only income he receives is the money from his books. That is why if you want to give to Raël, although you are not obliged, we will be passing a bowl around. We have never done this before. Thank you'" (Lindy 1993).

Another close-up look at the master-disciple relationship is given by Lesley Tannenbaum in her field report of the February 2003 meeting. It shows us what rewards Raël extends to his followers. Tannenbaum begins by describing the Raelians' oxygenation ritual and concludes with an interesting self-reflexive statement:

> Brigitte Boisellier sat on a stool and began to lead everyone through a meditation which seemed entrancing. . . . As I looked around the theatre, most of the Raelians had their eyes closed and the back of their hands resting on their knees, palms facing up. I felt surreal, almost scared to listen to what she was saying. Immediately after, music began to play, and young adults began to stand up and dance, making their way [up] on stage. . . . Everyone around us could feel the excitement, we were in awe of what was going on [since] I'm sure in [most of our churches] the sermons are not usually this lively. I was dazed by the whole afternoon, but I began to take notice when Raël was invited up on stage. . . . Raël began by describing how touched he was, and how he cried when he saw the young people up on stage dancing and enjoying life. He stated that it was OK if he were to die at any time, for he knew there would always be these people to carry on his teachings. "Even if I am not here, you will continue to teach others [the message]?" "*Yes!*" everyone shouted back.
>
> Driving home, I thought about the event I had just witnessed, and although I was deeply intrigued, I had a sense of anxiety as well. I was unnerved during the time in the theatre. . . . I had the feeling I was inside a room which resembled so much those scenes shown on television about cults. (Tannenbaum 2003)

Many of the students described how charisma is staged, that Raël always makes his surprise appearance right after the oxygenation exercise, when the audience is most relaxed and sensitized. Allister T. Roberts offers a vivid description of Raël's appearances in the February 2001 meeting:

> An Asian woman approached the stage, again to great applause. We were told, "make your body ready for a cosmic journey," [and] she continued, "Feel your body . . . feel your toes, your legs . . . your organs . . . your stomach, all the way to the top of your scalp. Can you not feel the warmth? Feel the molecules that make up your body." A noticeable collective sigh came from the audience. "Let's gather our energy, gather it. We are becoming a cloud, a big white puffy cloud of love. The cloud is filling the entire room. It's floating above the entire city, and at this very moment everyone in Montreal feels warm. This cloud is growing, be-

cause our love is growing. The love is now moving into outer space. Can't you feel it? It's traveling faster than light, straight to the Elohim. They are happy, because we have communicated with them, and they accept and share our love."

Slowly the lights returned and during the process, collection envelopes had been handed out. The seminar gave another collective sigh, and returned their hands from the outstretched position. A different Raelian Guide stepped onto the stage and announced that Raël himself was in our presence. The room sat up and began clapping, and soon enough, a small man wearing what looked like a white ninja suit, his hair tied in a topknot, much like a samurai, approached the stage. This was Raël. . . .

Raël had the passion and charisma of a true leader, able to sway them back and forth as he introduced his sermon, . . . able to make them laugh while maintaining his greater purpose. What was his greater purpose? . . . His explanation was long and drawn out and I soon fell asleep [due to] the soothing voice of the translator. Towards the end of his sermon I had apparently fallen into a comatose state as I was woken up by the prodding of a classmate [to meet] the scornful eyes of many Raelians in the vicinity.

Raël finished his sermon to an uproar of applause and a standing ovation, as an interpretive dancer moved in fluid motion to New Age music—something that was clearly a Raelian theme song. A Guide then announced the conclusion of the seminar, and told us we'd been blessed by Raël's presence, and we were told to disperse and spread the Raelian message. Our group [Palmer's students] were dazed, in a state of shock, afraid to speak, not knowing whether laughter or stunned mumblings would ensue. I openly welcomed the fresh air of outside, after being offered Raelian merchandise for the low price of $955. Having left the intoxication of the seminar, I had the chance to reflect upon that Sunday morning's event. I was shocked to see just how *friendly* the Raelians were, if not *too friendly*. This appeared to me [to be] a philosophical movement that appealed to "lost souls." I could not have been more thankful that the experience had ended, and yet still I feel a sense of better appreciation and understanding for the Raelian cause that will remain with me into the future. (Roberts 2001).

An excellent field report written by one of my Dawson College students, Max Grossman (1993), contributes valuable insights into how Raël and his bishops cooperate in constructing charisma. I include it here in its entirety.

Max Grossman's Account

On the third Sunday of November 1993, I [Max] arrived at Montreal's Holiday Inn Crown Plaza by 10:30 A.M. Although I was late, the meeting had not yet begun. Raelians were milling around the conference room and outer hall greeting each other . . . by kissing both cheeks, hugging, and patting backs. The men greet each other with as much physical contact as they give the women; . . . they were patting behinds and holding hands.

Around three hundred people filed into the conference room and sat down on folding chairs, facing a long table set with vases of flowers, a water pitcher, and glasses. A rumor was circulating that Raël might show up. The men outnumbered women and most were in the twenty-five to thirty-five age range. Most people were stylishly if not classily dressed—that is to say, they looked more appropriately dressed for a night in the clubs than for a Sunday morning meeting of a more conventional religion. Women wore makeup, tight clothing, and high heels, men and women alike had carefully styled hair, and appearance seemed to be important to them. Most . . . wore the symbolic pendant on a chain around their necks. Several of the men had long hair—the younger men wore it loose, and the older wore it in a small ponytail or growing at the nape of their necks.

The master of ceremonies was a tall red-haired woman who welcomed "Raelian members and guests alike" and then called on Lear, whom she introduced as having been initiated as a guide by Raël himself. [By 1993 priest guides were usually initiated by bishop guides, connected through a kind of chain of forehead holding to Raël himself, the "Guide of Guides." Lear was the youngest priest guide, so apparently Raël made an exception in his case.]

Lear then comes to the front of the room and takes the microphone. He is a young man with carefully styled blond hair, and he wears a large pendant dangling on his chest. First he tells everyone to relax, for meditation must be done in silence. The Raelians lean back in their chairs, and many lie down in the aisles, some with their heads on their friends' thighs. The lights were lowered, and soft instrumental music came on. Below is my loose translation into English of Lear's guided meditation: "Meditation is the link, the first and original form of prayer. Meditation sends vibes like radio waves to the Elohim. Close your eyes and breathe deeply. Feel the oxygen, imagine that you are the oxygen, feel it in every cell, nourishing each one. Breathe in life, exhale death!

"Concentrate on your sex organs, the cells that make up your sex, concentrate on the nerve endings which can provide pleasure when you free yourself of guilt, and the power your organs give you to reproduce. Concentrate on your fingers, your sense of touch, the sense that allows you to touch, communicate with objects and people around you. Travel up to your neck, feel your neck, which links body and spirit—the two are one." He continues on through the lips and tongue, the nose, and the sensual pleasures these organs give us.

Meanwhile, as I am observing things through my lowered eyes, I see Raël entering the room with a small entourage of excited young women and two men. He is dressed all in white but wearing an odd combination of clothing. His jacket is reminiscent of Star Trek, with flaps forming a V down the back—but he was wearing ordinary white sweatpants and white sneakers with it. He stands at the entrance to the room, primping—getting his jacket and hair adjusted by his girl helpers—while Lear continues to drone on soothingly. Everyone's eyes are closed; they are deep in trance or passed out on the floor and don't realize who has just come in.

Lear is saying: "Imagine a small bubble leaving your forehead and floating upwards, imagine that you are the bubble, floating higher and higher. . . . Feel the infinite movement within you and in the galaxy, the infinite energy of movement, feel that you are tiny, and at the same time a huge galaxy to those cells within you."

At this point, Raël moves in on the microphone, and Lear steps down from the stage. Suddenly, a new voice—and a ripple passes through the crowd. Some open their eyes; others keep them closed and smile to themselves. Raël tells them: "I have come because it gives me pleasure to be here. . . . I am relaxed and in complete harmony with the world." Everyone has by now opened their eyes and sat up attentively.[1]

Raël opens his sermon with question, "How is it possible to stay in complete harmony all the time, with everyone?" He goes on to say that people cling to their faults as part of who they are, but we can never achieve peace if we are defensive. He congratulates himself on being utterly happy always, because he has altered the negative parts of himself. His speech is choppy, and the ideas jump around. He speaks of the media, saying it forces certain ideologies on us, but no ideology or wealth can replace the happiness of pure being: "If we taught criminals to meditate, they would lose their criminal desire. If you lose the feeling of harmony you gain during meditation, it is your fault; *you* have *let* it go. Ideally, one would never have to meditate because one is in a constant state of elevation and happiness. The media propagates violence in our society. Television shows the hero shooting the gun, but it doesn't show the damage done to the human body, and the child only imitates the hero. Society generates the violence it then deplores, but Raelians are different. We have decided to live outside the cycle."

Raël then talks about change, how all decisions are immediate, made in an instant. Raelians must make that decision to be happy all the time now, *instantly.* "If it takes you ten years to change, it means it took you ten years to be ready for that instantaneous change! All good things come spontaneously—a laugh, a sneeze, an orgasm!" (The Raelians are laughing hysterically at this.) Raël then invites everyone to hold onto their feeling of harmony: "What the world needs is not a new political order, but a new spiritual order, where harmony and pleasure in being will bring about peace." He made a few more sexual jokes about the orgasm (which I didn't get) and concluded his speech by shouting, "And one day, we will ejaculate all the way to the stars!"

The Raelians broke into a storm of clapping, and within seconds all stood up and were cheering and jumping up and down. M—, the woman animator, then took up the microphone and introduced a man in his late thirties with hair slicked back into a short ponytail, also wearing a pendant with a protruding swastika. He informed us he had been able, during his tour of IsRaël, to meet Rabin, the Israeli prime minister, and to transfer documents concerning the embassy directly to him. A buzz of excitement vibrated through the assembly. He noted that one of Rabin's men had made a bad joke about them, but what is more important is that our name is known and recognized (applause). A few more announcements were made about a birthday party where a non-Raelian band would play for free out of respect for their religion. Raël's date of departure for his next world tour was announced, and many people whipped out pens and scribbled down the information so they could go see him off at the airport. Lear took up the mike again, and made a speech singing praises to Raël. He called him "the most enlightened man here, presently, on earth"—while the latter hung his head low, with a half smile, trying to look humble. Lear said we have been told to concentrate on the message and not on the messenger, but that in the process, we have somehow overly demystified Raël. We should cherish him, lavish him with gifts and luxuries. He joked that if Raël could find out how to send material gifts up to the Elohim, he would do it. Then Lear announced, for the very first time at any Raelian convention, that there should be a second donation made—not to the movement alone, but also to Raël. He called on his Raelian brothers and sisters to be generous and remember that Raël will not be around forever to guide them. Finally, he apologized to Raël for making this speech in front of him, but since he had been planning to do it, not expecting Raël's presence, he decided to go ahead and make it anyway. Then another man sat down on stage and performed a song he had composed in honor of Raël. During the song, I noticed a girl was sitting on Lear's lap, and he first had his hand up the back of her shirt, and then down her pants, stroking her behind. (Later he mentioned to me that the girl was his girlfriend.) Another man in the front row was massaging the shoulders of a girl sitting at his feet. The song received a standing ovation. The envelopes for the donations had been collected in a large basket, then M— reminds everyone that the Dawson students are here and would like to distribute some questionnaires or conduct interviews. The meeting was over.[2]

Reflections on Raël's Charisma

Theorists on charisma Weber (1947) and Wallis (1984) emphasize the notion that charisma is generated from the bottom up. In other words, a leader does not impose charismatic authority on passive acolytes, but rather the followers award their prophet that authority because it suits their spiritual and social needs. It is clear from my students' field reports that Lear and the guides prepare, amplify, and stage-manage Raël's appearances, and they educate the congregation in how to recognize and support charisma and in how to cultivate it in themselves.

Grossman had an interesting insight into Raël's appeal. He proposes that Raël is "Everyman." Like Christian, the protagonist of *Pilgrim's Progress,* Raël's very "ordinariness" permits his followers to identify with him and allows him to teach them profound lessons.

I wondered what made this man so attractive to these people, how does he inspire such awe and devotion . . . ? This was especially difficult to figure out since the group seems to stress that all people are equal, that there is no difference between the sexes, that they are all "brothers and sisters." The search for equality, yet the worship of their leader, is one of the many conflicting elements. . . . It then occurred to me that Raël's ordinariness and humility are precisely his charm. He represents their ideals exactly by not being particularly attractive, not very rich, not a superb speaker (or

> writer, judging from his books). He is an average man who had been chosen by above-average beings. His only power was that the message had been revealed to him, not to someone else. This tension was . . . accentuated in this meeting during Lear's speech about demystifying Raël and focusing on the message, but not the messenger, and at the same time calling him "the most enlightened man presently on Earth." (Grossman 1993)

Raelian Sexual Effervescence

Many of my students were taken aback by the Raelians' sexual exhibitionism and free-love ethic. Andrea Szabo (1993) writes that "a man commented on a woman's tattoo . . . and she took out her entire breast out of her shirt and showed the tattoo to [him] in a room full of people." Sonia Iasenza (1997) writes: "It was at this point when they were passing for the donations that I turned around and saw my newly found [Raelian] friend Stephane making out with the girl in front of him. This shocked me, because his girlfriend (at least I thought it was his girlfriend because I saw them making out before) was sitting right beside him."

One male student interviewed a middle-aged woman at a Raelian dance and describes how she "hit on him" at the conclusion to their interview:

> The more we talked, the more she got closer. I was about to leave and felt I had to thank her somehow, so I kissed her on the cheeks. That was a mistake, for she used that to kiss me on the lips, and then started to hug me. She was old enough to be my mother, so I kind of let her know that I was not interested. . . . She told me that was too bad, . . . we could have had a lot of fun together because she was very flexible, for she does yoga. I could have gone to the dance, for another lady (also about 40), gave me a ticket. She told me that she wanted to give it to someone good-looking. (Thank God I didn't let this incident go to my head with all these compliments. . . .) I guess it was my lucky day, for at least 15 women complimented me for something or another. Maybe it was the Raelian way of being friendly to all members. Maybe it was a way of recruitment, to make someone welcome. (Bujold 1988)

The Raelians' Anti-Catholic Stance

Over years of attending Raelian gatherings, my students and I have heard many anti-Catholic sentiments expressed: "Catholicism? Never! I never believed in that! It's a crock of shit!" a Raelian told my student Vince Mezzagno (1999). "I was Roman Catholic. But then I heard what the pope was saying, and he's a criminal!" another Raelian said (DiMaio 2001). One Raelian, a former Jesuit priest, said that the Roman Catholic Church was "racist," and that "the Vatican has known for a long time of the Elohim's existence but is withholding this information from their flock for fear [it would cause] a revolution" (Vendramin 1988).

This same ex-Jesuit hung around with my students after the transmission and kept them spellbound as he described with great gusto the details of his face-lift, hair-implant, and nose-job surgeries. "The Catholic Church stole my youth," he declared, his hand stroking the shoulders of his pretty Raelian girlfriend. "But thanks to science and to Raël, I have got it back again!"

The February 2001 Meeting

By the midnineties the venue and the tone of the meetings had changed considerably, and as a researcher I was not very happy about it. Meetings became more formal and stage-managed. In the good old days, Raël's presence was frequent and I could watch the bishops sitting at the front, interacting with each other, flirting, jostling, conferring, and petting their girlfriends. I could observe up close how they responded to Raël. The congregation had been smaller then, and there was lively interaction between the bishops behind the microphone and people from the floor. Sometimes I could watch decisions being made on the spot, new directions happening. Every meeting was exciting and taught me something about Raël, his guides, and the movement.

When their contract with the Holiday Inn expired, the Raelians moved their meetings to a quaint, art-deco, rather sleazy nightclub in the "gay village" of East Montreal. The entrance featured photographs of cabaret singers in drag and old comedians. The plush seats were worn out, the floors dirty. What bothered me, however, was not the venue, but rather the opacity of the research field. The Raelians were turning into an "audience NRM." The congregation sat in a dark theater and watched movies. Sexy girls paraded across the stage as a requirement for their training at the assistant animator level and made carefully rehearsed announcements in soft, ultra-relaxed voices. All the real action and planning now took place behind the scenes.

By 2000, the monthly meeting was moved to Theatre Gésu, an elegant theater inside a gray stone Jesuit seminary on Bleury Street. When the Jesuits realized to their horror whom they had as a tenant, they tried to break the contract, but the Raelians took them to court and won on grounds of religious discrimination.

When I entered the reception space on the third Sunday morning in February 2001, it was full of people who ranged in age from teens to fifties. An abundance of slender sexy women floated through the crowd, most of them angels, down feathers fluttering from chain or pearl necklaces. My students from Concordia University and Dawson College were already deep in conversations with Raelians. Two guards stood by, recognizable by their black outfits and cell phones held in readiness. One of them told my students that security guards were always present, just in case Raël decided to show up. It is a convention that Raël's presence at the meetings comes as a surprise.

I led my students past a row of tables where several older members sat selling Raël's books, the swastika medallion, and the sensual meditation tapes. We were encouraged to sign up for the weekend seminar coming up in April. Ushers directed us into the darkened theater's semi-circular rows, and we gazed at the banner over the stage: "Notre Religion c'est la Science!" (Our religion is science).

In a reference to the recent Valentine's Day, the stage was decorated with a tall white candelabra; two men and a women, semi-nude, swathed in white drapes, and wearing wings, assumed a series of stylized poses that told a story of courtship, rivalry, rejection—with a bisexual resolution. A home movie was shown of Raelians on the street offering hugs to passersby. (The anticultists will love that as an example of "love bombing," I thought.)

Then the lights went out and Raël's new personal assistant, a delightfully pretty Japanese guide named Shizue, crouched center stage in a white hooded robe, her long black pigtails hanging out, and talked the audience through the oxygenation deep-breathing exercise and the sensual meditation. She instructed the Raelians to send out love to the people walking by on the street, to the whole island of Montreal, and to the earth, and finally to send their love out across the universe until it was felt by the Elohim on their planet.

Then a screen descended and we watched a short clip of the Cirque de Soleil—two Chinese acrobats slowly balancing on each other's shoulders, swinging on trapezes, and catching each other as they flew through the air. They were young muscular girls whose slanted eyes, heart-shaped faces, and green gauze costumes reminded one of aliens—particularly as they seemed to defy the laws of gravity and the usual limitations of the human body.

"Why do they always show acrobats from Cirque de Soleil at the meetings these days?" I asked the priest guide sitting beside me. "It is because we admire these artists—so conscious and in touch with their bodies," he explained. Perhaps they choose these films to express the worship of the human body, its potential to become godlike or immortal through cultivating sensual awareness and mastering science. Also the film evokes the mystery of the other, the alien seen as an immortal androgyne, and the interaction between races.

The message here is that the human is infinitely malleable, can take many forms and colors. Through manipulating the body, we can fly off to new galaxies.

The Members

I have often been asked, "What kind of person joins the Raelians?" It is not easy to describe a typical Quebec Raelian, but three membership survey questionnaires address that question: a Raelian internal survey of 1988, my Dawson College students' survey in 1991, and my survey with Andrea Birchenough-La France in 2003.

Of 1,400 questionnaires distributed in the internal survey conducted by the Raelian Conseil Decisionel at the 1988 summer seminars in Quebec, 399 were returned. The results show that men outnumber women 2:1, and that the average age of members was 35, with 33.9 the median age for those in the structure, and 32.4 the median age of ordinary Raelians. Raelian occupations fall into four categories: 59 percent *travailleurs* (in the work force), 24 percent students, 13 percent "other," and only 5 percent *ménagères* (homemakers).

The survey of the leadership (*la structure*) indicates that the guides' sexual lifestyles (*plan sexuel-affectif*) are quite varied, with 28 percent *célibataire* (sexually inactive); 8 percent living in couples with "open" relationships with plenty of "extracurricular" sex (*plusieurs rencontres extracurricular*); 13 percent living alone with frequent sexual encounters; and 40 percent living in monogamous, or almost monogamous, couples.

The Dawson College survey, conducted by seven of my students who passed out questionnaires at a 1991 Raelian meeting in Montreal, received thirty responses out of three hundred participants. All respondents were from a Catholic background with parents who were low-paid, often blue-collar workers like filing clerks and telemarketers, janitors, elevator operators, bus drivers, and the like. In contrast, our respondents were upwardly mobile, aspiring to the middle class. Many were working in or training for the technologies and parascientific professions (lab technician, industrial technician, computer programmer, sound technician, dental assistant, paramedic, nurse, security guard in a psychiatric ward); twenty-nine of the thirty held an undergraduate degree or were in the process of earning one.

The third membership survey was coordinated by Andrea Birchenough-La France, then a student at Concordia University, and me. Together we wrote the questionnaire and enlisted my Concordia students to distribute it at the February 16, 2003, meeting at the Theatre Gésu. There were around 120 people at the meeting, and 12 of those were non-Raelians involved in our research. Fifty Raelians filled out the questionnaire (see the Appendix).

Birchenough-La France analyzed the results. Of the respondents, 38 percent were level 2, assistant animators; 28 percent were rank-and-file Raelians; 14 percent were level 1, probationers; and 14 percent were level 3, animators. None of the priests or bishops responded, probably because they were sitting at the front, actively involved in orchestrating the meeting.

Most members reported discovering Raelianism through a friend (26 percent) or through Raël's books (26 percent). The primary factor attracting them to the movement was Raël's philosophy (52 percent).

The responses concerning their level of education show that 22 percent held university degrees, including 4 percent who held master's and 2 percent (one person) who held a doctorate; 18 percent were graduates of a professional training program; 18 percent were CEGEP graduates (equivalent to junior college); 38 percent were high school graduates; and only 2 percent (one person) did not complete a secondary education. On the basis of my interviews with priests and bishops, they would have shown a significantly higher level in terms of education and professional career.

The responses to a question that asked respondents their parents' and their own occupations suggest that most Raelians today come from a middle-class background. The 1991 Dawson College survey, in contrast, showed that Raelians tended to have lower-middle-class or working-class parents. This confirms my impression that the Raelian Movement has become more upscale since I began my research in 1987, with an upwardly mobile membership.

The responses to the question regarding sexual orientation were quite consistent with the 1988 survey, showing that Raelians adopt a wide variety of sexual lifestyles.

Based on responses to the 2003 survey, the largest age group is 41–50

(40 percent), born between 1950 and 1960, the years of Quebec's "quiet revolution." The next two largest age groups are 31–40 and 51–60, both 18 percent. This statistic shows a maturation of the movement since 1988, when the Raelian survey found the median age was 33, and our Dawson College survey in 1991, which came up with 28 as the median age for women and 33 for men.

Males (76 percent) were more eager than females (18 percent) to cooperate with our research, perhaps because most of our student research assistants were attractive females. Although an "eyeball estimate" at the meeting indicated that males outnumbered females at the meeting, it certainly was not by 4:1.

Sixty-eight percent of our respondents were born in Quebec. While still high, this is a lower percentage than the almost exclusively native Quebecois membership I observed in 1988. This change reflects the expansion of the movement into other countries (foreign Raelians immigrate to be closer to Raël, or to live with their Quebecois lovers). It also reflects Quebec's increasing ethnic diversity over the last fifteen years.

Most members (72 percent) were baptized in the Catholic Church, fewer than the 97 percent baptized as Catholics in our 1991 survey (an admittedly small sample). The 12 percent baptized "Raelian" suggests these people had a secular upbringing or are second-generation Raelians. The 6 percent not baptized shows that newcomers from a nonreligious background are checking out the Raelian religion.

When respondents were asked how often they attended church during their childhood, 52 percent said they attended regularly, and 34 percent attended only a few times a year (Christmas, Easter, funerals, weddings, and the like). This finding is consistent with a question that asked "Are your parents religious?" to which 62 percent answered yes, 30 percent no, and 8 percent "no response." Only 10 percent never attended church.

The results of the question "Do you find any resemblances to / influences of Catholicism in the Raelian Movement?" were surprising: 48 percent said there were no similarities, and the 30 percent who said similarities existed noted only the similarity between the two churches' "structure" (bishops and priests). This question had the highest number of no responses (22 percent), which seems to indicate this is a touchy topic. The Raelians' anti-Catholic demonstrations and Raël's hostility toward the pope are well known.

Raelians tend not to be "spiritual seekers," according to the 2003 survey, for 86 percent were never involved in a new religious movement before joining the Raelians. Only 2 percent (one person) cited a previous NRM affiliation, and 12 percent did not respond. In this respect they are quite different from the members of Heaven's Gate and Unarius. Tumminia and Kirkpatrick (1995, 101) write that, "strictly speaking, Unarians are not converts. Potential members have already adopted the alternative worldview of the New Age philosophy, particularly acceptance of reincarnation and psychic awareness. . . . Repeatedly, those interviewed in Unarius describe themselves as 'seekers.'" The early Heaven's Gate (then known as Human Individual Metamorphosis or simply "the group") converts, as described by Balch and Taylor (1977), were typically "spiritual seekers." Balch and Taylor make the point that The Two's (Applewhite and Nettles) seemingly sudden and dramatic success in effecting instantaneous mass conversions can be explained by members' previous involvement in various New Age groups in the "cultic milieu," where they had already assimilated most of the key concepts preached by The Two. The finding that Raelians tend not to have a background in the New Age or the cultic milieu reflects Raël's rejection of—or perhaps lack of interest in—the occult (see chapter 1). I have observed newcomers of the "seeker" variety at meetings ask questions that attempt to apply Raelian philosophy to New Age or neotranscendental concepts; these tend to get sharply dismissive responses from Raël or the guides.

To give a simple answer to the question "What kind of people join the Raelians?" I would say that, in Quebec at least, the movement attracts young, attractive adults from a Catholic background that they have already rejected, who are upwardly mobile in society, ambitious in their education and careers, and individualistic and fun loving. Like many Quebecois youth, they reject conventional middle-class and Christian family values, live alone or with a partner outside wedlock, and postpone or veto reproduction. They tend to revere science and despise religious institutions, particularly the Catholic Church.

The 2002 international membership was fifty-five thousand, and in 2003, sixty-five thousand, but this number refers to Raelians who have been baptized rather than to active Raelians. I have seen guides perform the baptisms, then look around and ask if anyone else would like to come up. Giggling groups of teenagers egg each other on to volunteer for baptism as a dare. Many of these "members" are inactive or were never serious in the first place, and many others have dropped out. Of course, most mainstream churches inflate their membership figures and do not delete the defectors or the inactive members.

My students and I, who have been attending the Montreal Raelian gatherings biennially (at least) since 1991, have encountered a higher number of professional strippers than one would expect to find, say, at a Scientology, Hare Krishna, Mormon, or Unification Church gathering. At one meeting we counted four male strippers (fully clothed at the time, but they had mentioned their work in the course of our conversations with them). We also frequently encountered female strippers—introduced onstage or interviewed by my students.

One aspect of this movement that makes it so different from other NRMs is its encouragement of sexual minorities and sex workers. One student was told that a famous exotic dancer in the late 1970s, Lana St. Cyr, joined the RM and converted many of her fellow workers. This story was later denied by a Raelian bishop, who claimed that Lana St. Cyr was never on their membership list. A male stripper I met at a Raelian gathering seemed a bit wary of my request for an interview, insisting he was not a gigolo, but finally we set the record straight. He would meet me only at the pet store in the Atwater Mall (of all places), so as we sat between puppies and lizard cages, constantly interrupted by a squawking parrot, he explained to me the advantages for strippers of being Raelian. His agent booked him at nightclubs across the country, so he was constantly traveling. To wake up Sunday morning in a strange city, after a late night in clubs, he could look forward to attending the local chapter of the Raelians and tune in to a group of like-minded, sociable, and sexy friends. Moreover, Raël's heavy emphasis on avoiding drugs had helped many strippers he knew beat their cocaine and heroin addiction. He also claimed that Raël's insistence on the use of condoms had probably saved the lives of several of his more promiscuous co-workers. He said that "at least 75 percent" of male strippers were "either gay or bi" and felt profoundly alienated from the Catholic Church, which denounced their activities as sinful. They were delighted to find a religion that accepted and even celebrated their sexual differences.

Even people with AIDS were welcomed by Raelians and publicly introduced—or introduced themselves to us—at meetings. The Raelians held healing meditations for them in the late 1980s. Raël told a story at the 1990 summer seminar about a Raelian who had AIDS but managed to cure himself by fasting and meditating for forty days (note the allusion to Jesus). In 1997, I was introduced to the leader of the Mexican Raelian Movement, who was afflicted with AIDS and too sick to fulfill his duties, so his retirement was announced after a healing meditation was held in his honor. Another striking presence at the meetings is the drag queens, who show up in droves for the Raelian dances. It is difficult, however, to discern whether they are "real" transvestites or merely Raelians joking around, recapturing the hilarity of the cross-dressing party held annually at the summer seminars. I have also interviewed two Raelians who were transsexuals.

Another surprising phenomenon among the Raelians is that many of them undergo plastic surgery and love to talk about it, among them the ex-Jesuit priest guide described earlier. I observed an assistant guide make a sexual overture to the female priest guide I was talking to, and when she rebuffed him, he joked: "Wait 'til after I have my face-lift. I'll come back and try again!" Many of the older women in the structure are deceptively youthful in appearance, due to cosmetic surgery, strict diet, exercise, and perhaps the destressing effects of sensual meditation.

The Guides

The Raelians' international membership statistics have often been queried and are impossible to verify, but their statistics regarding the structure are quite reliable. The RM's internal survey of international leaders in February 1999 gives the following figures: Europe, 467 active leaders; France, 283; Switzerland, 60; Italy, 44. In the Americas there were 370 active leaders: Canada, 325; United States, 30; Mexico, 10; Chile, 5. Asia boasted a total of 539: Japan, 375; Korea, 120. Africa held 67 leaders, most concentrated in Burkina Faso (40) and in Cote d'Ivoire (20). Oceania had 45 leaders, the majority being Australians.

I have often sat watching the guides strut across the stage exerting charisma (quite considerable, in some cases) and wondered to myself: "Which one of the bishops will become Raël's successor? Who will be the next Brigham Young, the next St. Peter or St. Paul, of the Raelian Church?"

I asked the "Guide of Guides," Raël himself, this question in an interview on December 6, 1994. It was clear he had considered this issue carefully, for he immediately responded: "He will be elected by the guides at the top level. . . . The bishop guides—they will meet together and elect among themselves if I disappear. And also, while I am still alive, every seven years there is a meeting of the level 5 to reelect me or to choose somebody else. Until now, they look like they want to keep me in charge, but one day they can change it if I mismanage the Raelian Movement. . . . Yes, they can replace me."

SP: How are decisions made at the top level?

RAËL: I take their advice, but I am responsible. I take responsibility and teach to the guides to do the same. Listen to everybody, take the opinion of everybody, but make your own choice, alone, by yourself.

SP: What qualities do you look for when you choose your guides?

RAËL: Qualities in my guides? I look for harmony—very important, serenity, harmony, number one—also charisma. When they walk into a room, everyone look and have the feeling to speak with him. We are really family. The most important family is not the biological family but the family you choose, your friends. Of course the guides, the Raelians, are more my family than my biological family. We are in harmony, philosophically—and that is what is most important.

So I continued to wonder as I observed the bishops at the meetings. There were no visible signs of rivalry. I watched Lear at the summer camp climb on the back of Daniel Chabot's motor scooter and wrap his arms around Daniel's waist. I observed the male bishops horsing around, joking, pushing, and hugging each other—good-looking heterosexual men who were not afraid to touch each other to express their deep friendship.

There were several outstanding candidates for the succession. Daniel Chabot, the psychology professor, has a doctorate, is a dynamic speaker, and has written two popular psychology books praising Raël's method of sensual meditation and sensory education as a breakthrough in psychotherapy. For a while I thought it might be Lear, the handsome, stalwart blond artist who paints utopian friezes of naked humanoids picnicking in an alien Eden. He is the youngest Raelian ever to be made a guide and adopted Raël as his father figure shortly after his own father's tragic death when Lear was fourteen. Lear served as national guide, as Raël's personal assistant, and recently as his head of security. He had a special role as Raël's personal fundraiser. At one indoor meeting I attended, he was wearing a rather dramatic black felt hat. He announced, "If we love Raël, do we want to see him with a nine-to-five job, or will we help him do his work as our beloved prophet?" He then whipped off his hat and emptied his pockets into it—bills and coins—then leapt off the stage and ran around the room offering the hat to people in the congregation with a pained, sincere look on his handsome face. "For Raël!" he kept saying. "For Raël."

But in 2000, Lear was demoted by Raël on the grounds that he was not "in harmony" with his career as an artist (he had no time to paint because he was working so hard for the movement) and he left the structure, although as a Raelian he continued to attend the meetings. "It is still my philosophy, that hasn't changed," he told me. He returned in 2003 as Raël's head of security but recently resigned and is no longer in the structure.

Another outstanding candidate was Nicole Bertrand, the 2003 continental guide, who is a dynamic teacher, sexologist, and organizer of conferences, slender and attractive with a deep, charming voice. Daniel Turcotte, the former continental guide of the Americas (due to his linguistic abilities—he speaks French, English, and Spanish fluently) is now Nicole's assistant for the Hispanic countries. He founded and directs a flourishing massage school, has a weightlifter's body and a mane of reddish-brown hair, and exudes positive energy and enthusiasm in his speeches. All these bishops, male and female alike, are strikingly handsome and exert an aura of confidence and charisma on stage. Not one of them, however, possesses the unique credentials and abilities of Raël.

My question concerning the succession was finally answered at the Sunday, January 2003, meeting in Montreal. Three weeks after the Boxing Day announcement of the world's first human clone, the Raelians were riding high on the media blitz. Raël appeared at this meeting and formally appointed Brigitte Boisselier, a bishop, as his successor, expressing his gratitude for her efficient means of spreading the message as the director of Clonaid.

Interviews with Guides

Over the last fifteen years, I have collected many interviews with members of the structure, conducted by my students as well as myself. The questions we ask the guides tend to focus on their conversion to the Raelian religion, their perceptions of and relationships with Raël, and the impact of the summer seminars and Raël's philosophy on their sexuality. Rather than offer portraits of individual guides, I have chosen to organize these interview data thematically, under the themes conversion, sexuality, and relationship with Raël. My purpose is to show what the guides have in common and also to respect their wish for anonymity and privacy, difficult to maintain, since they are leaders and public representatives of the Raelian religion.

Reasons for Becoming Raelian

A recurring theme in these interviews was that guides were attracted to Raël's philosophy because it bridged the gap between the Catholic otherworldly faith they knew as children and the pragmatic, scientific worldview they espoused as adults.

1. Clonaid's press conference to introduce five surrogate mothers for the cloning projects. Reproduced by permission of *La Presse*

2. Raelians distributing condoms to Montreal high school students. Reproduced by permission of *La Presse*

3. Raël with Dr. Brigitte Boisselier, director of Clonaid, in Montreal, just after she announced the birth of the world's first human clone. Reproduced by permission of the *Montreal Gazette*

4. *(left)* Raël's angels dance down the streets of Montreal in the anti-Catholic "parade for apostasy" demonstration. Reproduced by permission of the *Montreal Gazette*

5. *(above)* Raelians carry banners denouncing the Catholic Church in the parade for apostasy. Reproduced by permission of the *Montreal Gazette*

6. Raël presents the model of the embassy in Japan, 1991. From *20 ans,* courtesy of the International Raelian Movement

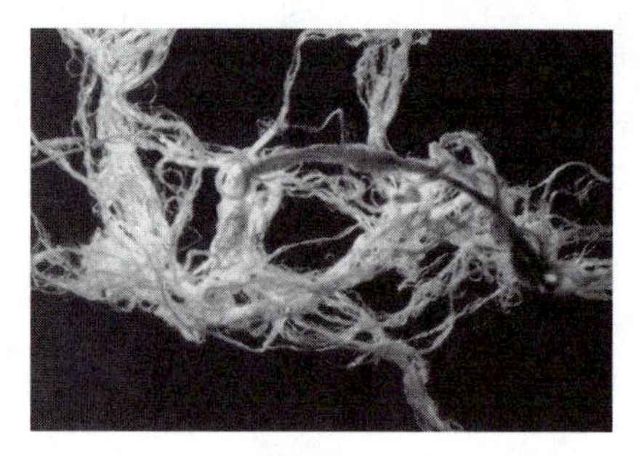

7. Angel hair. From *20 ans,* courtesy of the International Raelian Movement

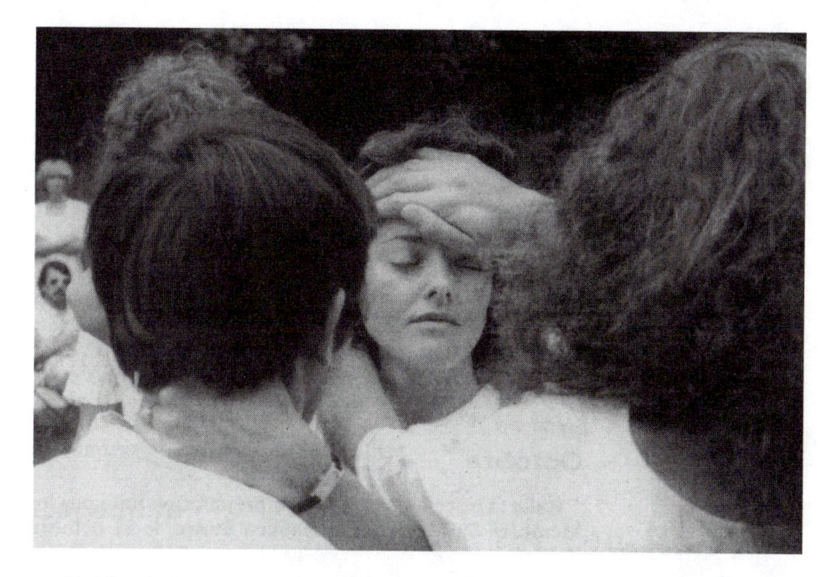

8. Ritual of empowerment for a new priest guide. From *20 ans*, courtesy of the International Raelian Movement

9. Raël in 1979. From *20 ans*, courtesy of the International Raelian Movement

10. The model of the embassy for the Elohim. From *20 ans,* courtesy of the International Raelian Movement

11. First international Guides Conference in Valcourt, Quebec, July 2002. From the *Apocalypse,* courtesy of the International Raelian Movement

12a and b. Raelians singing the "Hymn to the Elohim," ending with a joyful salute. From the *Apocalypse,* courtesy of the International Raelian Movement

13. Léon Mellul spreading the message in Tel Aviv. From the *Apocalypse*, courtesy of the International Raelian Movement

14. *(right above)* Raël, former pop singer, entertaining his friends. From the *Apocalypse*, courtesy of the International Raelian Movement

15. *(right below)* Raël with the race car sponsored by UFOland. From the *Apocalypse*, courtesy of the International Raelian Movement

UFO land
.com
linelTEX

16. Sophie, Raël's consort, dancing with Sean for the Raelian cabaret at Valcourt. From the *Apocalypse,* courtesy of the International Raelian Movement

17. Raël playing *boules* on the lawn. From the *Apocalypse*, courtesy of the International Raelian Movement

18. Jacket design to "spread the message." Courtesy of the author

19. Raelian car with the model of Raël's UFO and the embassy. Courtesy of the author

20. Exraël, Erick Llamarche, ex-member and outspoken critic of the Raelian Movement. Courtesy of Erick Llamarche

"Colette," a Raelian bishop, comes from a French Canadian working-class Catholic background. Her father was a salesman, her mother a homemaker with fourteen children. Two of her siblings are also Raelian. The interview was conducted by Danielle Lindy on March 18, 1994.

When I was young I went to mass and I was in all the things Catholic until I was sixteen. I was Catholic because my parents were, and I had no choice. But I was quite into it, because I liked being inside churches. I liked the music, the organ, and stained-glass windows. It was kind of peaceful. I had a good feeling when I was in church, but I was always frustrated with the teachings. I would ask questions but there were no answers. I was told to believe, but that wasn't good enough. I still wondered. I couldn't settle for just believing. I always kept in my mind that there was an answer and when I read Raël's first book I said, "Well, it's so simple." All those priests had told me was, "Well, it's a mystery."

I first heard about the Raelians in 1977. I was teaching math in St. Jerome and a teacher from my school came over to my place one night and said: "Look at that. You must read these books." I was surprised but curious because the first book was called *Le livre qui dit la vérité,* and I said, "Wow, hmmm, *la vérité,* well, why not?" I started reading it and couldn't stop. It was so funny and so simple at the same time—funny and simple. It was amazing. At that time I was dating a man who was also a teacher. I was always behind him saying, "Listen, Michel, listen to that!" And at the same time I had my studies, which were rational, mathematics and science, which have to do with logic, keeping me on the path, and I said "It's logical [the books] but at the same time it looks crazy." . . . I found that evolution was not a solid theory, there are a lot of "missing links" in the theory itself, and the other theory that God created man, well that's a different explanation or an enigma as well. Then I found out why the two look so apart, and I said finally, "Well, someone did it, a lot of them did it, but to human beings who examined the various possibilities. For evolutionists who deny God, it looks like it happened by itself." So, now I could reconcile the two theories about the origin of life with the logical theory about the Elohim.

I expected the Raelians to be in some way special, but they were just normal people. But I can understand it now because the book is so simple; it's written for people who are used to philosophy, everybody can understand it. And the strongest feeling was I had felt alone in my thoughts, but when I saw 150 people were there, I was so enthusiastic, I was not alone.

> It was a logical process, a choice which made me at peace with myself. I understood the Elohim created man in their own image from DNA and I didn't believe this without knowing. This process took me three years, and when the Elohim recognized me, I didn't feel anything, only certainty.

The paradox of Raël's god/man status—the tension between his unpretentious ordinariness and his extraordinary role as a prophet-messiah—was reflected in our interviews. Some Raelians stress his mere ordinariness: "Raël is an average person. He doesn't act any different than anyone else. I shook his hand and talked to him for a while. He's a very intelligent man who knows exactly what he wants out of life. He didn't appear to me as a 'special' person. All he wants to do is pass on information that he was given to us" (Jones 1988).

But other members' accounts of Raël were filled with passion and wonder. When I interviewed "Chantal" at the Holiday Inn in Montreal at the April 1991 meeting, she was a priest guide from a middle-class Quebecois family, a scientist with a Ph.D. and a successful career. She has since retired from active duty in the structure because she is married with two young children and the demands of her family and her career are overwhelming—but she remains a Raelian.

> I met Raël at age twenty-one when I was hitchhiking in Europe, in France. Some Raelians picked me up and took me to their campsite. I was attracted to the Raelians—they were harmonious, beautiful, radiating. I wanted to be friends with all those people. I had traveled alone and met a lot of people by the time I met them. They were camping, it was not organized like it is now. Not professional. I laughed at their beliefs. But in the months before, I had had experiences leading me to Raël. I had deep discussions about evolution. I wrote many pages in my journal. I found evolution impossible. It was too much by hazard. God was not possible, but there had to be some intention. . . .
>
> Then I saw a big flying saucer above my house. It was not a big surprise for me, I was already sure there were other beings out there. . . . I was very conscious of the danger of nuclear energy. I was in a state of alarm, feeling I had to find my way to help the earth. I stayed for two weeks and took the Stage de l'Eveil in 1978 at Perpignon, in the Paussac near Brantome. There were eighty people, all so beautiful! They gave me *Le livre* and answered all my questions.

For one year afterwards I traveled alone and had much time to think. I had to rethink all my theories. I had to be solid. My parents were afraid for me, but now they respect the path I have chosen. So, when I met Raël, it was like an electric shock! All the pieces came together like a big diamond in my head. It was so natural, so obvious. I wrote to all my friends, my family. They were surprised, they thought I was crazy, that Raël's message was a stupid invention. Then I felt upset; I realized I was alone. I met Raël three or four days before I read his book, then I went to him and said, "Are you sure the story you tell is true?" But I could see he had a positive intention to help people. I made a personal opinion [that] he says the truth. I met him many times and it confirms my opinion that he is sincere.

Anna Pascal interviewed "Madeleine," an animator, in December 1992 in Montreal. Madeleine comes from a wealthy old Quebecois family and is a successful businesswoman.

I always thought that ETs were existing. I remember when I was a kid my mother was asking me to do my prayers before I went to bed and I was talking as if I was talking to my brother. For me, [God] was a human being. He was not a spiritual wave of energy floating in the air or sitting on a cloud watching me. When I grew up, I stopped praying because my mother was not asking me to do it anymore. . . . And in 1985 there was a friend of mine who asked me to dinner at his house and then [I] saw these books of Raël on his shelf and I was really curious. "Wow! What's this? Extraterrestrials! That's really interesting!" He lent them to me, and I read those five books in the next week. So, for me, it really was a revelation. I thought, "This guy is wild!" And at the same time, I recognized myself. I felt that this was what I was always feeling without putting it into words.

At the beginning it was not easy, meditating and being with other people who had the same philosophy as me. Because a philosophy like that you always have a group of people who are a little bit fanatic about it, and you have the other people who think about the philosophy and live it in a very quiet way. I remember having a lot of nights chatting about it 'til four or five in the morning—about matter, about energy, about ETs, about meditating, going deep into yourself and feeling that you are made of the infinitely small, . . . it's a cycling. You know when you see a picture of a

> galaxy? Well, that is what we have inside of us. In other words, inside you have people living on another planet. . . . When we meditate and we are in harmony with ourselves, that's when the whole constitution will be happy. That goes down deep, though. A lot of people don't understand that.

"Wilhelm" a Raelian guide interviewed by Robert Unger in Montreal in April 1990, is from a Catholic background and is a family man and successful European engineer with a Ph.D.

> I went to a conference with a friend who was a member. I was attracted by the logical aspect of the message. We ponder over the origin of mankind. One idea is the theory of the Creation in seven days by an almighty and immaterial God. But, in the last fifty years a new theory developed which was almost as mystical: the evolution over millions of years entirely though chance. And neither of these I found satisfying and both of them rest on faith. . . .
>
> The message offers a third alternative, which is the creation of humanity and life by genetic engineers who came from another civilization. It does not contradict the other two theories; it unifies them, because there is an intelligent creator (actually a team of scientists) and there is also evolution, the result of decisions and experiments made by the genetic engineers, . . . but the evolution did not happen by chance, but in the minds of the creators.

"Yves," a Raelian animator, level 3, is a musician and a taxi driver. He was interviewed by Gamma M— on December 3, 1992, in Montreal.

> I play in [a] rock band, can't you tell by my shirt? But I've been a drummer for over ten years. In small clubs and places, the dark smoky corners of Quebec. My older brother brought home Raël's book. I picked it up and was fascinated. It was the message that first attracted me. I have always been fascinated by extraterrestrials. I was searching, . . . believed in another world, in other people to whom I could speak, but it was all in the imagination, a fantasy, and no one was talking about it. But then, when I stumbled upon the messages, I saw what they had done, there was a world more advanced than is described in many scriptures like the Bible that we call the "Elohim." I joined seven years ago.
>
> I was raised a Catholic but I have never truly practiced it. I went to church and those things because I was forced to, but, little by little, I

stopped practicing. Yes, I thought there was a God, who had a soul. There is too much emphasis on sin. That is how I was raised—it was how my parents were taught. All pleasure of the body is a sin! You must suffer in order to become happy! You must go down and hurt your knees in the church in order to get saved. Things like that are full of mystification. It never attracted me. It was too abstract. . . .

There is a difference between blind faith and intelligent belief. I was never into any particular religion, but I felt that there was some meaning or something to life, sort of like the code of ethics that I live by. When I read Raël's book, there was nothing in it that I couldn't agree with. And when I met the people in the group, they were really in tune with me, like they really understood what I was trying to figure out about myself.

I was married before I joined the movement, but I don't see her very much because she doesn't agree with my involvement in the movement. We haven't got a divorce because we still love each other.

The Helloim [*sic*]? I have never seen them, but I think of them a lot. It is during meditation, when I meditate [I] try to call upon, to make telepathic contact. I feel I sense the Helloim. I feel they're alive. I think of them indirectly. I could not tell you exactly, I could not show you visually or sensually, it is not palpable, it is something one feels.

How Becoming a Raelian Affects Your Sexuality

A recurring theme throughout our interviews with Raelians was how joining the movement revolutionized their attitudes toward their own sexuality. While media portrayals of Raelians emphasize the "orgies" at the summer camp, it is clear that for Raelians, this period of sexual freedom and experimentation is a delicate, sensitive foray into a primal realm of innocence. One guide, a thirty-three-year-old secretary and massage therapist who was undergoing a painful divorce at the time she joined, eloquently explained in an April 1988 interview with Jerry Evangelista her experience at the summer camp as an opening up of her sensuality.

A lot of people think that [it's an orgy]. . . . If it was like that I would never have joined the movement, because at first I was so shy! . . . I would just say hi to someone and I would blush drastically, I was so shy. I'll tell you frankly, it's not like that. . . . We fast for twenty-four hours, . . . we don't talk or eat or drink anything but water—we really get inside of ourselves. . . . After the twenty-four hours, we start eating again, slowly, and the food! Just the smell of it is great, . . . you can open up your senses, and if you

> do find someone appealing, if you feel like going with that person and sharing a beautiful evening or night with him or her, . . . and it could even be with another woman, but why not? It's beautiful, you're opening your senses, but you don't have to, it's not an obligation. If someone comes to you [and says,] "I'd like to sleep with you," and you don't want to, . . . you're allowed to say no, that's part of the respect, the choice you have.
>
> It's never happened to me like that. I've never had anybody come up to me and say, "Hey, baby! I'd like to sleep with you!" It's not someone you've never seen before. He's more likely to just come up and say, "I sincerely like you and I find you pretty." They're not going to say they want to sleep with you right away, because it's sensuality that comes out of it, not sexuality. Sensuality is when you eat or drink something delicious, or smell something nice, or when you touch something that's soft, and it's the same thing with a person.

Interviews with other guides indicate that the summer seminars had a profound impact on how they experience their sexuality and relationships. Chantal told me in our 1994 interview: "I have been for six years with my boyfriend. There were some things that shocked me in the beginning about sexuality in the Raelians, but we have always been an 'open couple' but always put respect and love in the first place. We believe in being clear and discussing our feeling about each other and other people, and are very conscious of our relationship. My boyfriend is a psychologist, not a Raelian, and we have a four-month-old baby."

"Andre," a Raelian guide interviewed by Lynn Roulston on November 20, 1994, at a Montreal café, told her that the summer seminar

> takes place somewhere beautiful along with nature, meditations, and practice nudity, because it is good to be comfortable with your sexuality. My first experience I did not know what to expect, but when I saw everybody nude it was very normal. Everyone's physique is different and beautiful in each way and is respected equally because we're all on the same level. I feel it is very good for the mind because we don't say, "Well, he has a bigger penis than me"—some people have a little one with the possibility to expand it as long as the other one. Sexuality is regarded as something we should explore and be in touch with our bodies.
>
> In the seminar we talk about everything—sexuality, philosophy, business, jealousy—and we tell you how to feel better in your career so when

you come back for another seminar you feel stronger, work better, and make more money. It opens your eyes and makes you realize if you don't like what you are doing, then make a change. It is beneficial on every level. We have course two hours in the morning and afternoon on Raël's teachings. It is a relaxed atmosphere, we laugh—it's like going to a people's university. You learn more in these two weeks than years in university because it teaches you about your mind, love, relationships, business, philosophy—all the things you are confronted with in life. We tell people how to communicate and interact with others better.

One night we have a game called a dating night when people get matched up. Another evening we have a cross-dressing dance; it's great—you can dress up like a woman with makeup, I love it! We also put on shows—some Raelians are performers—or we have parties. Sex is emphasized, but it's not compulsory, it's up to the people. Our movement is very affectionate and we like to show our love for each other. The meditations help your sexual life, especially if you do it every day. It builds up your energy and your senses. It works. You sense more, feel more when you touch, you caress differently, the sensation is totally different. When you are together with somebody in the movement one of the first experiences you have, you can see the difference. It brings you to another world, another planet. I am like a priest, but I can also have sex. It's great!

Madeleine told Anna Pascal in their 1992 interview:

When first I went to the meeting at the Crown Plaza, I felt a little bit strange, because in 1985 the society was less open about sexuality . . . and everybody there was kissing and touching everybody, and I felt a bit strange, especially being a girl, for the proportion there is a little bit less women. What does amaze me is that we see very pretty women in the movement and very good-looking guys, too. As long as we meditate, the people they open up and they change and they get more beautiful. They open up themselves and we see the transformation of the faces of certain people. It's amazing to see that from year to year. The media has focused very much on our sexual practices, but we do not advocate group orgies. In fact, we do not advocate anything at all except freedom of choice. Sexuality is one of many ways of expressing yourself, and the particular medium of expression is up to the individual. One should not be afraid of social taboos but should act on instinct, so long as one's choice does not

> infringe on anyone's rights or make them uncomfortable. You can spend your whole life as a heterosexual and then be attracted to someone of the same sex, once or twice in your existence. You should act on these attractions and not worry about being labeled "lesbian" or "gay." I have lived with the same man for four years, also a Raelian.
>
> We abhor jealousy—it is a disease that is very hard to get rid of once you catch it. We are free to sleep with others if we feel like it. Our own personal contract is to keep our house for ourselves and not bring others into our joint space. But if I were to go away on vacation for three weeks, he could be free to bring others into our joint space, and vice versa. The movement has a strict policy on condom use, and there are no exceptions. Raël has been arguing for the use of condoms for twenty years now. We even use female condoms for women who sleep together. I stopped using condoms with my steady lover, but only after we had been together a while and had been through many tests. It's not really about religion anymore, it's about . . . philosophy, . . . the philosophy of well-being, the philosophy of freedom, freedom of speech, freedom of what you want to be. If you are a woman or a man, there's no difference. You are a human being first. It's freedom of sexuality, not to feel guilty about having a different sexuality than what the neighbor [has] and living it in a really good way, within respect, and not hurting anyone around you.

These interviews indicate that while the Raelian social environment encourages sexual expression, in no sense can members be said to be "forced" to participate in sexual activities against their will. Of course, they may feel considerable social pressure to conform to the ethos of the collective, as in any religious congregation or youth club. But it was my impression that the people we interviewed deliberately chose to embark on the Raelian "free-love" adventure because it suited their own social, psychological, and sexual needs at the time. Long-term Raelians, after a few weeks or months of experimenting sexually, eventually make their own choices concerning their *plan affectif.* Most of the guides seem to settle down in stable heterosexual couple relationships (many with non-Raelians, interestingly enough). They do, however, continue to pay lip service to Raelian alternative sexual mores by declaring that their relationship is theoretically "open." In Raelian culture it is evidently uncool and un-PC to define oneself as 100 percent heterosexual or as monogamous. Several of our informants spoke of their heterosexual orientation almost apologetically, suggesting that in the future their innate homoerotic tendencies might surface.

Relationship with Raël

In their 1992 interview, Madeleine told Anna Pascal: "It was very impressive, because when you read the books and you know who he is, it's like 'Wow!' But he's a very simple man, very simple, and he has a good sense of humor. We laugh all the time. He comes for dinner and we laugh the whole way through. He's very down to earth and full of love and harmony. He touches you very easily. He says one sentence and you can think about it for days. He can only give us a little bit at a time, because the advanced technology the ETs showed him is too hard for us to understand. They made him understand by chemical education, and he was given all their knowledge in minutes. The knowledge of our highest genius is like the level of a simple child up there."

Andre told Lynn Ralson in their 1994 interview that he thinks of Raël "as a friend, and if I was going to have a best friend, it would be him, or a father, it would be him. We spent a lot of time together and never really talked about the philosophy. We talked about cars, we talked about women, because we are men. He is a great friend that has given me guidance, but one thing he will never say is 'I told you so.'"

Yves spoke of Raël in similar terms to Gamma M— in 1992: "Raël is like a brother, a friend. But in another way. He is the light that is radiating. I feel like he is a luminous being. He says things that were true without negative emotions or positive. I see Raël as a prophet, sent by the Helloim. I see him as truly like a direct line between the Helloims and me."

For "Donna," whom I interviewed at UFOland in July 2000, "Raël is the finest, the most precious person. To me he is a holy man, like Jesus' brother. I was his chauffeur in L.A., to and from his interviews. I was amazed at how funny he could be, he's just a normal, fun human being."

This theme of the tension between Raël's humanity, his inherent humbleness and human warmth, and his divine, extraordinary nature is reminiscent of the centuries-old debate concerning the wholly man, wholly God nature of Christ. Raël's celestial travels and origin imbue him with awe-inspiring authority that lends weight to his demands upon members' lives. But his mere humanity empowers his followers, who feel they also can be extraordinary one day. Thus, Raël is a perfect synthesis of Max Weber's "exemplary" and "ethical" prophets.

Chapter Six

Sexy Angels for Amorous Aliens

"The Order of Raël's Angels" was an explosive new revelation that had a profound effect on the role of women in the movement. Sex between aliens and human abductees is, of course, nothing new. But Raël reverses the scenario. Instead of emotionless aliens probing helpless humans painfully in their private parts as specimens of research, we find beautiful young women cultivating the arts of Eros and their seductive "feminine charisma" under Raël's tutelage so as to lure the aliens to earth to be their lovers—all in the ancient spirit of courtly love, or agape.

On December 13, 1997, Raël received a message from the Elohim that was manifested in the usual way, as voices speaking to him. He chose to guard his secret knowledge until the July 1998 (A.H. 52) summer camp held at Valcourt, Quebec. There he announced it briefly, almost casually, to the assembled Raelians, who were told they could pick up the text of "The Order of Raël's Angels" at the office. It caused a sensation among the assembled campers.

The Elohim had asked Raël to create a new order exclusively for women, the Order of Raël's Angels. This was to be a sort of secret society resembling the lay nuns of the Catholic Church. Raël was to create a training program to prepare women to receive the extraterrestrials when they landed, to act as hostesses, companions, and lovers to the alien visitors. Only Raël's angels would be permitted to enter the embassy, and they would function as liaison officers between the Elohim and the world's media, scientists, and politicians during this exciting time.

When the campers picked up "The Order of Raël's Angels," they found the aliens' message couched in a lofty tone suitable for godlike extraterrestrials: "The time passes and the Grand Moment draws near inescapably. We will be coming soon, it is time to prepare. We will arrive with a plethora of biological robot servants. We do not need humans to serve us. But we love our creation so much it would give us pleasure to see our Creation humbly offer to serve us."

The Elohim evidently wish to dispel fear, for they go on to explain that they come among us as equals and only at our invitation—to be demonstrated by the building of the embassy. Their intention is to hold formal audiences with the earth's governments; they regret their inability to spend time with each of us among their billions of creations (although they assure us that technology does enable them to follow the life of each individual). Then they cite Genesis 6:4: "When the sons of Elohim 'came unto the daughters of men and had children by them, they were the heroes of old, men of renown.'" They explain: "We wish to offer some daughters of men the chance to realize their dream; . . . we ask our last Prophet, Raël to set up a religious order of young women who consciously wish to put their inner and outer beauty at the service of their Creators and their Prophets when we arrive at the Embassy." The Elohim appear to be feminists: "Earth's civilization has demonstrated so much sexism, machismo, . . . it is only fair that women have the chance to be intimate with us."

Raël's Order of Angels is presented as a "religious order encompassing women of the Raelian religion who are legally of age. They will have the full-time responsibility of serving the Elohim, their Creators and the great prophets . . . Moses, Jesus, Buddha and Muhammad during their stay in the Embassy, seeing to their comfort at every level. Meanwhile, they will prepare themselves for this long-awaited day by being in the service of Raël the Last Prophet, and of attending to his well-being."

The document ends on a prophetic note: "Prepare yourselves, our return is imminent. Our love will accompany you through the earthly filter of consciousness while awaiting to see you again for eternity. In the meantime, take good care of our Beloved Prophet because you know that through him, there is a little bit of us among you."

To appreciate the radical nature of this sexual innovation, it is necessary to examine Raelian sexual mores since the 1970s. The first inkling of "free love" can be detected in Raël's second book, *Les extra-terrestres m'ont emmené sur leur planète* (1977a), translated into English in 1978 as *Space Aliens Took Me to Their Planet*. Raël (who was a married man and a father at the time) was touring the Elohim's planet when he was invited by a robot to sample alien sexual mores: "I found myself transported in front of a machine used for fabricating robots. A luminous cube appeared in front of me. . . . A magnificent young brunette with wonderfully harmonious proportions appeared in three dimensions; . . . a second woman, blond and heady [*sic*] this time appeared in the luminous cube; . . . a red-haired person and . . . a magnificent black woman, then a very slim Chinese woman." Since Raël was unable to choose between such splendid specimens of womanhood, he retired to his hotel suite with all six (one goes undescribed): "There I had the most unforgettable bath I have ever had, in the company of those charming robots, absolutely submissive to my desires" (Raël 1978, 252).

The Raelian community is seen by outsiders as an AIDS-free singles club for heteros, homos, and bisexuals. From a sociological perspective, it might be analyzed as a more extreme version of the liberal existential French counterculture of the 1970s, with Brigitte Bardot sunbathing in St. Tropez and the young vagabond Vorilhon singing in the sidewalk cafés of Paris. But it is also a deliberate attempt to mirror Elohim utopian society, where immortal geniuses cavort in nudist banquets on the grass, served by biological robot sex slaves, in eternal pursuit of personal pleasure and technological advancement. All of Raël's advice to his followers concerning their relationships and sexuality is based on his observations of the aliens' lifestyle during his one-day visit. (Raël's teachings on sexual freedom and the cultivation of the senses so closely resemble those of the French eighteenth-century socialist philosopher Charles Fourier that one begins to wonder if the latter might not also have boarded an Elohim spaceship.)

Raël's Philosophy of Sexuality

Raël advocates free love. "You will reject marriage which is only the proclamation of ownership of a person . . . one feels free to love, but when one has signed a contract, one feels like a prisoner, forced to love, and sooner or later, each one begins to hate the other." Raël even advises couples against trying to maintain long-term relationships by working out their problems or weathering rocky periods. Rather, in the absence of "harmony," they should immediately separate while they are still on good terms and remain friends. "You will live with the person of your choice for only as long as you feel good with them. When you no longer get on well together, do not remain together because your union will become hell" (Raël 1978, 285).

"The family is a dangerous sect," writes Raël, alluding to France's post–Solar Temple hysteria over "dangerous sects" (see chapter 3). He points out that only three or four groups committed murder, whereas "80% of crimes are committed in families" and "thousands of people are violated or killed at home by one of their own family members." Raël criticizes our society for endorsing marital violence and "encouraging its members to kill those they love" (Raël 1987b, 62–64). He particularly deplores the French *crime passionel* that allows a jealous man to kill his woman "for love," getting off "with five or six years in prison." Echoing the sentiments of the French free-love advocate Fourier, Raël insists that women should not be men's property. Fourier (1971a, 80) compares marriage to slavery: "Slavery is never more contemptible that when by a blind submission it convinces the oppressor that his victim is born for slavery. Civilized love, in marriage, is at the end of a few months . . . often nothing but pure brutality."

Raël also finds in marriage the potential for brutality: "The one who truly loves hopes his partner will meet someone who will give her even more pleasure. . . . The selfish person prefers to keep 'his property.' He prefers his companion to be unhappy with him rather than happy with someone else. And if this happens, he takes his gun to kill his 'loved one'" (Raël 1987b, 64).

Parenting and Children

Raelian society is not particularly child oriented, and Raelians are not sentimental regarding the joys of parenthood. Members of the structure rarely procreate (I know of only two exceptions). Certainly in Quebec, which has the lowest birthrate in Canada and one of the lowest in the world, Raelians tend to postpone childbearing indefinitely or limit their children to two. Raël's two rationales are to correct planetary overpopulation and to avoid parental responsibilities until "the individual is fulfilled," which can be achieved through the "fulfillment of your body" resulting in the "blossoming of the mind." Raël strongly advocates birth control and abortion.

Raël gives women permission to be unmarried mothers and sexually active single mothers: "To have a child does not necessarily imply being married or even living with a man. . . . Fulfill yourself as you wish without worrying what others may think; . . . welcome the men you like and they will serve as masculine role models for the child" (Raël 1978, 283).

Raël even gives women permission to dump their children, if they get on their nerves. "Thus, if you gave birth to the child you desired . . . and you no longer desire the child, you will be able to entrust him to society so that he may be brought up in harmony necessary for his fulfillment. . . . If the child becomes a nuisance, however slightly, he realizes it and his fulfillment is affected" (Raël 1978, 284).

When questioned about the prospect of having children, Raelian women express the kind of ambivalence shared by many young feminists ambitious to further their careers and maintain their independence in North American society, as this statement by a female priest guide indicates:

> This is a black and gray zone for me. I'm not sure about babies. There are level 3s and guides who have children, many children, but it's better not to go over two children . . . the environment. I heard Cousteau saying we are way too much on earth, that we will destroy our planet if we have more children. Very strongly I felt like having a baby one or two years ago, especially when you are in love you want to have babies. I am thirty-two so I don't have many, many years in front of me, maybe eight or so. But having a child takes a lot of your time and to me it's a very big responsibility. But I went back to school, I work a little bit, I cannot see being able to do these things, maintain my activity in the movement, and have a child. There are some who do it though—for me it's like superwoman. (Pascal 1992)

While there is a strong tendency among the guides to renounce parenthood, there is not a strict policy to ban babies, as the experience of a level 4 priest guide I interviewed proves:

> Raël decided this summer to name me guide. I was surprised because I was pregnant, but he said, "What is important is what you have in your head, not in your belly." I am very conscious that when I have the baby, my availability will not be the same as it will be in a few years. I will bring the baby to parties. As Raelians are working to be more and more conscious, they realize having a baby is a big responsibility. We agree with abortion. You need to have a really strong desire to have a baby when you can find so much meaning in your life in other ways. My boyfriend wanted a baby, and at first I said, "Maybe there is not enough meaning in your life." We have a very strong philosophy in the movement and refuse to make the same mistakes our parents did. I was level 3 before, and I would show my Raelian friends my ambivalence about having a baby and I received a lot of support. No one ever told me to or not to. When I did get pregnant, they were very happy for me.

The rank-and-file Raelians are just as likely as other Quebecois to have children. Raelians with children make no effort to transmit the message to them, true to the Raelian ethic of individual choice. If their children express a spontaneous curiosity, Raelians may lend them Raël's first book, but children cannot be baptized until age fifteen (the age limit keeps shifting), and even then they must first pass a test to prove that their choice was not due to parental influence or pressure.

Many religions that emerged out of the 1960s and 1970s counterculture placed a strong emphasis on procreating and socializing the second generation—especially when their first burst of success in proselytizing and finding converts among the youth of the counterculture began to wind down. This happened to the Hare Krishna and to the Children of God. But the Raelians, now in their thirtieth year, are not following this trajectory. Perhaps this is because the Elohim are expected to return in or before 2035, and adult longevity can be achieved through cloning—thus there is no imperative to rear a second generation of Raelians. But Raël is very pro-youth, and his movement defines itself as a youthful movement and has developed strategies to recruit teenagers. Raelians hold "raves," large drug-free dance parties with bands, that feature slide shows of UFOs approaching earth. They have given a lecture series on suicidal teens to convey the message that the body is all you have, so you'd better hang onto it—and don't be depressed, because the Elohim love you. Raël has organized a public platform for lowering the voting age to fifteen. Teenagers are encouraged to join the structure, prowl up and down the stage, and speak through microphones at the monthly meetings. This lends the movement a pro-teen or youth-friendly image.

Until 1998, gender roles in the Raelian Movement corresponded to the "sex unity" type (Palmer 1994). Women were considered the equals of men and endowed with identical emotional needs and intellectual abilities. Men and women were seen as independent, autonomous individuals, conceptualized as "biological robots" designed by extraterrestrial scientists and programmed to breed. As Raelians believed that we are living in the Age of Apocalypse with access to birth control and cloning techniques, however, the function of sex had changed. It was for pleasure, not reproduction, and traditional gender roles and the nuclear family could be dispensed with.

But in 1998, Raël suddenly created the Order of Raël's Angels. This event revolutionized Raelians' view of gender by placing an emphasis on women's unique qualities, thereby polarizing the sexes in the movement. It created for women a millenarian role—helping Raël prepare for the advent of the Elohim.

The way the Order of Raël's Angels was set up gives us new insights into Raël's character and his modus operandi as a charismatic prophet.

Raël, in selecting the candidates, was told by the Elohim to look for "religiosity, discipline, serenity, harmony, purity, humility, charisma, inner and outer beauty." The Elohim told Raël that physical beauty is important "because we, the Elohim . . . prefer to be surrounded by individuals of great beauty corresponding to the absolutely perfect original models of the different races that we had once created on Earth. Physical flaws are all due to the errors of generations past which have damaged our genetic inheritance."

On the heels of his announcement at the 1998 summer camp, Raël chose six girls on the spot to be his first angels. Raël's companion, Sophie, was awarded four feathers as a superior angel. Raël's former Japanese girlfriend, Lisa, he dubbed "the most feminine woman on the planet" and awarded her six feathers as an archangel. He explained, as one angel told me, that "the Elohim are more feminine than the most feminine woman, so in order to welcome them, we have to be very, very feminine." But other aspiring angels had to fill out a questionnaire, attach a photo, and explain their reasons for opting for this mission. To qualify, they had to be eighteen or over and test negative for sexually transmitted disease. They also should be beautiful.

"Beauty is not the body, it is the essence!" Raël told a journalist I later interviewed. "We become beautiful when we live the Raelian philosophy. All our women try to do their best, even if they are not beautiful. Like Brigitte here" (nodding toward Dr. Boisselier, the director of Clonaid, an attractive, elegantly attired woman in her mid-forties), "she does her best to look beautiful, but she is not so young anymore. But she does her best."

A later document compared the pink angels to the "pure and spotless Bride" of Revelation. The "calling" of the "Chosen Ones" is compared to "the spouses of Jesus," and they "will have no sex relationships other than with the Elohim or their prophets, and must undergo STD tests, and when the day comes for them to enter the Embassy and meet their Creators, when they reach the door that separates the human part from the Embassy," they must "put on a pure white linen gown that they will leave inside when they depart." A passage from Ezekiel 44:17 is quoted: "When they enter the gates of the inner court, they must be clothed with linen garments" (Raël 1998).

Researching the Angels

When the text of "The Order of Raël's Angels" appeared among my email on November 26, 1998, I did not realize it was meant to be top secret. I set about researching this new development and at first encountered no resistance. I met with Nicole Bertrand, a bishop (level 5), who provided me with data on the order. Next, I communicated with Sylvie Chabot, Raël's PR manager, to organize a field trip with my students to the next angels conference. But when I tried to negotiate follow-up research the next summer, I was told by Chabot: "No! The angels are secret!"

Still, I managed to gather much more information than any of the journalists who were begging me to share my findings with them (particularly a free-lance journalist for *Penthouse* magazine who kept phoning me, trying to elicit sexy details).

In February 1999, Nicole gave me a chart, "The Angel's List," that showed the world distribution of angels. There were 171 angels internationally. In the four levels, there were 105 trainees, 56 assistants, 8 angels, and 2 superior angels. Ten of them (all from North America) had golden ribbons. Gold-ribbon angels were chosen from the most beautiful girls. The majority (155) were white angels with a simple white feather: 41 in North America, 62 in Europe, 6 in Oceania, and 45 in Asia. There were only 6 pink angels: 4 in North America, 1 in Europe, and 1 in Asia.

By 2002, the age range of the white-feathered angels had broadened to between eighteen and seventy. Even some of the pink angels were older women. In 2002 there were 363 angels internationally, and only 12 were pink (see table 1).

TABLE 1
THE ANGELS IN JULY 2002

	Level	Pink Feather	White Feather	Gold Ribbon
Superior Archangel	6	0	0	0
Archangel	5	0	0	0
Superior Angel	4	2	2	0
Official Angel	3	2	10	4
Assistant Angel	2	4	100	8
Trainee Angel	1	4	198	8

The ranks of angels can be identified at the Raelian meetings by counting the feathers on their necklaces. Trainees have one feather, assistant angels have two, official angels have three, superior angels have four, archangels have five, and superior archangels have six feathers. The most beautiful angels wear a gold cord around their necks to show they belong to the ranks of the Cordon Doré angels. This sounds like French haute cuisine, but it is meant to be a sign that they will enjoy the honor of being the first to enter the embassy to greet the extraterrestrials upon their mass landing.

A later revelation clarified the angels' role in the movement. They were to recruit new angels and "instill a calling" in young women out in society, to save them from the "confusion of drugs, alcohol, or suicide." They were also meant to act as Raël's bodyguards: "For Raël's angels, the Elohim and their messenger come before everything else. They must be ready to sacrifice their lives for their Creators and their Prophet" (Raël 1998).

Raël gave an example in one of his talks, repeated to me later by a journalist: If an assassin tried to shoot him, an angel would lunge forward to shield him with her body, taking the bullet in her bosom to die in his stead. "I find that very beautiful," said Raël.

My students and I interviewed eight of Raël's angels on March 21, 1999, after the monthly Raelian meeting at the Theatre Gésu in Montreal. I had negotiated this research trip with Sylvie Chabot, who, besides being Raël's PR agent, is a superior (four-feathered) angel. I asked for student volunteers and hastily wrote an interview schedule as a guideline for my students (see Appendix).

As soon as the general meeting was over, the angels convened on the balcony of the Gésu for their own caucus meeting. It was very dark in the gallery, and twelve students had shown up—more than I expected, for two had brought friends. There were only six angels present, two pink and four white. Each angel found herself surrounded by three or four students firing questions simultaneously, so I told my students to back off and take turns. I sat with the angels' "mother superior" and asked her general questions about the order.

It soon became evident that the angels had been primed for our visit. They spoke "officially" as ambassadors for Raël, and the interview data were not rich in individual anecdotal material. This was not ideal as far as social science methodology was concerned, but we took advantage of the conditions available to us and gathered valuable data concerning the angels' backgrounds, aims, and religious mission.

The angels were all Quebecoises, all baptized Roman Catholic. What the angels had to say we found fascinating.

The first thing we noticed was that our informants tended to downplay the angels' apocalyptic function: "Our goal has always been to welcome the Elohim," they said. Asked if the order's existence means that the Elohim are coming sooner than expected, they replied cautiously, "It's a possibility." The notion that the authenticity of the belief is less important than one's well-being kept coming up in the interviews.

A forty-three-year-old pink angel explained that she wore her medallion to work, but put on her pink feather necklace only for Raelian meetings. "I hope the Elohim arrive soon, so that I can fulfill my duties as a pink angel. But I will not be disappointed if I do not see them within my lifetime. Even if I am on my deathbed and they have not arrived, I will be happy because I have dedicated my life to something I love" (Bishin 1999).

Asked how they would prepare for the Elohim's arrival, one angel replied, "By becoming more harmonious, more refined, more aware of my surroundings."

Their two stated goals were to "make Raël comfortable" and to "spread the message among women." When we asked how they would go about making Raël comfortable, a recurring reply was, "I would bring him a glass of pure, clean water." (One of my students looked puzzled, took me aside, and said, "I don't understand why Raël needs so many women just to make him comfortable.")

"How do you go about attracting women to the movement?" I asked the superior angel, who explained: "We organize special events to spread the message. When I speak to a stranger, I always choose a woman. We have a *sondage* [survey form] we give out and invite women to fill it out. They must ask themselves, 'In my religion, can I be a bishop, a priest?' Then they realize only in the Raelian religion can they do this."

When I asked about their weekend training seminars with Raël, she was rather vague: "Raël shows us how to develop qualities of charisma, of love." When I asked what "charisma" involved, she replied: "To listen more than speak. . . . When we meet people, be nice with them, listen, ask questions."

The other angels were not very specific concerning training activities, but they mentioned "meditation and prayers to the Elohim," "experiencing ourselves," and "exchange."

When we asked about their feelings regarding Raël, the response was more forthcoming: "I consider Raël to be my guide, my awakening, the most important person on Earth. He is my father, my teacher." "He is a simple man, full of love and compassion. He shows us how to be honest and love others. We angels have a good relationship with Raël." "He is a kind of pope who must be respected. But unlike the pope, he is very free."

A pink angel, thirty-two, explained that her role was to give Raël massages when he was in town (she is a trained massage therapist) and occasionally to cook for him. She also helps in the preparations for Raelian parties (Bishin 1999).

A twenty-one-year-old two-feather white angel said: "I have not been intimate with Raël, but I spent an evening alone with him, talking. I have a boyfriend; we've been together for almost two years. Our relationship is based on respect and freedom, we don't believe in monogamy, and I am comfortable with this, so long as we are open with each other and avoid hypocrisy. I have three close friends among the angels. I have never had sex with a woman, but I respect others' choices and I participate in the Gay Parade every year. Sometimes I will hold hands with my girlfriends" (Drolet 1999).

When asked if the Order of Angels had changed the role of women in the movement, she responded: "It brings femininity and refinement to the Raelians, and it removes machismo. The angels cultivate good feminine qualities, like being gentle, delicate, and refined. These qualities are manifested in the way we walk, eat, our odors, and other small everyday details."

When asked what they liked about being an angel, what the appeal was, one white angel replied: "I like the fact it's just for women, the teachings are different, and it's a new development." Another replied: "My role is to continue in my work, and I would enjoy to climb higher in the structure, in the Order of Angels—but that is for Raël to decide. What I like most about being a Raelian is the concrete action, the human rights issues we fight for, and all the opportunities for sharing and exchange. I consider my real family are the Raelians with whom I share the same philosophy."

"I like the fact it brings me closer to Raël," a pink angel responded. "I have more chances to be with him. I feel closer to him now."

We asked the angels about their relations with each other. "I'm real good friends with them, sort of like sisters, and I get along with them very well." "We have the best relationship ever. It is very deep and committed. We are connected to each other spiritually. There is no jealousy between us. We have unconditional love for each other."

"Nancie," a twenty-one-year-old Quebecoise who holds a CEGEP diploma and supports herself as an art model, is a pink angel. "I am saving myself for the Elohim upon their arrival and I am bisexual," she said. "I have chosen to become an angel because it's what I wanted to be. It has always been inside me to be an angel." Asked about her duties, she replied: "Well, I must meditate, usually thirty minutes a day, I try to follow Raelian principles and take care of the prophets, and we cannot smoke, drink, or any such things."

Pink angels must reserve their sexuality for the Elohim, but they may have sex with Raël, since he is currently the only prophet and Elohim half-breed on earth. They may also have sex with each other. My female students seemed to be impressed by the angels' dedication. One student brought a friend who said to me, "I wish *my* life had such a strong purpose!" But my male students were more skeptical. Stephan Piech (1999) wrote that "their religion seems harmless, but . . . it seems to me that since the pink angels can only have sexual experience with Raël or the Elohim, and since the Elohim do not seem to be coming back for about 25 years, therefore Raël seems to have at his dispense [*sic*] a lot of young women—however, who am I to judge?"

What was interesting in the interviews was the evident appeal of the order for young ex-Catholic women. Apparently, the notion of an order struck a familiar chord, evoking childhood memories of nuns and the romance and mystery of the cloister. One attractive forty-three-year-old with a high school diploma, formerly a devout Catholic, noted: "When I was young, I was raised as a Catholic and would have given my life for Jesus. When I heard about the Elohim, I made the decision to follow them and give my life for them, if necessary. When I met the Raelians, nineteen years ago, I was on the verge of suicide, I was in an unhappy marriage and had a small child. When I became a Raelian, it gave me the strength to leave my marriage and get my life together. It was a difficult time, for I lost custody of my baby, but I was able to pull myself out of my depression and move on." A secretary, she worked for McGill University to support her son, now grown up. She applied to be an angel as soon as the order was established, and then opted to be a pink angel: "It is my dream come true, one I have had since childhood."

The other pink angel explained her vow of celibacy in an interview with Jamal McIntyre (1999): "It's like the Catholic nuns who reserve their sexuality for Jesus." She described her *plan affectif* as "single, celibate, but also bisexual." When she became an angel, "everything changed automatically" with her male friends and lovers. "They did not see me as the same person anymore. I tried to make them happy by doing other things, and they tried to accept my beliefs."

Nuns or Sacred Prostitutes?

While the Order of Angels claims to replicate the Catholic convent, on closer examination, the role of a Raël's angel bears a closer resemblance to the sacred prostitute in the ancient world than to the nun. To fulfill their sacred mission, Raël's angels are expected to be sexy and seductive. Two recent events make this clear.

The first event was Raël's birthday celebration. On October 6, 2000, Raël turned fifty-four. His birthday celebration was held at the hay and fiberglass headquarters of UFOland in Valcourt. I was not present, but my student Pamela Naymark (2000) went and submitted a field report to me. As she described it, the large hall was decorated with flowers, streamers, and candles, and everyone sat around circular tables for the banquet. When Raël appeared, ushered in by his bodyguards, all rose to honor him. Then the angels lined up on each side of their prophet's path, "dressed—or rather undressed—in a just sexy, provocative way—scarves, thongs, miniscule bras," and as Raël ran the gantlet, they threw rose petals in the air.

"He smiled and seemed to enjoy it," Naymark reports. "Then, at the table where I was sitting next to an angel, Raël came up in the middle of the meal and thanked her and complimented her on her decorations for the hall. When he left, she was crying—crying with joy. 'He is so humble!' she kept saying."

After dinner, there was a cabaret and toward the end, the angels all got up on stage, stood in a row, and danced. "They were gyrating their bums and grinding their hips—It was the sexiest dance I've every seen, sort of like strippers—what you'd see in a strip club. Then they all sort of collapsed on the floor and pretended that they were having a lesbian orgy! Everyone was clapping from the tables—they loved it. Suddenly, Raël stood up and made a beeline for the stage. He tore past me—actually I was in his way and he shoved me rudely so I fell in a heap! He's quite small, I noticed, very wiry. He leapt up onto the stage and dived into the middle of the orgy and pretended to join in, and everyone was screaming with laughter and clapping and cheering" (Naymark 2000).

While this story merely describes some light-hearted fun at a party, it does say something about the angels' role and their charismatic relationship with Raël. It is perhaps significant that in the angels' newsletter, *Plumes d'anges,* their formal greeting is "Hellorgasm!"

The second event was the singular incident of the "lap-dancing angels." A letter was posted on the Web by a French anticultist, Frank Muhletaler, on April 25, 2002, that relates a sex scandal.[1] Muhletaler claims he received this information from an anonymous European ex-angel who was "scandalized by the event." Her story was of several European angels who came to Canada to see Raël and supported their stay by dancing in the clubs of Quebec and Ontario, where, as lap dancers, they could make between six hundred and nine hundred dollars a night. (One Raelian I interviewed, who works in nightclubs, told me that in Quebec lap dancers receive only ten dollars for a dance, whereas in Ottawa and Toronto they receive a twenty-dollar tip at the end of a dance that lasts between three and five minutes, depending on the song that is played—"some clubs edit the song so it only lasts three minutes." Lap dancing is currently the most lucrative work for exotic dancers and strippers, he told me, and it is not taxable.)

The trouble began when one of the regular girls at the club resented these foreign visitors' doing so well and alerted the Immigration Department. Three girls were arrested and interrogated for several hours. Two held tourist visas that did not permit them to work in Canada, and the third held a student visa. The two tourists were released with a formal injunction to desist from working and to leave the country when their visas expired. But the third angel faced more serious consequences: She was expelled from the university.

Muhletaler claims he double-checked his source of information by phoning Canadian immigration, and he suggests the girls returned to Montreal to discreetly resume their "underground activities." The tone of Muhletaler's letter is an odd mix of salacious double entendre and virtuous indignation. He complains that "Raël earns his pennies partly through the (semi) prostitution of the angels, but unlike the usual pimps, he does nothing to protect his girls when they are in trouble." (What useful defense Raël might have offered in the circumstances, Muhletaler doesn't say.)

I found the angel phenomenon interesting. While anticultists would predictably interpret their behavior as evidence of brainwashing, and feminist scholars and psychologists would no doubt view it as an example of the sexual exploitation and degradation of women, there are more insightful explanatory frameworks.

Peter Worsley in *The Trumpet Shall Sound* describes ritual obscenity among the cargo cults of Melanesia and then examines their social function: "If we examine the many cases of sexual excess, erotic communism, morbid asceticism and all the other labels pinned to ritual obscenity and sacrilege, it becomes clear that we are not dealing with unbridled lust or ascetic perversion. We are dealing with the deliberate enactment of the overthrow of the cramping bonds of the past, not to throw overboard all morality, but in order to create a new brotherhood with a completely new morality. . . .

Sexual communism and sexual asceticism, both so common in millenarian movements, are thus two sides of the same coin—the rejection of outworn creeds" (Worsley 1968, 251).

The angels' training drill would appear to be a more intense continuation of the ritual breaking of taboos that takes place at the summer seminars. These include confessions of sexual deviancy, the Betty Dodson group-masturbation exercise, and sex play based on avant-garde psychotherapy from California. In Butterflies and Flowers, for example, an exercise practiced at the Quebec summer seminars, one person lies down, naked, and becomes the "flower," so that a group of people hover over him or her and make complimentary remarks on his or her beauty and good qualities. If the "flower" offers permission to be touched, they then begin to massage and stroke the person, continuing to express positive feedback, and if the flower invites sexual contact, then some people in the group may explore that direction. Another "taboo-breaking" exercise was reported by an Italian researcher who participated undercover at the Raelian summer camp in Alby, France, in 1992. She described how she walked through a corridor lined with holes in the wall. The campers were instructed to place their hands into the holes—where they touched the genitalia of men and women. The idea was to rid them of guilt, shame, and rigid preconceptions regarding male and female sexuality.

It seems the purpose of these drills is to unite the angels into a new sisterhood—the first step toward forging an alternative system of ethics and creating a fortress against the outside world.

It is also important to examine the effect this ritual breaking of taboos might have on an individual's commitment to the group. The exercise just described, and indeed many of the techniques practiced in the Raelian seminars, like Butterflies and Flowers, conform to Rosabeth Moss Kanter's theory of commitment mechanisms.

Kanter describes six types of commitment-enhancing patterns found in "successful" utopian communes ("successful" is defined as lasting twenty-five years or more), and one of these is the commitment mechanism of "mortification." Most, if not all, religions have mortification practices, such as public confession and ritual humiliation, which reduce the individual's sense of a private unconnected ego. Kanter notes that sensitivity-training groups employ mortification processes that "can be a sign of trust in the group, a willingness to share weaknesses, and one's innermost secrets with others. People often come to such a group . . . deliberately seeking the identity change involved in mortification. They may call it 'personal growth' instead" (1972, 103).

From this perspective, one might argue that the angels' training corresponds to the commitment mechanism of mortification, since these young women are sacrificing their private sexuality on the altar of alien gods. This act would foster simultaneously a narcissistic sense of sexual autonomy and a communal sense of sexual sharing that would serve to distance the angel from her boyfriend and discourage "dyadic withdrawal." It would also increase the angels' tolerance toward same-sex expressions of their sexual feelings. Indeed, several ex-Raelian men have complained that their girlfriends, once they joined the angels, lost interest in pursuing their relationship.

Some historical insights are gained from comparing the Raelian Movement to the Oneida Perfectionists, one of the most famous free-love religious communes in U.S. history. This intentional community, founded in the 1830s by John Humphrey Noyes, settled in Oneida, New York. The commune was based on the utopian ideals of sharing, equality, striving for individual perfection (freedom from sin), and a kind of free-love system called "complex marriage" (Foster 1981).

While the Raelians are not communal, there are striking affinities between these two millenarian movements. Both discourage procreation and aspire to a human this-worldly immortality. Both espouse the "sex unity" view of gender and undermine conventional sex distinctions in labor, dress code, and social and religious life. Both leaders, Raël and Noyes, equate marriage with the selfish hoarding of private property. They are both sexual mystics who speak of the sexual act with a sense of the numinous or sacred, as a means of communing with God or gods.

The Oneidans regularly held what might be described as Victorian versions of the "lemon session" (satirized by Tom Wolfe in "The Me Decade"). These were called "mutual criticism" and involved members of the commune taking turns sitting in the center of the circle while other members pointed out their flaws and recalled moments of selfishness, particularly "selfish love" or possessive displays of romantic feeling toward individuals of the opposite sex. Victorian travelers' accounts (Nordhoff 1966, 292) indicate that mutual criticism was a device for discouraging exclusive sexual relationships or close interpersonal bonds that might threaten group cohesion. The historian Lawrence Foster explains it as "a form of social control which helped to prepare the way for complex marriage and the close community life associated with it" (1981, 98–99).

The revelation of "The Order of Raël's Angels" provides new insights into the logistics of Raël's charisma. The first time I read this revelation, received by Raël from the extraterrestrials in June or July of 1998, I was impressed by its strong resemblance, both in tone and in style, to Joseph Smith's revelation of the Celestial Order of Marriage.

In many ways the Order of Raël's Angels imitates the Mormon women's auxiliary organization, the Relief Society. Both offer women a separate society where they can perfect themselves as women according to religiously based ideals of femininity. As a Mormon teenager, I attended role-playing exercises of the Relief Society in which the aim was to learn to be a better wife and a more caring mother, or to offer suggestions on how to curb profanity in the workplace. Workshops were offered on how to dress attractively but modestly, how to cook and can food, how to help your children with homework, how to welcome your husband when he arrives home from work, among others. Mormon women develop deep cooperative friendships inside this society. These enrich their daily domestic lives as stay-at-home wives and mothers.

Raël's angels have a similar nurturing role to play, not with their husbands and children (which they don't have) but with Raël and the expected visitors. They cook for Raël, massage him, bring him glasses of pure mineral water, decorate UFOland's halls for his parties, welcome him when he returns from his world tours at the airport; they accompany him to his races, where they dress seductively and cheer him on, in a role resembling a rock star's groupies. Angels cultivate close friendships and occasionally lesbian relationships among themselves, which enrich their social life within this UFO subculture, where they are regarded by male Raelians with high esteem.

Of course, it is important and only fair to emphasize that Mormon and Raelian morality could not be more different. Relief Society training strengthens the biological family and reinforces dyadic loyalty between husband and wife. This in turn strengthens the Mormon Church, which exalts the nuclear family, marries couples for "time and eternity," and preaches that even God has a wife, Heavenly Mother. The Raelian religion exalts the atomized individual, who cuts his or her ties with ancestors and the biological family and is self-made in the image of the extraterrestrials.

Nevertheless, both of these women's auxiliary organizations are examples of what Rosemary Reuther calls "conservative romantic feminism," which "stresses the differences between male and female as representatives of complementary opposites" (Reuther 1983, 105). Just as nineteenth-century female Christian reformers sought to extend women's domestic role into public life through peace marches and moral reform, as represented by the slogan "A new broom will sweep up city hall," so Raël's angels are in training to counteract machismo and aggressive tendencies, and to teach humankind to be peaceful and stop war.

The superior angel certainly sounded like a conservative romantic feminist in our 1999 interview: "We are not feminist, not aggressive or against society. Woman can have her place and keep her femininity. For her, it is important to express love, to be a woman. Before, we were insisting to have our place in society. Now we don't have to be aggressive or masculine, to be a good leader as a woman. We can be sweet."

Raël described the Elohim as being "more feminine than the most feminine woman on earth," and his previous girlfriend, Lisa, as "the most feminine woman on the planet," although "Lisa is only 10 percent feminine compared to the Elohim." The Elohim he described as "doux, suave, no rough edges." This meant that women were now superior to men in the movement, closer to the "gods," with greater access to Raël.

Cultivating feminine qualities became an urgent, apocalyptic exercise. Raël told me in our 1994 interview that "to escape destruction, humanity must stifle the masculine principle. That is why we have that exercise in cross-dressing at the summer seminars, and we encourage gays, who fall in between the masculine and feminine."

Raelian women I spoke to were acutely aware of the implications of this shift in their role. Brigitte Boisselier, who was wearing the white feather of an angel when she lectured to my class in 1998, said: "It seemed at first we were going backward, to be more like women in the churches—a nurturer. But it gives us a new way to develop our spirituality."

The ultimate aim of both Mormon and Raelian women's training is otherworldly. Mormon women are preparing for heaven by cultivating their nurturing qualities, looking forward to the future when their husbands will be gods with their own kingdoms in heaven, and they will be queens and mothers to their children, who are "sealed" to them for eternity. Raël's angels are cultivating their feminine, nurturing side so that they will be worthy to enter the embassy, greet the Elohim and the prophets, and serve them as their liaison officers with earthly dignitaries and journalists, and as their companions, caretakers, and lovers. And the hope of being chosen for cloning holds the promise of immortality.

What is the function of this order for Raël? In my view, Raël is a sexual mystic comparable to Thomas Lake Harris, Bhagwan Shree Rajneesh, David Berg, and Adidam (Da Free John). All these leaders chose to surround themselves with a mystical erotic circle of adoring females as their assistants, administrators, and helpers.

Adidam lives on a Fiji island waited on and adored as a living god by his four beautiful white-robed *kanyas,* "the circle of women practitioners who have given the gift of lifelong love and devotion to Heart-Master-Da-Love-Ananada, and whose purity of practice is a gift of inspiration to others" (Da Kalki 1990, 38). David Berg went into hiding and surrounded himself with beautiful topless secretaries who worked with him on his *Mo Letters.* Bhagwan Shree Rajneesh created a "Ma-archy" of "supermoms" to be "the pillars of my commune" and during his three-year vow of silence sat on his throne at the evening *darshan* surrounded by beautiful dancing girls—mediums who were "receptive to my energy." It is understandable that an inspired male prophet, struggling to build a whole civilization from scratch, often reviled and persecuted by society, would want to retreat into a haven of protective, nurturing, unthreatening, ornamental young women—as opposed to dynamic young male competitors. A circle of women can provide the inspired, persecuted heterodox prophet with precious moments of entertainment, relaxation, and refreshment in the midst of his busy schedule.

Religious movements—particularly unconventional ones—often exhibit strange and alien patterns of sexuality. The Mormons were infamous for polygamy in the nineteenth century, the Oneida Perfectionists practiced a kind of group marriage called "complex marriage," and the Shakers renounced sex altogether (Foster 1981). New religious movements, especially those that are communal, often discourage the intimate dyadic bond between husband and wife as threatening to group cohesion, and replace marriage with experiments in free love, celibacy, polygamy, arranged marriage, rotating partners, and other exotic relationships. Journalists have pointed to these radical departures from monogamy as proof that the leader is a sexual deviant, a megalomaniac, and an exploiter of women. Sociologists and historians, however, stepping back to look at the larger picture, have argued that new religions provide forums for experimentation—in gender roles and family life, among other arenas—for men and women dissatisfied with or damaged by the conventions of "normal" family or sexual life, due to upheavals in the structure of the family or shifting gender roles. They have tried to understand these radical, spiritually based sexual practices within their social and historical contexts, and to analyze them as symptoms of social change (see Foster 1981; Aidala 1985; Palmer 1994).

UFO religions provide us with fascinating glimpses of alternative, indeed "alien," forms of sexual expression. All our assumptions concerning the nature of man and woman and the forms and function of conjugal and parental love are challenged as these groups embark on radical social experiments and the ritual breaking of taboos. To emulate extraterrestrial sexual ethics is to embark on a quest to solve the mystery of our human origins, to explore the link between flesh and spirit, and to redefine the boundaries that separate human, animal, and machine.

A survey of other contactee-prophets shows a concern to deconstruct gender and discover true androgyny, as if the fountain of youth, the secret of immortality, and the power to travel across the galaxy somehow lay behind and beyond the original human's tragic fall into dimorphism and sexuality.

The founders of the Unarius Society, a small group based in El Cahon, California, met when Ernest Norman gave Ruth a psychic reading and informed her that in a past life she had been the pharaoh's daughter who found Moses in the bulrushes. Ruth married Norman and became her husband's helpmeet, stenographer, and typist as he channeled messages from "Space Brothers" on Mars and Venus. Upon the demise of Ernest Norman in 1971, Ruth assumed leadership and, still in psychic communication with him, proceeded to channel new visions from other planets and prophesied the descent of thirty-one starships from the galactic federation in 2001 to usher in a golden age of "logic and reason." Coming out in 1973 as Uriel the archangel, Ruth Norman organized her cosmic wedding to the archangel Michael, with her top aide (and eventual successor), Antares, standing in as the groom. The wedding and coronation festival were held in a California ballroom, where the seventy-three-year-old Ruth, in her wedding dress festooned with glowing lightbulbs, was crowned by the celestial form of her departed husband and retitled "Queen Uriel, Queen of the Archangels" (Tumminia and Fitzpatrick 1995).

Heaven's Gate provides another example of a charismatic duo—what Robert W. Balch (1982a) referred to irreverently as a "folie à deux." Bonnie Nettles and Herff Applewhite formed a celibate duo engaged in spiritual innovations; they interpreted Herff's psychotic aural hallucinations as messages from extraterrestrials and forged a new eclectic theology combining Bible fundamentalism with Star Trek tales and theosophical doctrines (see chapter 1). They organized their followers to travel around in male-female celibate partnerships that mirrored the leaders' relationship. Herff resolved his struggle to subdue his sexual desires by opting for castration surgery—and convinced several of his male followers to follow suit. The death of Nettles in 1984 led to a theological crisis, since the most basic aim of the group was to overcome physical death by transforming the body into a superior androgynous, immortal, extraterrestrial body. When Herff in 1997 led thirty-eight followers into mass suicide in San Diego, their aim was to "drop the vehicle" (the body) and ascend in spirit to meet Nettles, whom they believed to be piloting the UFO spotted in the tail of the comet Hale-Bopp (Balch 1982a, 1995).

Summum is a small, obscure UFO group in Salt Lake City that offers mummification services for clients who wish to preserve their bodies after death. Their founder is Amon Ray, the Egyptian sun god (called Corky by his followers). A former Mormon elder, married with two children, Corky astral-traveled to an alien planet in 1975, where he beheld a golden pyramid. Inside he encountered beautiful extraterrestrials who taught him the secrets of the universe by placing him inside a crystal shaft that flooded his mind with "concepts" which enabled him to grasp the "underlying principles that create my world."[2]

Summum somehow got permission in a Mormon state to brew sacrificial wine inside the golden pyramid on Corky's suburban estate in Salt Lake City. The group supports its spiritual work through operating gumball machines. One of their sacred texts, *Sexual Ecstasy from Ancient Wisdom,* offers instruction for married couples in lovemaking, masturbation, semen-retention techniques, and attainment of a "permanent orgasm" with the help of an ancient Egyptian ointment called Merh they sell on the Internet.[3]

The underlying quest that all these quite disparate departures from conventional sexuality share is the quest to overcome death. They seem to be responding to the rapid secularization of our society. As our faith in the traditional religious pathways of transcendence diminishes (due to the corrosive effects of the scientific worldview on spiritual belief systems), there seems to be a need to forge new patterns of transcendence based on new conceptions of the flesh and the consciousness, and the relation between them. New-minted magical technologies are handed down by extraterrestrials to contactee-prophets, who impart them to their followers—techniques that manipulate the flesh, exploit sexual energy, and harness invisible forces from far-off planets. These new technologies take various forms: cloning, mummification, Tesla energy towers, uploading memories into computers.

UFO religions perform the ancient rites of sex magic in new "scientific" guises. When contactees or abductees have sexual relations with aliens, whether angelic or demonic, one is reminded of the shaman's marriage to his helping spirit, the Taoist monk's semen-retention exercises, babies kidnapped by fairies in Celtic lore, and Aleister Crowley's thelemic magic. This ancient lore helps us understand Uriel's geriatric wedding to an extraterrestrial, Raël's night of lovemaking with biological robots, and Herff Applewhite's castration so he could board the spaceship. As weird, incomprehensible, and shocking as some of these strategies are, it is clear that their common aim is to extend life, to stimulate the life force within, and to seize the prize of immortality.

Raelian sexuality is driven by that quintessentially religious desire to overcome the limits of the human body and to yoke the individual's consciousness with the whole universe. The Raelians' ultimate goal is to live forever.

Millenarian Implications

When a Raelian friend first told me about Raël's angels, I asked him if this meant the Elohim were returning sooner than the expected date of 2035. He replied: "Definitely! I have heard it going around that they will return within five years, or, at the latest, in fifteen years." Certainly this seemed to be implied, for why otherwise would a cadre of beautiful girls train to please the aliens socially and sexually if they wouldn't show up until these girls were in their late fifties and sixties? And yet, in our interviews with the angels, they were cautious about making overly specific predictions. Since 2000, when cloning fever began to dominate the Raelian agenda, the angels have been relegated to the back burner. The Order of Angels today no longer denotes an intensification of millenarian expectation.

One angel over fifty explained to one of my students that her age did not disqualify her to be an angel, since "the Elohim know how to clone a uterus"—with their scientific expertise, they could make her young and beautiful again. One guide even recently suggested that the angels were just an experimental model for future generations of young angels who may be the lucky ones chosen to enter the embassy.

One might ask how Raël, or indeed the Elohim, came up with this Catholic–New Age synthesis. Angels appear to be an anomaly in a UFO religion that rejects the notion of the soul and replaces the transcendent realm of heaven with UFOs and edenic planets.

But Carl Jung has called UFOs "technological angels." The celestial origin of Space Brothers, as well as their message-bearing function and redemptive actions toward humans, have led to a close identification between benign aliens and angels. But since the 1950s, "the redemptive theme has been supplanted by the abduction theme" (Lewis 2000, 26). Abduction narratives in the wake of Whitley Strieber's 1987 novel *Communion* feature emotionless "grays" who subject kidnapped humans to painful operations and probing of orifices—usually sexual in nature. "In these stories extraterrestrials play the role of demons—that is, fallen angels" (Lewis 2000, 26).

Raël has reversed this narrative and the role of aliens as fallen angels. It is now human females on earth who are the "angels." The clinical, painful sexual experiments perpetrated by emotionless grays have been replaced with the romantic expectation of erotic encounters with the Elohim reminiscent of the courtly love tradition. Rather than await abduction and probing, Raël's angels study the art of love so as to lure the handsome visitors down from the skies and seduce them. This narrative is quite consistent with the Raelians' postmillennial, human-centered vision of the end of time. The fact that humans are no longer passive victims in this narrative but take an active role in the human-alien relationship says something about Raël's insistence on individual choice and human accountability, and his vision of the godlike potential in humans.

Chapter Seven

"Enemies Within!"

All religions must deal with the problem of evil. Most emergent religions meet with opposition, and each must find its own way of understanding its enemies and of coping with critics.

Journalists have often asked me, "Are the Raelians a *dangerous* group, like the Heaven's Gate, like Jonestown? Do you see them as potentially violent—or suicidal?"

I say no and try to explain Raël's zero-tolerance stance regarding violence. I mention that the Raelians deplore suicide. After all, they believe the body is all you've got, and they aspire to live forever in the flesh. But after the Solar Temple perpetrated their 1984 mass suicide, followed by Heaven's Gate in 1997, rumors abounded that this or that "cult" was secretly plotting another spectacular mass suicide.

The Raelians even found it expedient in the midst of the media blitz over Heaven's Gate to issue a press release condemning suicide (as did The Family, the Rosicrucians, the Hare Krishna, and Mandarom). As one member put it: "If those idiots want to kill themselves, well, that's *their* problem. We Raelians love life, we enjoy our bodies. We want to live forever!"

I am often asked about Raël's "control" over his followers. I usually point out that unlike members of communal groups, Raelians are free to pursue their own independent lifestyles. Raelians are nonsectarian. They integrate well into the larger society. Unlike the Jehovah's Witnesses, Raelians aspire to higher education and better careers and avoid heavy-handed missionary tactics. Raelians can drop out or "sit on the bench" as long as they like without censorship or shunning. No one is pressured to tithe—only the small annual membership fee is obligatory. Many rank-and-file Raelians drink wine and smoke marijuana or cigarettes, knowing it is against the rules.

But a much more rigorous standard applies to the guides. They must avoid recreational drugs, caffeine, and alcohol; they must take care not to "deform" the message; and they must behave as exemplary representatives of the Raelian religion.

Within the movement, criticism of Raël or of his guides is not permitted. While some ex-members and anticultists have suggested that this prohibition contradicts the principles of free speech and democracy, one must remember what a difficult task the Raelians are undertaking. Raël exerts the kind of social control over his flock that a film director exerts on the set, or a martial arts instructor exerts whipping his *dojo* into shape for a tournament. Those who volunteer for these disciplines presumably understand that control is necessary to accelerate learning and get the task done.

"So, all you've told me is positive," one journalist complained. "I'm going to ask you now, is there a downside, a dark side to the Raelians?" I gathered that he'd just been talking to ex-members, and I suspected they had warned him that I was a naïve "cult apologist"—or possibly on the payroll of "the cults" to say nice things about them.

Enemies "Out There"

Do the Raelians have a dark side? Compared to other millenarian new religions, their worldview is refreshingly upbeat, optimistic. The threats they fear are pragmatic, the ones we all fear in the "real world"— nuclear war, oppression of ethnic and religious minorities, overpopulation, deforestation. Even Satan, the dissident extraterrestrial who voted against science lessons for humans (Raël 1987a), is not exactly "evil"—he just has a pessimistic view of human nature and doesn't think we should be awarded the power of free choice.

Thus, Raël's theology lacks that sense of Manichaean struggle, the "us and them" mentality found in the prophecies of Asahara (Aum Shinrikyo), Jim Jones (Jonestown), or The Two (Heaven's Gate). It is exactly this paranoid mentality, the demonization and dehumanization of the outside world, that has proved to be a contributing factor to a group's potential for violence (see Wessinger 2000).

A survey of other UFO religions reveals that the Raelian Movement is quite an anomaly: It lacks evil extraterrestrials. The Elohim appear to have no enemies in the universe, and humanity's worst enemy is itself. To grasp the implications of this idea for a deeper understanding of Raelian culture, it is useful to see how evil extraterrestrials operate in the belief systems of these other groups.

Heaven's Gate insulated members from the outside world because of their "obsession with spirits . . . attachments to the human level that took

the form of doubts, desires, memories, . . . and interfered with salvation" (Balch 1995, 139). The Two preached that evil aliens called "luciferians" walked among us, assisting in the human entrenchment in ignorance and unconsciousness. Heaven's Gate practitioners believed themselves to be the "righteous remnant" who would be carried away aboard a spaceship; they saw ordinary U.S. citizens as going about their daily middle-class existence mired in a soulless, "plantlike" pursuit of materialism and sensuality—unaware they were living in a garden about to be "spaded over." Ashtar Command prophesied an imminent mass landing of starships in the mid-1990s that would usher in an age of purification involving an orderly evacuation of human beings worthy to enter the "light." When that prophecy failed, a mythic narrative was revealed that explained the delay was caused by evil extraterrestrials: Decades ago, a group of cadet trainees defected from the Ashtar Command and set up an evil renegade extraterrestrial government who made alliances with rebellious entities "operating on the lowest planes closest to the earth" (Helland 2000, 38).

An African American UFO religion, the United Nuwaubian Nation of Moors, has a racialist version of the "righteous remnant." Dr. Malachi York-El, their charismatic leader, has since 1993 presided over Tama Re, an Egyptian-style theme park (the FBI calls it a "compound") in Eatonton, Georgia. The Nuwaubians were preparing for the mother ship from the planet Illyuwn to arrive in May 2003 to collect 144,000 chosen ones and transport them to the planet Rizq—until the "compound" was stormed by FBI agents in May 2002, and York was charged with 116 counts of child molestation.

In his book *Are There UFOs in Our Midst?* York narrates a myth of warring tribes of extraterrestrials whose cosmic battles account for the black-versus-white race wars on our own planet. The evilest aliens are the "reptilians," eight feet tall with dark green scaly skin. They are from Draco in the six-star constellation Orion and have been covertly interbreeding with humans for centuries. The aliens we know as "the greys" are "really a crossbreed between humans and reptilian species" and "are being used as slaves by the reptilians" (York 1995, 67). For York, the benign extraterrestrials are the Anunnaqi. These are gods or angels who are "dark reddish brown in skin complexion with large dark slanted eyes, with kinky or woolly hair" (101). They will arrive on the mother ship to "reap the small harvest of 144,000 human souls and relocate them for advanced schooling . . . in the event of a natural disaster" (107).

Unarians believe in evil aliens, also from the constellation Orion, who tortured their prophetess Uriel for a thousand years. "Their negative state was brought about by the use of electronic devices" (Tumminia and Kirkpatrick 1995, 94). Charles Spaegal, Uriel's successor, was once an evil tyrant suitably called Tyrantus, the "commander of doom" who waged war on other planets and conducted atrocious experiments on humans (breeding, mutilation, transplants, and such).

While Raël does not speak of evil aliens, he does occasionally introduce a dark discordant note into the symphony of his unfurling revelations. There is a faint hint of threatening aliens in the message of March 14, 1978, transmitted telepathically from Yahweh to Raël at midnight: "Beware! It is not impossible that other Aliens will make contact very soon, . . . people we have also created scientifically in another part of the Universe. . . . Tell them the truth as revealed in the message . . . contained in 'The Book Which Tells the Truth'" (Raël 1987a, 11).

So, on occasion, Raël's revelations contain fleeting hints of a conspiracy theory or a cosmic battle to explain current political events. But then the idea is dropped, and these mordent themes are never developed into a coherent theodicy. They do, however, provide momentary drama and suspense for his audience.

ENEMIES AROUND US

Raël's enemies hail not from outer space, but from our own planet—the pope, the French anticult movement ADFI, or the odd troublesome journalist (like Christophe Dechavanne). While Raël does not perceive the surrounding society generally as polluted or demonic, he does identify certain enemies. Shortly after the cloned-baby excitement died down, Raël sent out via the *Contact* newsletter in February 2003 an "important warning" to his followers, "The Abraham Project." In the letter he warns that "it is highly probable that I may be the victim of an assassination in the near future. The fact that I am mentioning it today is one way to try to stop it. . . . As one of our highly-ranked spy [*sic*] told us, . . . the American secret services linked to the CIA and their French equivalents, have a secret department called the ABRAHAM PROJECT that is in charge of political assassinations of people who are too 'disturbing,' by mentally ill people."

Raël explains that these crazy assassins are groomed by audio systems planted in their walls "seemingly coming from God asking them to kill." When the time is ripe, they will receive a visit from an agent disguised as a "celestial messenger" with "fluorescent eye lenses, white wig or luminous stones," who will give them a firearm. Raël then accuses George Bush and Jacques Chirac of plotting to assassinate him because he "preaches atheism," "is the creator of a dangerous sect," and "is responsible for cloning."

Raël demands in the letter that if his assassination is accomplished, investigations be made "up to the highest levels so that the services of the Abraham Project are unmasked and especially the presidents who initiated them."

At the same time, Raël reorganized his bodyguards to provide maximum security. He appointed Lear as head of security, but they had a falling out, and Lear left the structure. A bishop told me that "once you have left the structure twice, you will never be let back in!" Raël replaced Lear with one of the world's top Savate artists, Salem Assli. (Savate is a kind of French baroque kickboxing.) Raël told Assli he did not expect him to avert bullets but simply wanted him to design the best security system against assassins.

Another of President Bush's nefarious plots was unmasked on www.rael.org in February 2004. We are told that a new "ultra secret" American weapon designed to "assassinate political and religious leaders" who dare to criticize the U.S. government's policies has been installed on geostationary satellites. These satellites, disguised as observatories, are fitted with "high precision cannons [that] emmit [*sic*] extremely cancerous rays" aimed at the residence of "the person they wish to eliminate" so that within a few months we will hear of "well-known critics of USA policies who suddenly die of cancer." When I asked a Raelian bishop what the source of this information was, she replied, "I have absolutely no idea!"

It is difficult to know how to interpret these developments. I am inclined to see them as Raël's attempt to drum up commitment and support from his followers during the lull after the media dismissed the cloned baby as a hoax. They might also be interpreted as a strategy to stave off the experience of cognitive dissonance or prophetic disconfirmation. Just as Uriel responded to the galactic federation's failure to show by blaming her students for lynching her in a previous life (see Tumminia 1998), Raël takes the blame for the putative "hoax" off Clonaid and himself by blaming his political enemies for the clone's disappearance. He says in his letter that "George Bush . . . pushed his brother, Florida governor, to launch a subpoena against BB [Brigitte Boisselier] as she announced the birth of the first cloned baby in that state."

But cloned babies and CIA plots aside, the most serious opposition to Raël's mission comes from within his own ranks. These "enemies within" include dissident members, rival contactees and would-be prophets, and ex-Raelians.

Enemies Within

Raelianism has generated other reform movements that have spun off to form schisms—parallel movements whose members bypass Raël and call upon the Elohim directly for guidance.

Similarly, Mormonism was racked with schismatic forces after the assassination of its prophet, Joseph Smith. Brigham Young, Stanley Rigdon, and others claimed the mantle of prophecy and led their flock in different directions (Foster 1981). The Children of God (now known as The Family) also weathered a series of upstart prophets in the mid 1970s who challenged the authority of David Berg.

There are three types of members who exit from new religions, according to David Bromley: defectors, apostates, and whistleblowers. Defectors leave quietly, without public disputes or external attempts to criticize or reform their former religious organization. But apostates take an oppositional stance toward their former religion, and their leave-taking occurs in a highly polarized situation. Each side in the conflict—apostates, as well as their former religious group—constructs a narrative of the conflict that labels the other as quintessentially evil or subversive (Bromley 1998, 37). Whistleblowers expose a perceived injustice or "evil" in the NRM they have just exited and ally with secular authorities in the larger society. The whistleblower's narrative exposé of the NRM may influence future relations between the minority religion and its host society.

We find all three types of leave-taking from the Raelian Movement.

The Rival Prophets

Some ex-Raelians might be categorized as heretics or "counter-cultists" (Introvigne 1995)—meaning their reasons for leaving are strictly ideological. They are preoccupied with correcting Raël's theology and launch countermovements over what might appear to outsiders as abstruse theological nitpicking concerning the true nature of extraterrestrials.

One example is Pierre Andre Bouchard, a self-proclaimed prophet who published a tract, *A la découverte des veritables Elohim* (In search of the real Elohim) with a vanity press, Les editions nouvel art de vivre, in Montreal in 1977. In it, he propounds his own alternative biblical interpretation of the Elohim and Raël's creation myth. The RM handled this heretic by ridiculing him and dismissing his ideas as "delirious" in one publication: "Maitre Pierre of confused spirits, who addressed the Raelians in a delirious mystico-esoteric prose developing the idea that the extraterrestrials were angels sent by God!!" (*20 ans,* 52).

Another "heretic" and rival prophet emerged out of the highest rank of national guides in the 1980s—Victor Legendre. A double apostate, Legendre was a former Catholic priest from Quebec who rose rapidly to the peak of the Raelian structure as bishop and national guide of Canada; he resigned his post in 1992 and left with his girlfriend, "Louise," level 2 in the structure.

There was a striking discrepancy in the accounts I received of why these two left. I tried to contact them for an interview and was approached by their "friend," who informed me that Legendre and Louise did not wish to speak to me directly, since I "did not speak French." They had authorized this friend as a go-between to tell me their story.[1]

The "official" story that appeared in the Raelian record, *20 ans des pioneers* (118), was as follows: "Victor Legendre vient de demissioner de son poste de Guide National du Canada" (Victor Legendre has been dismissed from his post as National Guide of Canada). A Raelian priest guide's understanding of the whole affair was conveyed in an interview conducted by Anna Pascal (1992):

> I know very little about this, but the national leader resigned . . . because he was torn between the movement and his love for a woman. The woman was very implicated within the movement, she was level 3, . . . and somewhere she took a wrong turn. In the end she was saying she was the prophet, that Raël was not the only one who was contacted by aliens—that she was too. She had a special message for us that we had to listen to. . . . For me there is only one prophet and that is Raël, he makes too much sense. The way I have improved my life, the happiness I have now, through all the things I learned from him, I'm far more productive and far more serene with myself than seven years ago. And this is, for me, even if the whole thing is not true, if Raël was not the real prophet, he gave me so much joy in my life that it doesn't matter if it's true or not. And she talks about very mystical things, she can lift tables or things like that that are not possible. So, the national leader loved her very much and then Raël made her leave, . . . he expulsed her, so it was not possible for [him] to see her. He had a big conflict there, he could not be with the messages and Raël and also with her, so he resigned. His love was stronger than the Message.

Forty Raelians in the Legendre/Louise camp were told to leave at the same time.

My informant, the "friend" mentioned earlier, conveyed the apostate couple's version of the rift. The following is an extract from our taped interview at my house in June 2001.

> [Louise] was accused of making a schism, of wanting to start a new movement. It all started because she was against the theory put out by one of Raël's right-arm men, Daniel Chabot. He wrote that on other planets, AIDS and plagues were a way to weed out the bad elements of humanity, sent on purpose by superior extraterrestrial scientists. She thought that showed a lack of love, of compassion. She was sure the Elohim would never say plagues were a *good* thing, and those who catch them deserve to die! So she spoke out against the theory, and he heard about it. She was going to go to the Conseil des Sages [Council of the Wise] to complain officially about the theory, but he beat her to it.
>
> He [Chabot] put her out of the movement, without any protest or trial. We were told she claimed to get direct revelations from the Elohim that contradicted Raël. It was a lie. She never did [claim that]. [Chabot] used her book against her—she wrote a novel—but it was just a novel.
>
> When I heard the story they were telling about her, I said, "What?" I started to laugh. I tried to contact her, but nobody would give me her phone number. "Why?" I asked. "Why don't you call her up and verify the story?" The movement is like a little Quebec village—everybody talking behind themselves [*sic*]. Nobody bothered to verify, nobody defended her.
>
> She was insulted publicly by Raël. He said, pointing to her, "She's not beautiful! Some women, when they come into the movement are not beautiful, but after a while they begin to look nice. But not her." Victor got fed up with her mistreatment. She was his girlfriend, and she is a wonderful person. She has a wonderful heart. So he resigned. The leaders covered up by saying officially, "Raël l'a renvoyé!" [Raël sent him off.] But it was not true. When Victor left, a lot followed him. They didn't like what was happening. You can't discuss or protest, you can't have different ideas. If you do, it's interpreted as aggressivity [*sic*] toward the prophet and his guides. There is no democracy. They just say, "Leave if you're not happy!"

Legendre and Louise today are more than apostates; they are rival prophets who have formed a schismatic (albeit miniscule) movement parallel to the RM. They distribute a newsletter called *Les Apôtres des derniers temps*

(The Apostles of the last days). They argue that the Raelian Movement went off the rails and that Raël, although originally serving as a mouthpiece for the benevolent Elohim (from Lucifer, the political party that promotes free choice and scientific knowledge for humanity), was later taken over by Satan, the rival party of their planet that plans to institute a fascist government on earth and bring about a mechanistic, predetermined, and collective salvation for humanity.[2]

The Apostles of the Last Days prefer to maintain a low profile in society, although they do occasionally try to reach out to Raelian members, hoping to reform the IRM, expose Raël as the puppet of evil extraterrestrials, and rescue misguided souls. It is interesting that they have moved away from Raël's radical materialistic worldview and have incorporated apocalyptic strands from Quebec's ultramontane Catholicism, such as Virgin apparitions and guardian angels.

The Defectors

Most ex-Raelians I have encountered exhibit neither rancor toward Raël nor regret at joining the movement. Many admit they learned some valuable lessons in the IRM, had fun, and met wonderful friends. But one unusually eloquent interview of a defector, conducted by Dawson student Daniela Camplese in 1992, offers some profound reflections on the unforeseen emotional costs to members' marriages that becoming a Raelian can entail. Rosabeth Moss Kanter's (1972) theory of "commitment mechanisms" found in utopian communes seems applicable in this case. Kanter identifies six patterns that enhance the members' commitment to the whole group. One of these, "renunciation," demands that the exclusive bond between couples be severed or weakened through embracing polygamy, celibacy, or free love. The purpose is to prevent "dyadic withdrawal" and integrate the husband and wife as brother and sister into the fictive family provided by a spiritual community.

Daniela Camplese's informant, "Maria," was born in 1951, married at eighteen, and moved to Montreal from El Salvador with her husband. "I had no higher education nor profession when I arrived," she commented. Maria enrolled in French and secretarial courses and since 1979 had worked as a receptionist for a textile company, where she met a Raelian woman who introduced her to the movement. "She soon became deeply involved," Camplese writes. "Maria, who is very pretty, rose quickly in the Structure to Animator. In 1980 she had her first baby girl who has recently been baptized Raelian. In 1982 Maria introduced her husband to the movement, who at first refused to be convinced by their ideas, but after a few months became involved."

The involvement of this couple in the IRM soon broke up their marriage, and today Maria is an embittered ex-member, as she tells Camplese in this excerpt:

> The liberated kind of love that is practiced within the movement contributed to the separation of me and my husband. From the first day, I believed and respected the Raelians' methods and ideas. I thought I could be like them, until the day I discovered differently; the day my husband left me and my daughter for a lesbian—a pretty, young Quebec girl. That day I knew what jealousy is all about. Jealousy is synonymous with ownership, and this is one of the things that Raël is against. At first everything was OK because my husband had no idea of what I was going through—my experiences with members of the group, both male and female. I am not a lesbian, but I did have previous experiences with women which I didn't feel comfortable talking about. Most of my good experiences were with one man I met at the summer camp. When my husband finally joined, he was shocked to learn the truth and thought I was crazy. The first meeting my husband went to, he told me that the women were "sluts" and the men were all gay and "perverts"—like most visitors tend to think. He was in some way outraged to learn that his own wife cheated on him. He became involved with someone else in the group as a form of revenge for what I did. When my husband realized that he could have more than one woman, many girlfriends at the same time, he became more actively involved than me, and no longer thought that I was crazy, but told me it was good for us to open ourselves in this way to others. "Bullshit!" I used to think, even then. But I believed in this way until the day he broke my heart. When he started seeing other women, many differences came between us. That is why we separated. I did not realize how much I had hurt him by seeing other men, but I just did not see it then, while I was "cheating" on him. This cheating was only friendship then. Today I regret that I ever became involved to such a point, although there were many advantages—like many trips to different parts of the world paid by the movement under working circumstances.
>
> After all the pain I went through, and still feel today, this experience answered many of my questions. Through experimenting in the movement, I finally found myself. Many years ago, when I was in high school, I would surprise myself staring at girls, the way they were, the way they talked, et cetera. I admired many among them and many times I asked myself how a guy felt by being their boyfriend. I asked myself if any of those

> girls had the same weird and stupid thoughts I had. To tell you the truth, I was scared to find a girl just like me and to define myself as a lesbian, especially in the kind of society that I was brought up in.
>
> But when I joined Raël's movement I was able to answer this question that bothered me during my adolescent period, and many years after I learned to look with the insight of me, of [Maria]—and there is much more inside me than what I thought. Personally I think that it is an experience that all of us should go through in our lifetime, because we positively define ourselves and learn a lot about us, we find more confidence in ourselves. If you are not the jealous type, and single, it is the right religion for you! (Camplese 1992)

Maria's experience was a complex one, and her reaction ambivalent. While she regrets the demise of her marriage, she appears to have internalized Raelian sexual values, and she acknowledges that her time spent in the movement was one of extraordinary personal growth.

A quite different ex-member perspective came from "Héloise," one of the early leaders in the IRM. Within the movement, only Raël is permitted to communicate with extraterrestrials, and this defector left because she had her own notion of the Elohim and found it impossible to accept Raël's authority. Her story provides a fascinating glimpse into the evolution of Raël's leadership and the nature of his relationships with his followers.

Héloise is from the Saguenay region of Quebec. Her parents were middle-class professionals who baptized her in the Catholic Church. Héloise joined the IRM when she was sixteen, in 1980, and by eighteen she was a level 3, animator. In an interview with me in July 2003 in Montreal, she explained how Raël's message fit into Quebec's ufology milieu in the 1970s and 1980s.

> I was seeing UFOs since I was 7, I grew up in the Saguenay, and in the '70s, when we would see UFOs. Our local newspaper had a picture of a UFO on the bridge in Chicoutimi. We even had a joke—when the electricity went off (and it did quite often) we'd say, "Beware of the UFOs!" So I've always known we are not alone in the universe. We are monitored, helped by higher beings—I've always felt that—that's why I joined.
>
> When I went to my first Stage [summer seminar] Raël promoted me to animator. Raël was very nice . . . he was funny! We joked around, he was not taking himself too seriously at the time. I found him very sincere and trying to do his best. I felt he was saying the truth.

I believe Raël is psychic. In 1988 I came to the meeting to sing a new song. I am a singer and I told Raël, "I have a new baby!" (meaning my song). Raël put his hand on my belly and stopped like that for two or three minutes. He knew I was pregnant, and I did not know it myself yet! He *is* psychic, definitely! When we looked at each other, we felt a connection. He was coming in my dreams and we were playing together like children (our friendship was never sexual).

But he changed. He disappeared for a while—that was in '84. When I saw him at the seminar in the summer of '84, I was shocked. He was very, very thin, he had shaved his beard and hair—it was frightening, the change in his appearance. He told me what had happened. He said there had been a *chasse des sorcières* [witch-hunt] in France. He was caught and imprisoned by the police and questioned over and over again. He was locked up in prison and suffered from lack of sleep, He did not eat well, and he got very sick and almost died. He was taken to hospital and had an operation. So, he was deeply traumatized. He told everybody at the time, "I'm not dead yet!"

While he was in France, I had a dream. I saw him looking at himself in the mirror, shaving his hair and beard. He looked very sad, and I knew he had cut himself off from the Elohim at the time. That was my dream before I saw him changed.

So then he took a leave from running the movement. But the year after that, when he came back, he had completely changed his personality. He was more dictatorial, more greedy—in fact, all those things the French journalists accused him of being, which he was not before. When I met him the year after, we talked and he said that he wanted to be my guide. I found him very arrogant and cold. "But I want to see my friend" (because he was my friend before). "No, I don't want to be your friend, I want to be your guide," he kept saying. I started laughing. "Don't be my guide!" I begged. We used to tease each other all the time. We had a competition with jokes—to see which of us is going to tag down the other person with a joke.

But he refused to play with me, to joke around anymore. So finally I said, "I am not interested. I am my own guide." I heard people say, "The Raël we know is dead. This is someone else." I felt that too, and I didn't like this new guy. He was arrogant! In the early days he used to tell us, "If one day I tell you I am infallible, just push me aside!" Today, I hear people are told to kneel in front of him! The Elohim said, "Don't do that to us. We are your equals." The Raelians would not do that if they listened to the messages. Now people are controlled by fear: "If you don't listen to *me,*" Raël says, "you won't be re-created!"

In *Le livre* Raël says, "Don't look at my finger, look to where it is pointing! I am only a messenger." But today all Raelians look straight at his finger. They bow to him, kneel in front of him. Even *he* is looking at his own finger!

After that, I noticed the movement went through a moral degradation. Suddenly *appearance* became very important. The new Raël liked flattery, money, and beautiful women. The people at the desk had to be beautiful. You needed to look great, you needed to have money. Before that it was not important. Before it used to be the Elohim who chose the level 5 [the bishops]. They [the bishops] would live a special experience on their own, where the Elohim would directly tell to them, and then they would tell Raël. This happened to Victor Legendre, to Rejean Proulx, and also to Katsumi.

But now, Raël names the bishops. And they are self-centered people who love power. The eternals must care more about others than themselves, and must be elected before they can be an eternal. There are no elections in the Raelian Movement, not for the guides, not for those who are to be cloned [the clients of Clonaid]. The trouble is, Raël is not living up to the standards of the geniocracy. The Elohim re-create those who deserve, but Raël only clones those who are rich.

Raël fell into the trap of Satan, the guard dog of the Elohim. He is the one who tests the egos of people to protect our creators. The best way for them to verify if we understand the message and can apply it to our lives, is to make Raël go off track. And see what happened!

As you can see, it's pretty disturbing what happened. We are under a test—to see who follows their own consciences, their own heart, and are not blinded by fear. Everyone knows in the heart what is right and wrong.

Raël no longer shows us the love of the Elohim. It is pretty cold in there. Like the angels—why are there no male angels to serve the women? It's sexist! It's not in the messages. The Elohim never asked for sexual slaves to serve the guides and themselves. It's very wrong to make women believe they are chosen and to use their loving natures to enslave them. Where is love in all this—true love? It's only sex. It's willing prostitution of the worst kind—empty, with no exchange of the souls.

The Whistleblowers

There are two outstanding whistleblowers whose grievances focus on what they perceive to be the IRM's financial mismanagement and excessive control over members' lives. They are Jean Parraga (see chapter 3) and "Gaspard."[3]

Gaspard, an ex–Jehovah's Witness, enrolled in a Raelian summer seminar, then declared war on Raël: On June 1, 1995, Gaspard posted a thousand copies of his letter to Raelians concerning the slow progress of the embassy, "Poeme à la Louange des Elohim" (Poem in praise of the Elohim). In this letter he objects to the purchase of the Valcourt estate and the building of UFOland with members' donations, which he felt should be dedicated exclusively to building the embassy.

Gaspard's letter accused Raël of mismanagement: "Why was there no progress in building the embassy?" Gaspard suggests the embassy fund was redirected into Raël's expensive hobby of car racing. He goes on to criticize the social control methods exerted over members by the guides, and Raël's insistence on absolute loyalty, as in "The Test of Satan," a questionnaire campers filled out demonstrating their uncritical fidelity to the movement, its leadership, and its goals.[4]

Raël offers an interpretation of this conflict in a letter entitled "Enemies Within!" in the IRM newsletter (Raël 1995). He suggests that Gaspard and other "enemies within" are undercover operators sent by the Catholic Church to "destroy or weaken the Raelian Movement" who, "under the aspect of false liberation or reformers of the Guides' actions, . . . recently sent out letters trying to instill doubt on some subject among our brothers and sisters in the world."

Gaspard had alleged that the IRM was facing financial collapse because Canadian guides had invested all the money collected to build the embassy in the Valcourt property instead, where UFOland was under very slow construction. Raël insisted that he took full responsibility for the decision to invest some of the IRM's funds in the UFOland project: "I had already decided a year ago to create in America a huge center for the diffusion of the messages and a training center for the guides as the one that exists in Europe in Eden. . . . Instead of building a replica of the Embassy, which would have cost nearly 2 million dollars, I decided to lend 1.5 million to the Garden of the Prophet and to install the UFOland project in the hotel along with the American seminar."

Raël also noted that ten years earlier he had invested $1 million in the European summer camp, Eden, located in the south of France. He promised that, "as soon as the Elohim announce that the moment has arrived to build the Embassy, if it is necessary the total property of the IRM will be sold to finance the constructions." Raël noted that his bishop Rejean Proulx had "made a management error" in regard to the Garden of the Prophet and consequently was demoted from his high level of continental guide of the Americas.

Raël spent an hour talking to Gaspard on the telephone, trying to smooth over the situation, and was incensed when he discovered that Gaspard had taped the conversation and given the tapes to a journalist, who wrote an exposé of Raël in *La Presse.* On June 22, 1995, Raël made a stern announcement: "On behalf of the Elohim, I have, on June 22 49 at 09.00, Quebec time, cancelled the transmission of the cellular code of [Louise] and [Gaspard]. This sanction, the worst that exists, is final" (Raël 1995).

This act was called "demarking," a reference to the mark in the forehead or "third eye" where the Elohim note a person's DNA code. It was a new rite of exclusion, at once excommunication and damnation, for it revoked the potential of physical regeneration in the future.

The Career Apostate

The most visible apostate from the IRM is Erick Lamarche, who renamed himself Exraël in ritual opposition to Raël, and wears a Raelian swastika medallion obliterated by a large *X.* He is engaged in writing a book attacking Raël's philosophy whose working title is "The Elohim Are Sick." One of my students encountered him in her social circle and announced her intention of interviewing him for a research paper, then dropped out of college. I followed up by phoning Exraël to arrange an interview.

Exraël met me at the door of his apartment, wearing only shorts and his large crossed-out Raelian medallion. He is an athletic, extroverted, thirtyish man with a strong Quebecois twang and dead-white skin from working in a nightclub. I sat down at his kitchen table next to a sprawling beanbag of a blue alien, a "gray" with large slanting plastic eyes. The wall displayed a plaque of the Raelian symbol obliterated by a bold *X.*

Exraël poured me a glass of orange juice and expressed anxiety: "How do I know you are not an *espion* [spy] for Raël?"

I explained I was a sociologist and religion teacher and was writing a book on the history of the RM. "You too!" he responded and told me about his book in progress, a theological work in which he attacks Raël's ideas, pointing out logical inconsistencies between different passages. He showed me a passage in *The True Face of God* in which Raël denounces racism based on skin color, then says: "If you have to be racist, be racist against stupid people! Discriminate against fools whatever the colour of their skin" (Raël 2003, 188). "That's still racism!" Exraël exclaimed. Then he showed me pages

142–143 in *Acceuillir les extra-terrestres* (Raël 1979) where the extraterrestrials threaten all those who oppose their beloved prophet. "When they die they will be re-created and suffer eternal punishment!" explained Exraël. "The Raelians oppose capital punishment, so what's this? Eternal suffering and punishment? Is this logic?"

Exraël's background corresponds in many ways to the notion of a typical Quebecois Raelian. He was baptized Catholic, grew up a fatherless child (like Raël), and was raised by his mother, who worked, among other jobs, as a bank secretary. He works as an *animateur* (a sort of DJ and host) in a nightclub, presenting the exotic dancers to the public. At twelve he discovered the pleasures of masturbation and was disturbed that sex was a sin in the Catholic Church. At fourteen he read Raël's book and became immediately Raelian. "I believed!" He saw Raël on TV; "I began diffusing the message to everyone around me five years before I officially became Raelian!" At nineteen he was baptized by Raël, himself: "It was on Ste Helene Island, I was so happy! I looked up into the beautiful cloudy sky with tears in my eyes and said, 'Elohim! I recognize you as my fathers! And I really want to help Raël construct an embassy to welcome you.'"

Exraël showed me his security badges from his first Sensual Meditation seminar in 1989, when he was a skinny mustached youth, and his notebooks from jotting down Raël's lectures. "For me, that was a week of paradise, and I was sure I'd found the true religion and I fell in love with my religion—peace, harmony, love, eternal life. We were in nature, camping, and Raël was so intelligent—he speaks well. Tabernouche! [a blasphemy]." At twenty-one, he attended his first seminar for members who wish to join the structure. One year later, he became an animator's assistant [level 1].

He was deeply involved in the movement from 1989 to 1992. Then he took a break and returned to the structure in 1998 and worked with the technical support team that organizes the meetings and rents space and sound equipment. Every Saturday for many months, he sold Raël's books on the street and from door to door: "I was out there in thirty-below weather. I used all my intelligence to justify Raël, every one of my brain cells to defend his theory!"

Nonetheless, he continued to break the rules by smoking cigarettes and drinking beer secretly with his old high school friends. "Because of that, I always kept a distance from the Raelians, so I was never 100 percent integrated in Raelianism."

Exraël considers Raël to be "a false prophet" because his first and fourth books claim it is his "priority of priorities" to create an embassy—"But this is bullshit!" Exraël described a series of developments in the movement that caused him to become disillusioned.

In February 1999, during the time that he was most involved in the structure, a memo came out from Raël's racing team announcing that Raël had just won third place out of sixty-five competitors in the Fédération Internationale de l'Automobile. "Now he feels more confident than ever in all of us," the memo proclaimed, "so much so that he is racing once more. It brings so much happiness and excitement to his life. If it is within your means, I would invite you to contribute to Raël's Racing Team fund. Anything will help; . . . look at it as an investment."

Exraël did not approve: "Raël knows he is immortal. He has all eternity to do this shit! Now there are more urgent things . . . what about all the starving children in the world? Our money was given to build an embassy. The guides would say, "It's good publicity for the Raelian Movement." But, vrooom! Raël zooms past at 250 m.p.h. What was that? You call that good publicity? I would go to the meeting and see a hat on the table begging money for Raël's Racing Team. Oh, wow! If I put in a dollar, maybe the Elohim will like me?"

Exraël showed me a photograph of Raël in his race car, captioned "Le prophète le plus rapide de l'histoire de l'humanité!" (The fastest prophet in the history of humanity).[5] "You know," he said, "Raël used to be a street musician who put out a hat for money. He was a vagabond who played guitar, he used to sleep on the street. Now he is doing that again, begging with his hat."

Exraël defected for three reasons. First, he was in agreement with Gaspard; he too felt that the original goal, the embassy, was postponed for more trivial projects—Raël's racing team, for example.

Second, he was upset when the Order of Raël's Angels was announced—not at first because he felt that the girls were being sexually exploited, but because he was felt it wasn't fair. "I wanted to be an angel. It was unfair! Why only women?" He felt the Elohim were guilty of reverse sexism. "When it was announced at the seminar, we were told we could pick up the text of the revelation at the office. When I read that passage, that the angels should be willing to sacrifice their own lives and professions for Raël and their creators—it really bugged me! Is this the religion I'm married to? I asked myself." During his last Raelian seminar in 1999, he requested a private audience with Raël, but was kept waiting for four days and in the end only got to speak to Lear. "And while I was waiting, I saw a guide go up to a very pretty girl who was new—she wasn't even a Raelian—and tell her that Raël found her interesting and would like to arrange to meet and talk with her."

Third, Exraël disliked what he saw as the IRM's new focus on materialism—although he admitted there was very little pressure on members to give money if they did not want to. He himself had paid only $1,100 in membership fees over ten years. But he objected to the "new traditions"—some of which cost money.

> Suddenly in the 1998 seminar we were told that bowing to Raël should become a tradition like in other religions, to show our respect. There's too much worship of Raël. In his first book he warned us about that: "Don't look at my finger, look to where it's pointing!" he said. Now we buy him race cars and his beautiful $350,000 condo! Then it became a "tradition" to wear a djellaba at the seminar. It cost twenty dollars, although we were not told before to bring twenty dollars to the seminar. Look, is this worth twenty dollars? [He showed me a skimpy white robe.] Everyone has to wear it. I asked one of the guides about it. He said, "It is not an obligation, but it is suggested." So, when I went the next year, for a whole week I dressed in black. I was the little black sheep among four hundred people—they spotted me! What's happening with this guy?
>
> And you know something? For the seven days I was there, for the first time in my life, I did not have a hard on! I was traumatized! Too much blood going to my head. My brain was popping, I felt isolated. I was waiting for a sign. I kept looking at the sky. I had prayed to see a UFO since I was five years old, and even more by being a Raelian. Please, Elohim, give me a sign! Show yourself to me, because, it's not going very well for me down here! And I never saw a UFO! What the f—?

Exraël complained that Raël was becoming enamored of money and power.

> Raël used to be very anticapitalism, but in one of his speeches he praised Bill Gates, saying it was good to have Bill Gates around, he paid his taxes, created jobs, and even should get richer; . . . he seemed to be saying capitalism is good!
>
> Then the very last morning of the stage, Lear spoke for a long time. His argument was based on the principle of giving money to Raël. "Wouldn't it be nice to see Raël in a Ferrari!" he said. "Wouldn't it be nice to see all the bishops behind him with their own Ferraris?"
>
> So, in the afternoon there was a question period. Anyone could get up and ask Raël a question. I was in the chair with adrenaline stress. Do I really want to ask this question, but I really have to ask it. So I stood up in

front of the mike and said, "Raël, all week long we have been taught that happiness lies in being, not in having possessions—*être, pas avoir* [to be, not to have]." Raël nodded. "That is so." "But I am perplexed," I said. "Lear was talking all morning about wouldn't it be fun for you and all the bishops to have a Ferrari."

There was a silence for at least eight to ten seconds. Then Raël answered, two times in a row, "It's Lear who said that," pointing at Lear. Then we were all going to the meditation, and four Raelians came up to me and one of them said, "It took guts to ask that question!" and one of the bishops stood near us and watched us carefully.

So, when I came back from the seminar, it was a really dark period for me. I was crying, banging my head on the wall. I painted my cubicle at work black. I was in a deep depression. I was starting my disintoxication of the Raelians' beliefs.

Raël stole my youth, my adolescence, from me! Raelianism isolates you from the world. People think you're bizarre. Some of the beliefs scare people—that you shouldn't marry, sleep with as many people as you want, that jealousy is wrong. My friends ask me, "Are you crazy to give all your money to build an embassy for extraterrestrials?"

Exraël's apostasy career started when he appeared on a French TV2 *envoyé spéciale* in January 2000. "Ten million people watched me. All Raelians who speak French know about me." Since then he has also appeared on NBC, CBS, FOX, and TQS and made the cover of *La Presse* in January 2003. Exraël occasionally stands outside the Theatre Gésu during Raelian meetings, passing out flyers advertising the anticult Web site of Frank Muhletaler and his own, created with the help of a Swiss friend, www.escape.to/exrael. He argues with every Raelian he meets, pointing out what he considers to be contradictions in Raël's philosophy. ("They usually say 'F— you!' and walk off.")

Exraël is active in the ex-members' informal network. He receives newsletters from Les Apôtres and talks to the other ex-Raelians occasionally. The last time I spoke with him, he was disturbed about a lawsuit launched by the IRM against a French ex-Raelian and former angel, Dominique St. Hilaire, who had been interviewed on TVA by Paul Arcand, and he noted that an article by me was among the court documents used against her.

Exraël concluded our interview by describing his ultimate dream. "One of my biggest fantasies is to be on the same TV program as Raël, and to ask him questions [making a grandiose sweep of his arm]—Raël and . . . Exraël!

I am one of the most perfect guys to ask him questions; I have been following him for twenty-one years! My goal is to create the Exraelian religion, to stop the spread of Raelianism, because it is a disease—just like all of the other religions, I think. Raelianism is a psychological virus that is easily transmitted to young people. It separates them from society. Karl Marx called religion the 'opiate of the people' and that's what it is—a dangerous addiction!"

Bromley's "career apostates" typically make a noisy exit from the group and create rituals to facilitate their transition to mainstream society (1998, 38). Exraël fits this model, for he confronted Lear in public, appeared on television to criticize his former religion, then transformed his work cubicle into a ritual mourning space by painting it black and changed his name to invert his identity and fashioned a new symbol—the crossed-out medallion.

As Max Weber (1947) observed, new religions based on charismatic authority must undergo institutionalization if they manage to survive long enough. It appears Héloise and Exraël left the IRM because they could not accept changes that made the movement a more impersonal, regimented environment. Raël, like many prophets before him, gradually escalates his charismatic claims as a test of faith that weeds out the less loyal or adaptable among his followers. Héloise, Gaspard, and Exraël were deeply committed to the original vision and goals expressed in *Le livre* and were unwilling to accept the new—to them unjustified—permutations and the resulting loss of intimacy with their leader. It is clear that the IRM has become increasingly intolerant of nonconformists and malcontents and ruthlessly exiles those who challenge Raël's authority. Exraël's courage in dramatizing his dissent despite the overwhelming pressures to conform during the summer seminars is impressive. But no rival prophet of any stature has risen from the apostates' ranks. It takes an extraordinary aggregation of attributes, dedication, and single-mindedness to launch a new religion—and perhaps a little help from the Elohim?

If the power and relevance of a new religion can be measured by the quality of its apostates and rival prophets, the IRM scores high. I was impressed by the intelligence, sensitivity, and persistent spirituality of the apostates and ex-members I encountered. That a handful of apostates—but not Exraël—still worships the Elohim (whose nature they have redefined), and still exerts considerable effort trying to oppose Raël and reform the Raelian Movement for years after leaving it, surely says something about the profound impact of the Raelian organization on people's lives.

Chapter Eight

Cloning Around—Hoax or Heresy?

Raël's angels are still waiting to usher in the Elohim, but they have already put their bodies on the line to usher in the world's first human clones—as surrogate mothers. This sacrificial act caught the imagination of the media, which finally began to treat Clonaid's claims seriously.

In the autumn of 2000, I received an intriguing message on my email. The Raelians were holding a press conference to present fifty women who had volunteered to be surrogate mothers for the cloning experiment. I invited my students at Dawson College to accompany me on what promised to be an exciting research venture. Their response was enthusiastic.

On Thursday, September 21, 2000, I met my students at the Maritime Plaza Hotel in Montreal. Fourteen had shown up with a bevy of excited, inquisitive friends, eager to start researching. Unfortunately, the Raelians had booked a tiny conference room. I had been warned by Raël's publicity agent that there might not be room to seat my students, since journalists were the top priority. After some last-minute negotiating, I was able to gain access for three students, who squeezed in to take notes while I waited in the hall with the others. Two bodyguards stood around and chatted with us until their cell phones rang, calling them to duty.

There were lots of Raelians around, slender longhaired Francophones wearing the swastika and Star of David pendant. They greeted us warmly, starting conversations that kept getting interrupted when another Raelian arrived on the scene. Then they would break off in midsentence to greet him or her with an ecstatic hug. Beautiful girls teetered in and out of the ladies' washroom on high heels. We watched an abundant blond in a pink mohair batwing sweater and tight slacks moodily circle the hall, as if she were a singer warming up before her cabaret performance. We later realized she was Anoushka, one of the cloning mothers.

Suddenly, Raël was poised in the doorway, impressive in his samurai topknot and white padded suit, closely flanked by his white-garbed bishops and bodyguards. He strode purposefully through the hall toward the press room with theatrical speed and intensity, right past my gaping students, and his troupe marched on his heels in military formation.

The field reports my Dawson students submitted on the press conference described Raël sitting at a long table flanked by six women.[1] Two male bodyguards stood off to the side. Raël opened with a dramatic announcement: "The goal of the Raelians is to help humanity attain immortality!"

He declared his intention was no less than to "liberate humans from death." He spoke of how he had been "dreaming of cloning for twenty-seven years." Raelianism, he explained, was "more of a philosophy than a religion," which "blended technology with spirituality." Raelians would "raise science to the next level, so as to realize humanity's dream of eternal life."

"Those who choose to accept it shall live forever, those who are against it—let them die!" was his battle cry.

Raël then spoke of Clonaid, explaining how he had founded the company three years ago after he heard the pope's reaction against cloning. Until now Clonaid had been no more than a consultant company where one's DNA sample could be taken for future use, but now the company was ready to clone.

Brigitte Boisselier stood up. She is a pretty Frenchwoman in her midforties who holds two Ph.D.s in chemistry. She moved to Canada after she was victimized by the recent wave of anticult hysteria that gripped France in the wake of the suicide-homicides of the Solar Temple. When she came out as a Raelian on television in 1997 and spoke in defense of cloning, she was fired from her job in Lyons as director of research for a chemical company. She then moved to Quebec, where Raël promoted her to the rank of bishop. He had already appointed her director of Clonaid, and on arriving in North America, she embarked on a series of lecture tours and media interviews to promote Clonaid's goals and drum up clients.

Boisselier announced that the first of Clonaid's clients to begin the cloning process in earnest were an anonymous American couple whose ten-month-old had died as a victim of malpractice in a U.S. hospital. They would use their compensation money to finance the cloning operation.

She claimed the lab was currently being built, as the funds had been available for only one month. The scientific team consisted of two biologists, a gynecologist, who would remain anonymous, as well as Boisselier herself, a biochemist. The DNA would be extracted from blood samples taken before the baby died. Boisselier assured the audience that as the technology advances, the risks decrease, and that the team would be paying close attention to safety procedures throughout the process.

Five of the fifty cloning mothers sat beside Raël. They were introduced to the press by name: Anoushka, Marina, Jade, Jocelyne, and Sylvie. They ranged in age from twenty-two to thirty-four and were all very pretty. Each girl wore the feathered necklace of the Order of Raël's Angels. (I found it interesting that none of the journalists mentioned this in their news reports the next day.) When the journalists demanded to know their motives for volunteering, they gave three answers: They wished to experience being pregnant without the lifelong task of parenting; they wished to make the couple who had lost their child happy; and since the Raelian religion was all about science and technology, they were simply confirming their religious beliefs.

"They are not paid to do this," Raël added. "They just want to give the wonderful gift of life to someone else. They're doing it because they are true Raelians."[2]

Raël went on to explain that the Raelians were against war and violence, that they are pro-life. He predicted that genetically modified food would put an end to world hunger. He emphasized his strong support for new scientific advancements and the importance of maintaining science's link to human spirituality. He condemned "primitive religions" like Christianity for stalling human development. "There are no such things as miracles, only different levels of technology!" He expressed his hope that the baby would be alive by Christmas 2001, and that the public's views on cloning would change as a result.

"This baby will be proof that there is no miracle of birth!" he concluded triumphantly.

When asked, "Why Christmas?" Raël responded, "It is a symbol of a new century, a new beginning for technology to take its place."

Raël claimed that cloning was the way the Elohim had created us, and that it is the way humans will achieve eternal life. He suggested that people stop criticizing him and pay attention to things that are actually harmful and kill people. "I am simply trying to create and extend human life, not make nuclear weapons. People often ask if the Raelians are a dangerous or suicidal group—but why would we be suicidal if our goal is to clone and live forever?"

Since, to date, the surrogate mothers have not been used, one might ask what the function of this event was. One might analyze it as a test of loyalty, as a strategy to "one-up" Clonaid's rivals in the race to clone—and of course as a publicity stunt. And perhaps it is better that the angels, eager to lend their beautiful young bodies to a controversial human experiment, were not needed. A surrogate mother to a clone would have to go through an ordeal. She would be pumped with hormones so that her ovaries, normally the size of an almond, swell to the size of a walnut. She would be injected twice daily, her blood drawn so that her hormone levels can be tested. Research on animals has shown that many cloned embryos die in the womb in the third trimester, the result of faulty attachment between the placenta and the wall of the uterus. Most of the embryos are oversized and suffer from inadequate nutrition. And most of those that come to term display genetic abnormalities.

One of my students, Jasmine Noel (2000), concluded her field report on a prophetic note: "During this conference there was no mention of outside obstacles to overcome. The governments have not interfered so far, and they have had no problems with the law. It will prove interesting to see how people react to this project."

Jasmine turned out to be quite right. Within a year, a controversial drama erupted.

Clonaid—A History

In February 1997, Dr. Ian Wilmut, the embryologist, and his colleagues at the Roslin Institute in Scotland announced they had just produced a lamb named Dolly. She was the first mammal ever cloned from an adult cell.

The very next month, Raël held a press conference at the Flamingo Hilton in Las Vegas and announced he had created a new company, Valiant Venture. Backed by a group of investors, Valiant Venture offered cloning, via Clonaid, for grieving or infertile parents and gay couples for the price of $200,000. Clonaid's Web site advertised other services, such as Insuraclone, which would store cells of children who might be cloned in the event of an untimely death. Also featured was Clonapet, for wealthy pet owners and racehorse owners ("a very promising market, considering the outrageous prices paid for champions").

The Bahamian government froze Valiant Venture's offshore bank account. Raël later told journalists that the Bahamian-based company was little more than a post office box, according to Aaron Zitner in "Clones, Free Love, and UFOs," which appeared in the *Los Angeles Times* on March 6, 2002.

Brigitte Boisselier began traveling around Canada and the United States giving public speeches on the benefits of human cloning. She claimed in

March 1999 on Clonaid's Web site that they had opened an office in South Korea and were negotiating with scientists there. She began to hint at Clonaid's secret labs outside the United States and claimed she had set up a six-member research team of scientists and doctors—two biologists, two biochemists, and two physicians—one an expert on in vitro fertilization.

The specter of human cloning had already raised concern, both religious and bioethical. As early as 1987, the pope had denounced cloning efforts as "dangerous experiments" that showed "lack of respect for life" and were "harmful to human dignity." He urged governments to ban the cloning of humans, because people "have the right to be born in a human way." Raël said he took pleasure in opposing the pope, *son enemie jure* (his sworn enemy), according to *Le Journal de Montreal* on March 12, 1997. Other religions objected that cloning humans is akin to "playing God" and were concerned that a cloned human would lack a soul. President Bill Clinton had his National Bioethics Advisory Commission devote a whole day to testimony from invited religious leaders on the ethical implications of cloning. The commission called for a moratorium on federal funding of human cloning research.[3] Since Dolly, cloning experiments on mice, goats, and cows have had success rates as low as 1 percent. But Raël was optimistic.

"I was the first to talk about it twenty-seven years ago," said Raël, presumably referring to the Elohim's promise to "re-create" worthy humans, and his firsthand experience on the aliens' planet, where he witnessed his own re-creation in a vat. But, he explained, cloning is "just the first step" in his plan for immortality, laid out in his 2001 book *Yes to Human Cloning*. The clone is a sort of twin, he explained, and the next step is to make the clone undergo an "Accelerated Growth Process" to become an instant adult. The final step, uploading and downloading the individual's memory, will result in "eternal life in another, identical body" (Raël 2001b).

Raël at the U.S. Senate

March 28, 2001, was a triumphant day for Raël and all Raelians. He appeared before the widely publicized congressional hearing on human cloning. Boisselier was invited to speak on behalf of Clonaid, but she insisted she would attend only if her spiritual master were asked to speak. Canadian newspapers showed Raël in his customary astronaut-like suit and topknot, standing in front of the domed and pillared porch of the U.S. Capitol, his right hand raised as he was being sworn in.

His unconventional dress excited much comment. Aaron Zitner wrote a year later in his *Los Angeles Times* article: "A star-shaped pendant around his neck, his hair gathered atop his head in a bun, the white-suited leader . . . told lawmakers they should no more block his plans to clone human beings than they would stop . . . other medical advances." The *Ottawa Citizen* noted that Raël "was given all the respect due to a mad scientist when he appeared before a subcommittee that seems bent on banning human cloning."

Raël testified that Clonaid was planning to clone a dead baby in the near future. Then he discussed the relationship between science and religion. "Science destroys superstition and supernatural beliefs. This is why religion is always the enemy of science and of progress, and tries once again to stop science whenever it can." He suggested that we should let all religious people refuse the medical assistance and benefits of surgery, antibiotics, abortion—and cloning—and then they will die out, leaving only enlightened atheists who will enjoy immortal life. He ended on an historical note. "If religion and superstition, that are no different, have power over science, we live yet in the dark ages. Don't make the mistake of burning Giordano Bruno again!"[4]

No one paid attention to his speech, but it says a great deal about where the Raelians stand on the frontier between science and religion. It also demonstrates that, in his quest to gain social recognition and respect for his "church" in a secular society, Raël was shifting ground, attacking religion, and tactically reformulating his movement as a "scientific philosophy."

The Mark Hunt Story

Clonaid's first serious client approached Brigitte Boisselier in August 2000.

Mark Hunt was a lawyer and an ambitious politician, with a Hunt for Congress office in Charleston, West Virginia. He was forty years old, had been a member of the West Virginia legislature for five years, and was a candidate for election to the U.S. House of Representatives.

The Hunts were devastated when their hospitalized baby, Andrew, born with a congenital heart defect, died at the age of ten months in September 1999. They sued the hospital for malpractice and were awarded a large compensation by the court. Hunt kept his son's cells frozen and embarked on a quest for cloning services, hoping to create a "genetic twin." He contacted Boisselier through www.clonaid.com, and they made a pact in August 2000. Hunt invested $500,000 in an unregistered company, Bioserv Inc.

By December 2000, Hunt had arranged to rent an old high school science lab in Nitro, West Virginia. Earlier that year, Boisselier had been hired as a chemistry professor at Hamilton College near Syracuse, New York. She gave

many press interviews in which she justified human cloning and predicted a cloned baby would be born by the end of 2001. She was soon being investigated by the prosecutor for the grand jury in Syracuse, who was gathering evidence for a possible indictment against her based on the premise that cloning violated drug laws. The Food and Drug Administration (FDA) had also begun to "spy on her" (personal communication). Boisselier told a journalist she suspected the FDA was using the grand jury to get her phone records and discover the location of the secret lab, as well as Clonaid's list of clients. Boisselier in turn threatened to sue the FDA, claiming it had no jurisdiction over cloning.

The caretaker of the high school that housed the lab was a man named Casto. He looked after the building, which was currently used as a community center, with a daycare center and a senior citizens' club. Casto was watching television one evening when he saw Boisselier being interviewed on CNN. He realized he was caretaking a cloning lab and became alarmed. The community center was his responsibility, and "I didn't want any trouble," said Casto, according to a journalist I interviewed. He was worried about anticloning protestors, riots, and dangerous materials on the premises. He called the police, and they called in the FDA.

The FDA arranged with Boisselier to visit the lab at Nitro. They seized its equipment and experimental material, but they found no incriminating evidence—no human eggs, only cow eggs. So they struck a deal with her and Mark Hunt. In return for keeping secret the location of the lab and the identity of the father/sponsor, all cloning activity would cease until the "legal picture was clear."[5]

But Boisselier was not cowed. She was caught up in a whirlwind of publicity and continued to speak out boldly on television in favor of cloning and was featured in many news reports and magazines. Boisselier had become the darling of the media; in photographs in the top magazines and papers, she wore sexy avant-garde clothes, with her face heavily made up. Some journalists were flattering (the *New York Times Magazine*'s Margaret Talbot called her "pretty" in "The Lab of the Human Clones" on February 4, 2001), but others suggested that serious scientists don't dress that way. (One reporter described her as wearing a white silk suit that displayed her "abdomen.")

The next summer, a reporter from the *Sunday Times* of London showed up in Charleston. He had figured out the location of the lab from information Boisselier had supplied in her interviews with the media, mentioning a lawyer, a former legislator with a ten-month-old baby who had died in a hospital of a congenital heart defect, whose parents had won a malpractice suit. When the Hunts sued the hospital, there had been a public fund-raising effort to help cover their legal costs. Boisselier had even read out the letter from the anonymous father: "I am a successful attorney, a former state legislator, a current elected official, a husband, a son, a brother, but most importantly, I am a father. We didn't know what to do and couldn't accept that it was over for our child. . . . I decided then and there that I would be never give up on my child. I would never stop until I could give his DNA—his genetic makeup—a chance. I knew that we only had one chance; human cloning. To create a healthy duplicate, a twin of our son. I set out to make it happen."[6] The reporter managed to track down Hunt through an Internet search and flew to Charleston. He spoke to Hunt's relatives and visited the lab in Nitro, where he warned the locals that dangerous work was going on, that it was likely someone would bomb the building. Casto begged Hunt to close down the lab.

Boisselier continued her work as ambassador for the Raelian religion, granting interviews to the media and claiming that the cloning work had moved to another secret lab outside the United States and was forging ahead.

Hunt became disillusioned. He changed the locks on the Nitro lab and decided to make a public statement. He announced he was breaking his ties with Boisselier and Clonaid and referred to her a "press hog."

Later, in an interview with ABC's *Downtown* host, Hunt talked about how he had interrupted the work at the lab. The television crew followed him as he walked through lab, talking about what equipment was installed. There was a computer, a telephone, a Brita water purifier, a microscope, a centrifuge, a micromanipulator, and an incubator.

Mark Hunt spoke in the ABC interview of the profound grief that led him to his involvement with Raël's Clonaid project: "For parents, nothing can be worse. It was devastating. We cried, we prayed, . . . you can't imagine the absolute misery. It's more than depression, it's physical pain." He sought to explain his unconventional quest in traditional Christian language: "For the first time in human history I/we didn't accept death as the end. Not since our Lord and Savior, Jesus Christ, spoke to Lazarus and told him to 'come forth' from the grave has a human been able to bridge the great gulf of death. . . . I hoped and prayed my son would be the first."

Meanwhile, the prosecutor in Syracuse continued his investigation of Boisselier and her Clonaid company, under suspicion of defrauding its clients. Mark Hunt was approached, but he was not interested in suing, for Clonaid had returned his investment. The FDA never did find out who the other clients were. Boisselier claimed in interviews that she had no intention of breaking the law and would simply move the project to a country where cloning was not illegal. "We still have two thousand on the list in the U.S.," she boasted in the ABC *Downtown* segment.

But the question of whether a serious cloning project had been underway in the Nitro lab was still unresolved. Casto, in interviews shown in *Downtown*'s film clips, protested that the lab was ill-equipped, and that he had observed no research activity going on: "I'm in the building every day of the week, I tell you, there was nothing going on." The incubator had never been turned on, and the refrigerator was empty when the FDA came. Casto claimed Boisselier had come in perhaps three times and stayed only a few minutes each time. She would sit at the computer or talk on the phone. "She was a nice lady; . . . she told me, 'I'm just making sure things are OK.' There was nothing going on in there, I know that for a fact. I never did see the four scientists."

Casto had been upset at the way the *Sunday Times* of London had portrayed the building as small, dingy, and dirty, as he prided himself on keeping it clean. He has since resigned as caretaker and now works for the East Bank Police Department in Nitro.

Long after the Hunt scandal had died down, the "Cult that Clones" still had an impact on public policy. During the first week of August 2001, the U.S. House of Representatives voted to ban all forms of human cloning. The lower house was also considering a bill that would impose a ten-year jail sentence and a $1 million fine on anyone who practiced cloning. President George W. Bush said he would sign the legislation if the Senate passed a similar measure. Raël was still in the picture as the debate on cloning continued in the House of Representatives, for Senator Orin Hatch and Representative James Greenwood mentioned Raël in the congressional hearings of January 2002, in their attempts to build a case for a law banning reproductive cloning.

Aaron Zitner argued in his *Los Angeles Times* article that Raël might have unwittingly provided the catalyst for a draconian legal clampdown on the most significant scientific direction of our era. Zitner claims that scientists are now being told not to pursue avenues of research like stem-cell therapy that could save millions of lives and extend human life in the future.

The Race to Clone

Soon after the Hunt debacle, Clonaid found a new wealthy client—an Israeli businessman—as Tamara Taubman reported in "Attack of the Clones" (*Ha'Aretz Daily,* September 11, 2002):

> In 2000 a rich Israeli businessman diagnosed with terminal illness stopped taking medication. He is 58 and childless and wants to leave something of himself behind, and has become obsessed by the idea that this something should be a cloned child, one who is genetically identical to himself. He sees his premature death as an unfortunate "mishap" and believes his genes deserve a second chance. Five years ago he would have made an endowment of a new children's ward in a hospital, or a cultural center named after him. Today, since the genome is being dubbed a culture hero and the "book of life," he wished to perpetuate his genes. Eighteen months ago he saw the Clonaid Web site, and invested 1 million ("they say"), at any rate he made a deal with the raelians who direct this project.
>
> Is the desire to perpetuate yourself through cloning a case of "bio-megalomania"?

Raël mentioned another serious client during his "Yes to Cloning" launch in Britain at the February 21, 2002, press conference. Clonaid's scientists had started work on cloning a terminally ill elderly man. He had no family and had agreed to stop taking his medication as soon as the surrogate mother, a Japanese Raelian, became pregnant with his clone. At this point there were three thousand clients on the Clonaid list.

In 2002, it looked as if the race to produce the world's first human clone was nearing the finishing line. There were rumors in the media that Russian and Chinese teams of scientists were also in the cloning race. Dr. Panagiotis Zavos had told the U.S. Congress in May 2001 that five groups were racing to produce the first cloned human baby. The Raelians' chief rival, Italian gynecologist Severino Antinori, announced in May 2002 that three women from his clinic were pregnant with cloned embryos. In late November, Dr. Antinori claimed that a female client in his clinic for infertile couples was carrying a cloned embryo and was expected to give birth in early January.[7]

Close on the heels of Antinori's announcement, Brigitte Boisselier preempted him by claiming that Clonaid not only had several pregnancies in progress, but also that the implants of her blastocysts had taken place *before* his, in February–March 2002, although miscarriages had occurred, "as they do in test tube conceptions." Boisselier claimed that in the examination of the miscarried blastocysts, no abnormalities were detected. She did not reveal how many miscarriages had occurred, or how many embryos remained viable. Clonaid's vice president, Thomas Kaenzig, was more specific, claiming the company was engaged in cloning "10 to 20 clients."[8]

The effect of all this publicity was that the Raelians were considered serious contenders in the human-cloning race. Professor Don Wolf of the Oregon Regional Primate Research Center says: "When you look at the critical prerequisites for cloning—money, eggs, a surrogate womb, determination and patience—the Raelian group has them all."[9]

The Annunciation of Baby Eve

On the day after Christmas—Boxing Day—2002, at the Holiday Inn in Hollywood, Florida, Boisselier held a press conference to announce that Clonaid had succeeded in producing the world's first human clone. "She is born. She is fine. We call her Eve," she said, reassuring the journalists that the baby was "healthy." When interrupted, she objected: "Let me speak. This is *my* day."

Her ecstatic deportment was hardly that of a sober scientist. One journalist noted: "Perhaps mistaking the venue for the other Hollywood, she launched into an Oscar-style acceptance speech."[10] Nor was she dressed like a scientist. The media mercilessly scrutinized her "flaky" appearance, her heavily applied lip liner and long bleached white-silver-copper hair. Some journalists waxed quite hostile and ignored the fact that Boisselier happens to be an attractive woman with Parisian chic. One journalist went so far as to rudely describe her triumphant smile as "showing her browning teeth in meaty gums."[11] The *Montreal Gazette* featured an unflattering photo taken from below and placed it on the page beside a picture of cloned pigs ("This is no accident, believe me," a friend who teaches photo journalism at the college level assured me.)

Boisselier introduced Dr. Michael Guillen, a former ABC science editor, who promised to oversee the testing by a top-level international team of independent scientists. But over the next few days, the testing was postponed repeatedly, and no scientific evidence was forthcoming.

The world's response to Boisselier's Boxing Day statement was ambivalent. The media cooperated enthusiastically with Boisselier's bid for fame and Raël's mission to preach the message but reacted to their announcement with skepticism and horror. The Raelian religion became a target of ridicule. The reaction of reputable scientists and bioethicists to the notion of a "cult" meddling in a scientific enterprise that would have a profound impact on the human condition was one of disgust and outrage.

Boisselier next appeared on BBC TV's *Breakfast with Frost* on January 4, 2003. She explained that, although she wanted DNA testing, she would not rush the parents, even if she had a contract with them. She claimed that three more cloned babies would be born by late January or early February, the five out of ten implantations that had survived. She labeled the public outrage "the yuk effect": "When a new technology arrives we have disgust, . . . then fear, then doubts, then you slowly accept. Probably in five years from now, people will say, well, this is okay."

Raël and his bishop seemed to be having the time of their lives as they rode the crest of a "global media blitz," as journalist Tu Thanh Ha put it, for at least three weeks.[12] And perhaps some of the journalists' hostility derived from their suspicion that they had "been had."

Then Guillen stepped forward and made a rueful public statement: "It's entirely possible Clonaid's announcement is part of an elaborate hoax intended to bring publicity to the Raelian Movement."[13]

The notion that Raël and Boisselier were milking the media as calculating performers was supported by one offstage moment on January 28. Simon Boivin of *Le Soleil* reported that Raël whispered to Boisselier off-camera during Pierre Maisoneuve's talk show: "It is going well; . . . too bad the last phrase didn't get in. We have to make the folks cry. We have to make women, mothers, reach for their handkerchiefs."[14]

But it is interesting to note that when Dr. Antinori's clones failed to materialize, first in October 2002, then in early January 2003, the doctor's Roman Catholicism was never an issue. Nor was Dr. Panagiotis Zavos's religion (presumably Greek Orthodox) ever targeted.

Then an unexpected attack from a new quarter bent the story line. A Florida lawyer, Bernard Siegel, filed a petition seeking a guardian for "Eve," asking that her unknown parents be summoned before a Florida court in Broward County for a hearing January 22. He said he wished to protect the interests of the child even though no one had seen her.[15]

Clonaid's vice president, Thomas Kaenzig, a Swiss Raelian, was summoned to this hearing to reveal the whereabouts of the baby. He testified by telephone from his Las Vegas home that the company was not incorporated anywhere and had no board of directors and that Boisselier kept him "largely ignorant about its operations." He said he didn't know the location of Eve. He refused to answer most of the questions and was threatened with contempt of court by Judge John Frusciante, who then ordered him to appear in court Wednesday, January 29. Kaenzig said he had Boisselier's word that "the child is being taken care of." Frusciante, a family-court judge, replied, "Parents of starved and abused children tell me that every day."[16]

Raël also went on record claiming ignorance. As he told Daneen Brown of the *Washington Post* (January 17, 2003): "I don't know where and I don't know with what person [the baby is]. I don't know the family. I don't know where is the laboratory. I don't know the scientists. I know absolutely nothing. I just learned, like everybody else, when she announced the birth of the child."

It would appear then, that only Boisselier knows the truth. This leaves us with four possible scenarios:

1. BB is telling the truth. Baby Eve et al. really exist, are healthy, and are being kept undercover by their parents for sensible legal and humanitarian reasons.

2. BB is the author of a hoax, a "scientific joke," as Raël put it, perpetrated to spread the message, to please Raël, and to facilitate her own rise within the Raelian hierarchy.

3. BB told the truth initially, but then backed off. Appalled by the public's overwhelmingly negative reaction, she decided not to follow up on the tests and allowed her scientific breakthrough to be dismissed as a hoax. Another possible reason we must consider is that Eve during her first two days appeared to be a healthy baby, but within the next two days developed complications caused by genetic mutation. Thus, Boisselier may have decided it would be unwise to allow the team of scientists access to her. A sick, deformed, or dying baby is no longer a triumph, but a tragedy—and one with unpleasant legal consequences.

4. BB was sincere but was conned. Given the covert, extralegal status of Clonaid's enterprise, an unscrupulous scientist seized his or her opportunity. Boisselier trusted this person and was in regular communication by email but could not personally oversee the nine-month lab experiment, since she was under surveillance by the FDA and possibly the FBI. She possibly oversaw the implanting of the blastocyst and relied on the scientist for news of its progress. Thus, when she was told of a successful birth, she held the Boxing Day conference—only to be left holding the bag.

Personally, I find the fourth hunch ties up more loose ends, although I have no hard evidence to support it.

"Baby Said to Be Clone Will Vanish, Raelian Announces," read a January 23, 2003, headline in the *Toronto Globe and Mail.* Boisselier held a press conference in Toronto to declare that the American parents of the still untested Baby Eve planned to vanish forever, and "I will not have contact with them anymore." The reporter, Graem Smith, conveys his skepticism: "The president of a firm that doesn't formally exist said . . . she still can't prove her 'human cloning company' has cloned any humans." He notes snidely: "Ms. Boisselier chose one of the city's most expensive conference rooms to declare that her costs have been rising."

If one were to pursue the hoax hypothesis, it is interesting to recall a hoaxlike precedent in Raelian history. The tale of the Teesdale inheritance bears many of the lineaments of the Baby Eve story (see chapter 2). In both cases there is a competition (for the inheritance and for the world's first clone) that Raël wins. The "prize" in each case is a specimen of superior alien technology (an alien artifact and a cloned human). Both conveniently vanish. An apparently old and reputable law firm turns out to be bogus in the Teesdale case, just as Clonaid, described for six years as a "private company," turns out to have no legal standing. Although the first "hoaxer" was never exposed, if one were to ask who would gain from the Teesdale charade, the answer would have to be—Raël. To win the prize of alien artifacts would support his charismatic claim to be the Elohim's chosen prophet. In Weberian terms, this might be interpreted as an example of "charismatic display."

The only two suspects are Jacques Vallée or a ring of hoaxers who gained nothing from the exercise. Jerome Clark (1998) argues that, while Vallée started out as a serious scientific investigator of UFO phenomena, by his fourth book, UFOs had become just one of many guises of a chameleonlike invisible order formed to shape and direct human consciousness. In *Messengers of Deception,* Vallée fits "sects and cults" into his conspiracy theory: "UFOs are real. They may be in fact terrestrial-based manipulating devices. Their methods are those of deception: systematic manipulation of witnesses and contactees; covert use of various sects and cults" (1979, 21). Vallée points to several NRMs, especially Heaven's Gate (and this was *before* their mass suicide), as dangerous organizations that use traditional religious themes and adverse social conditions to dupe gullible people. But Clark notes that "for these sweeping speculations, Vallée offers little of evidence" (1998, 436). Thus, it is not unreasonable to imagine that Vallée may have concocted the whole story to support his conspiracy theory regarding UFOs, and to discredit Raël.

The Raelians' Reaction to Baby Eve

On Sunday, January 19, 2003, I bumped into a group of Raelians in Montreal's best vegetarian restaurant, le Commensal. They welcomed me enthusiastically, saying, "We're having so much fun these days!" They had just come from the monthly gathering at Theatre Gésu, where Raël had dropped in for a surprise visit after his whirlwind of publicity. He had made two momentous announcements.

First, he claimed his mission was "50 percent complete." He was referring to his mandate to spread the message. "It's done. I've informed the entire planet of my message." The remaining "50 percent" is building the embassy. "It's so important that the message should be brought to humanity by a baby," Raël added. (My Raelian friends said it was also significant that the baby was female.)

Raël's second announcement was that he had appointed Brigitte Boisselier as his successor. He expressed delight that she had found such an effective means of spreading the message. Then he made an extraordinary admission: "If Brigitte has done it, she has achieved a wonderful thing and should receive the Nobel Prize. If it isn't true, it's the most beautiful scientific joke, . . . but in any case, whether true or false, it has allowed us to communicate our message to the whole planet. I want to thank Brigitte eternally for it, and when I say eternally, I mean it."

The obvious way to interpret this statement is that Raël is protecting himself in case of a legal suit. He is publicly declaring he had no part in the "hoax." But, at the same time, he is compensating Boisselier for the risk she took to promote the message in such a dramatic way. The theological import of "when I say eternally, I mean it" could be that the Elohim have decided to re-create Boisselier when she dies—so her salvation is assured.

One Raelian mentioned that Boisselier had been consulting a lawyer the day before, so it appeared a lawsuit was pending. When I asked about the future of the Clonaid Company, they responded: "Clonaid is not a company. It is a project! It was never a company. It is only a Web site—but the real name of the company *behind* the Web site—that may never be known." I was surprised, as I had always heard it referred to as a "company."

The *Calgary Sun* confirmed their story, although the January 20, 2003, headline, "Raelian Founder Admits Report of Cloning Could be False," overstated the case. But Raël has planted, or rather watered, the seed of doubt.

"But what about Dolly the sheep?" I asked. "What about all the abnormalities in cloned animals?"

"That's not a problem for *us,*" responded Michel Beluet, the former director of UFOland. "The Elohim told Raël that they specially designed humans to be *easy to clone*—not like the other mammals."

It surprised me that my Raelian friends, as we sat around the table munching delicious Commensal salad, couscous, and ginger tofu, seemed to be absolutely certain, even blasé, about the ubiquitous presence of clones. "You notice that Antinori is keeping very quiet right now," one of them said. "He predicted a baby for early January, but he doesn't want legal problems, and his clients don't want their baby taken away." They even suggested that Baby Eve was not necessarily the first. "There are cloned children right now walking all over the earth—sure there are! In a few years they will come forth and be known."

"We're having so much fun right now," said a guide. "We are out there doing our *diffusion* [missionary work], and when pretty girls stop on the street to talk to us, I lean forward and say, 'Can I have one of your hairs, please?' holding out tweezers and a plastic bag. They freak out and run away. They think we can clone them on the spot!" We all burst out laughing.

Miraculous Babes in Science and Religion

Miraculous babes appear and disappear like bubbles throughout the history of heresy. Prophets have placed high expectations upon infant avatars, divine boys, and new Eves to usher in a new age.

Joanna Southcott, an English prophetess of the 1770s, received a revelation that she was the "woman clothed in the sun" of Revelation 12. Announcing at age sixty-four that she would bear a son named Shiloh who would rule over the new age, her belly swelled as several doctors confirmed her pregnancy. As her followers eagerly awaited a virgin birth, her false pregnancy subsided and within a few months she sickened and died. Then a new prophet arose among her following, George Turner, who stepped into the breach and reinterpreted her prophecy. He claimed the unborn babe, Shiloh, had been taken directly from Southcott's womb by angels and ascended to heaven. Shiloh would reappear at a later date, he assured the Southcottites, to inaugurate the new millennium and rule over the earth (Melton 1985).

Baby Eve appears to be yet another miraculous babe who mysteriously fails to materialize. Unlike Shiloh, Eve is not the product of a biblical superstitious miracle—rather she is a miracle of science. And yet her miraculous quality derives from her being the product of a technology that does not yet exist—except on a far-off planet. But she baffles the world because she cannot be dismissed as a mere religious fantasy, since human cloning is a plausible forthcoming event on our scientific horizon. If she turns out to be a media hoax, she must be *more* than a hoax. She is prophecy recast in scientific language—a prophet's playful revision of apocalyptic expectation.

And Raël is a prophet. For Raelians, he's the last prophet of the Age of Apocalypse that commenced in August 1945 with the bombing of Hiroshima. We are living in emergency times, warns Raël, where humanity's only hope is to learn to use scientific knowledge for creation, rather than destruction. Raël regularly hears extraterrestrial voices that instruct him in important matters like how humanity originated and how to save the planet from a nuclear holocaust. Raël is the prophet of the world's first "scientific religion."

Dr. J. Gordon Melton of the Institute for the Study of American Religion in Santa Barbara says groups that confront the failure of a predicted event to materialize typically take one of two routes: postponement or "spiritualization." The Seventh-Day Adventists have postponed Jesus' imminent return, whereas the Jehovah's Witnesses (like Southcott's group) claim it already occurred, albeit on an invisible spiritual plane, but will become physically manifest "before that generation passeth away."

The Raelians cannot "spiritualize," since they do not believe in a spiritual realm, neither in God nor the soul. Indeed, the only hope for immortality for a Raelian resides in his or her unique genetic code. Hence they must postpone.

So for the sixty-five thousand Raelians who still await the visible signs of the allegedly cloned babies, this is more than a "cult hoax" or even a scientific breakthrough. This is a moment of hushed apocalyptic expectation. This cloned baby girl, Eve, represents an epiphany in Raël's oral prophetic tradition.

"We call her Eve," said Boisselier, evoking Raël's ufological interpretation of Genesis, where extraterrestrial scientists arrive on our barren planet and set up a laboratory to concoct the first humans—baby Adam and Eve—from their own DNA matter. Thus, the cloned girl is a confirmation, a reenactment of the Raelian creation myth of our extraterrestrial origins.

This new, third Eve (like the second, who was the Virgin Mary) not only confirms the past, but also ushers in a new era. For Raelians, her birth implies that they don't have to wait passively for the UFOs to descend—they can rise up to meet their alien creators.

To date, Raelians have made little progress in preparing the world to greet the aliens. Despite their widely publicized message of peace and tolerance, they have failed to set up a geniocracy or to stop war and nuclear testing. Thus, their dilemma is: How can we prepare the human race to be worthy to receive the Elohim?

Cloning was the answer. Cloning was still in that twilight zone of semi-legality, semi-respectability, semi-possibility. There was the Internet, a new tool for powerless, renegade groups to communicate their worldviews and advertise their services. So Raël founded Clonaid, which offered cloning services to its investors as soon as the technology became available.

For Raelians, the apocalyptic message in human cloning is nothing less than Neitzschean: Man has become God! Since in Raël's radically materialistic worldview, there is neither God nor soul, cloning means that the human race is undergoing "Elohimization." Raelians will succeed where Heaven's Gate failed—in transforming human bodies into superior, extraterrestrial flesh. When and if the Elohim return to earth, the Raelians look forward to meeting them face to face, as proud, accomplished sons and daughters. One might speculate that this takes the pressure off the need for the aliens to show up at all. If humans can evolve into virtually immortal advanced technocrats, we could even venture out into space to meet them. (I do not mean to suggest that Raël is thinking along these lines, for the complex, creative mind of an inspired prophet is beyond a sociologist's ken.)

At this juncture, it appears that Baby Eve may become one of the unsolved mysteries in the annals of ufological lore. The world's media has dismissed her as a "cult hoax," but Raelians will always award her a major apocalyptic role in their "scientific religion."

If yesterday's magic has become today's science, then tomorrow's scientific discoveries can be appropriated by a futuristic new religion as today's magic. And magic is what our contemporary churches are badly in need of—magic that is impervious to relentless disconfirmation by the encroaching secular worldview and scientific method. The magic of extraterrestrial technology and tomorrow's scientific advances must offer a special satisfaction for people who are "religiously musical" and yet anticlerical. Is seems reasonable to assume that committed atheists who are hopelessly secularized yet suffering from the existential angst of living in a world devoid of order and higher values should find in Raël's "scientific religion" a solution to their dilemma.

Chapter Nine
"Science Is Our Religion"

The Baby Eve announcement evoked an astonishing display of international rage and revulsion. To understand why, it helps to look at how the world's religions are responding to the specter of human cloning. Then we might see that the Raelians stand out as the only religious group that believes that human cloning is morally sound and theologically correct

This point was made by Rev. Eileen W. Lindner of the National Council of Churches' biological technology project.[1] Although religious bodies disagree over stem-cell research (rabbis voting in favor, Catholic priests against), they unanimously condemn human cloning. A survey of the major faiths supports her view.

The Catholic Church has always condemned human and technological intervention in the natural reproductive act within marriage, which is part of God's order of creation as defined by the divine doctor, St. Thomas Aquinas. The pope sternly condemns cloning, predicting it will lead to racism, human exploitation, and murder. "Therapeutic cloning would be a new and terrible form of slavery," Archbishop Renato Martino warned the ad hoc subcommittee at the International Convention against the Reproductive Cloning of Human Beings, which met in New York in September 2002. "Regrettably," he added, "it cannot be denied that the temptation of eugenics is still latent, especially if powerful commercial interests exploit it. Governments and the scientific community must be very vigilant in this domain. The distinction between reproductive and 'so-called therapeutic cloning' are unacceptable to the Holy See. Human cloning could usher in a new form of racism." As the archbishop explained: "Here is a new form of racism, for the development of these techniques could lead to the creation of a subcategory of human being, destined for the convenience of certain others." He argued that human cloning with a view to obtaining organs for transplants is not morally acceptable—even when the proposed goal is good in itself: "These techniques involve the manipulation and destruction of human embryos." He concludes firmly: "Based on the biological and anthropological status of the human embryo, and on the fundamental moral and civil rule, it is illicit to kill an innocent even to bring about a good for society."[2] Cardinal Anthony Bevilacqua of Philadelphia warned that cloning "reduces human beings to mere products of a manufacturing technique. . . . The child is produced and wanted, not for his or her own sake, but because he or she will carry traits that someone else values" (zenit.org).

The Protestant churches are more worried about the social effects on families and cloned children in the future than about insults to God. Paul Ramsey, a Methodist ethics professor at Princeton, published the article "Fabricated Man" in 1970, which anticipates much of today's bioethical debate (zenit.org).

The United Methodist Church, at its general conference in 2000, expressed concern over the "social and theological ramifications of human cloning; use or abuse of people, exploitation of women, tearing of the fabric of the family, the compromising of human distinctiveness, the lessening of genetic diversity" (zenit.org).

The Conservative Lutheran Church of the Missouri synod decided cloning was a "fundamental assault on the created order of God." But the Lutherans seem to accept the notion that human cloning is inevitable. Since "human clones will walk among us" soon, they admonish Christians not to assume that "some people are not more human nor less human because of their origins" (zenit.org).

Rev. Eileen Lindner sums up the position of the National Council of Churches by denouncing human cloning as a kind of "idolatry": "Talk about graven images. . . . Where you have a superhuman, that's a kind of quintessential idolatry" (zenit.org).

Representing the Southern Baptist view, Rev. Richard Land warns us that "sooner or later we are going to be presented with horrific images of human tragedies coming out of these laboratories" (zenit.org).

Conservative Judaism's Committee on Jewish Law and Standards noted it had taken 272 attempts to produce Dolly the sheep, and "it would be quite another thing to create and kill multiple human beings with major birth defects" (zenit.org).

Within the Jewish faith, there is wide diversity of opinion and a strong pro-science position. Israel's Knesset does not exhibit the same moral repugnance as the papal see. The legislative body rejects reproductive cloning but seems favorably inclined toward stem-cell research. A "cloning law" was passed in Israel in 1998 that temporarily prohibits cloning as a substitute for existing fertility treatments. This prohibition expires in 2004. The wording of the law implies that there is no intrinsic moral problem with cloning per se, merely a technical problem because the method is not fail-safe. Michael Ravel, however, an Israel Prize laureate who is on the bioethics advisory committee of the National Academy of Sciences, is favorably disposed toward reproductive cloning. He says that cloning, if it's ever made safe, will not harm human dignity. On the contrary, he argues, if it will help infertile couples, it would mesh nicely with the commandment to be fruitful and multiply.[3]

Many secular scientists, like Rudolf Jaenisch, a biologist at the Massachusetts Institute of Technology, are opposed to cloning on scientific and humanitarian grounds. Jaenisch points to the high failure rate in animal experiments that produced "a veritable gallery of horrors," such as aborted fetuses, immune deficiencies, congenital malformations, and premature aging. He noted that while a small sample of cloned animals did survive for several days, many of these suffer from pneumonia, liver diseases, obesity, and accelerated aging.[4]

The Raelian Position on Human Cloning

The Raelians have one advantage in this global debate—theological certainty that suits the modern condition. Their doctrines concerning the nature of god(s) and humanity and their creation myth dovetail neatly with the scientific ideology of progress, experimentation, and the quest for knowledge. In the global debate over the ethics of cloning, we have two opposing stances, two incompatible worldviews—the scientific and the religious. Only the Raelians can declare with certainty that god wants us to clone. Only the Raelians feel that to produce the world's first human clone will confirm rather than betray the myth of Genesis.

This philosophical view is echoed by Vardit Ravitsky, who earned his Ph.D. at Bar-Ilan University: "The genetic revolution and the project to interpret the human genome has changed our thinking—a step toward unravelling the secret of life itself. The idea of self-perpetuation via perpetuation of DNA has tremendous symbolic and emotional weight. [It implies] a metaphysical faith in the power of genetics."[5]

Raël elaborates on that innate symbolic value. He promises his audiences virtual immortality through the replacement of body parts with cloned tissue. He does not address the ethical dilemma this practice will raise. At what point should the original person opt to die and let the clone carry on—or does one simply continue to replace the heart, liver, skin, until the lines between the original and the clone become indiscernible?

The pope's objections to cloning, birth control, and abortion are all based on the belief that humans were created in *imago Dei*. Thus, to obstruct conception, to abort, and certainly to clone is to oppose the divine will. For Raelians, cloning will fulfill the divine will. If the first little Adams and Eves were created in a laboratory from the aliens' own DNA, to clone is to emulate the gods and to become godlike. To clone human beings and body parts for increased longevity is one step toward "Elohimization."

Dr. Massimo Introvigne (founder-director of CESNUR, the Center for Studies on New Religions, in Turin, Italy), although famous for defending new religions, expresses a staunch Catholic's moral repugnance for the Raelian cloning agenda: "From a Catholic perspective, the Raelian doctrine reminds us of the 'machine-man' of certain philosophers of the Enlightenment, and represents modernity in all that is brutally anti-Catholic. From the moral point of view I am convinced that human cloning . . . is reprehensible and illicit, and that the Raelian principle, according to which everything that is technically possible is also licit, destroys morality. Unfortunately, this view is not only held by Raelians."[6]

The Issue of Ensoulment

The deepest objections that religions have to accepting clones as fully human has to do with their beliefs concerning ensoulment—the process whereby a human receives his or her soul. According to Catholic doctrine, God infuses a soul into the embryo before birth. St. Thomas Aquinas stated that this divine act occurred two weeks after conception in the case of male babies, and four months after conception for females. In Jewish theology, a baby receives its soul when it draws its first breath. (Consequently, Jews are less inclined to condemn abortion as murder.) But at what point does a clone receive a soul? If we do succeed in producing clones, and we accept them as fully integrated members of our society, does not this threaten to undermine our belief in God as the divine creator? Will clones be baptized and pray to God, thanking him for life's blessings?

Raël does not have to worry about the knotty issue of ensoulment. Since humans are mere matter "made of atoms and dust," the problem of how a clone gets a soul is irrelevant. But for the great religious traditions, cloning raises the most profound question of what it means to be a man, a woman. Will clones have souls? Will they be truly human? From the Raelian perspective, a human being does not possess a soul. All he or she has that gives life order and meaning is his or her unique genetic code. Raël claims this genetic code is the key to immortality, to omniscience, to virtual divinity. When Raël founded Clonaid, he was obeying the gods, and humanity was (unwittingly) taking the first step to becoming closer, even equal, to the gods.

Scientific Heresy and Technological Utopianism

Raël is not only blaspheming traditional religions, he has committed an act of heresy, as far as the scientific establishment is concerned. A scientific breakthrough was broadcast, but no proof was forthcoming, rendering the theory unfalsifiable. "The University of Pittsburgh School of Medicine findings throw fresh doubts on claims by the Raelians that they successfully cloned a baby last year," writes Tom Spears in "Human Cloning Impossible" (*Ottawa Citizen,* April 11, 2003). These Pittsburgh scientists note that primates' cell machinery makes their cloned embryos produce the wrong number of chromosomes in a "chaotic" jumble. This means the clones do not survive through pregnancy and makes therapeutic cloning "extraordinarily difficult"; reproductive cloning "may be impossible." When I discussed this with a Raelian, he responded: "But that's not a problem. The Elohim told Raël that they especially designed humans to be easier to clone than the other primates."

Raël's views on cloning do resonate with certain pillars of the scientific establishment. Indeed, Raël's philosophy of science might be analyzed as a *parody* of some of the strands of technological utopianism in the scientific community.

Dr. Richard Seed, famous for his role in the cloning of Dolly the sheep, offered a blatantly religious justification for cloning during his interview on National Public Radio's *Morning Edition* on January 7, 1997: "God made man in his own image. God intended for man to become one with God. We are going to have almost as much power and knowledge as God. Cloning and the reprogrammation of DNA is the first serious step in becoming one with God."

As we enter the twenty-first century, we are still part of that thousand-year-old tradition in which scientific advancement is grounded in religious expectation. The Enlightenment ushered in the secularization of society. Intellectuals of the eighteenth century assumed that science and the pursuit of reason would soon overcome blind faith and superstition. Religious authority was relegated to a primitive past, and technology to a glorious future. The two worldviews appeared to be incompatible and polar opposites, since the scientific worldview is a logical outcome of a more advanced stage of human development and knowledge.

But David Noble, in *The Religion of Technology,* argues that today we once again find science and religion intertwined. It appears the Enlightenment interrupted this unhappy marriage only temporarily, or obscured it with secularist polemic. Noble asserts not only that science evokes powerful religious emotions, but also that science has itself *become* a religion, a "church" with its own clerical caste, its arcane rituals and articles of faith. "The technological enterprise has become suffused with religious faith," Noble insists. He points to the religious preoccupations that pervade the U.S. space program, the creation of artificial intelligence, and genetic engineering. He dubs this phenomenon "scientific perfectionism" and states that "we demand more than mere convenience, comfort or survival, we demand deliverance, . . . liberation from the sufferings of mortality. We demand the recovery of man's lost divinity" (Noble 2001, 6).

This new faith is deplorable, even dangerous, says Noble, considering our "utter inability to think and act rationally about this presumably most rational of human endeavours" (6). Noble's purpose is to disabuse us of our "otherworldly dreams" that lie at the heart of the technological enterprise. He pleads with us to direct our use of technology toward worldly, more human and humane, ends.

I would argue that the Raelians are at once a proof of and an exception to the "religion of technology." The Raelians are significant because they bridge the cultural and cognitive gap between science and religion. On one hand, they are proof that religious aspirations are the fuel that drives our mastery of scientific technology. On the other hand, they are trying to forge a philosophy of science that will mitigate humanity's violent impulses and preserve the human rights of minorities. The Raelian religion rejects the notion of a transcendent realm, thus arguing for a more pragmatic use of technology to serve the physical needs of humanity.

Raël's response to the terrifying implications of apocalyptic-driven nuclear theology is to replace the otherworldly aspirations of Christian fundamentalism with this-worldly pragmatic concerns. The authority of the Bible prophecy tradition is replaced by extraterrestrial mandates. In a strange way,

Raël's movement combines the militant anthropocentric atheism of secular humanism with the strict reverence for religious authority found in Christian fundamentalism.

Thus the Raelians are essentially postmodernists. They are radical individualists who embrace differences, who stand up for minorities, who passionately advocate freethinking, free choice. And yet they defend *Le livre qui dit la vérité* as the literal truth. There is no room for metaphorical thinking, psychological interpretations; no individualistic hermeneutics are tolerated in Raël's community. Even the Catholic Church is softening its fundamentalist stance on the afterlife, for the pope in 1988 conceded, "Hell is not a real place." But in Raël's books, the planet of the Elohim is a real place, Eden was a laboratory, and the creation "myth" has become fact. The miracles recounted in the Bible are evidence of superior alien technology, and St. John's Revelation is about to come true.

Raël claims that his very existence is a response to the abuse of scientific knowledge, that the Elohim, appalled by Hiroshima, decided to send us a prophet to warn humanity to stop war. His mother, he tells us, was a fifteen-year-old farm girl living near Vichy who was beamed aboard an alien spaceship, impregnated, and released with her memory of the event erased.

Raël expounds a new kind of secular humanism based on the dictations of extraterrestrials, who are in turn super secular humanists, godlike in their scientific knowledge, in their physical longevity, and in their cosmic mobility. The message is a call for the faithful to have faith in the inherent goodness and common sense of the ordinary human being. It is possible to overcome humans' propensity for self-destruction, the Elohim assure us. They've been there, done that. Humans have the potential to learn to use the tools of science to protect, enhance, and extend human fleshly life—because the Elohim have already succeeded. They are our role models, our older brothers who offer hope that we too can make intelligent, rational choices that will overturn our urge to self-destruct and the paralyzing fatalism of nuclear theology.

Raël makes us uncomfortable because his "religion of science" represents an extreme position, almost a parody of our scientific pursuit for human perfection. Raël's utopian technological society in the future is so absurd, even dystopian, that one begins to wonders if in fact Raël is not a utopian philosopher, but rather a social satirist. His recent book, *Oui au clonage humain: La vie éternelle grace à la science* (Yes to human cloning: Eternal life thanks to science), embraces technological advancements and shows us surrealistic visions of the future that threaten our deepest assumptions concerning what it means to be human.

Raël extrapolates freely on how computers, cloning, and genetically modified foods could transform human society for the better. Whether he intends his fantasies to remain in the subjunctive world of science-fiction fantasy, or whether these ideas are meant as serious propositions, is not clear. What does become apparent is that Raël is taking the mickey out of his disapproving audience.

Yes to Human Cloning could be mistaken for a deliberate parody of a predominant faith of our age—"the religion of technology." Raël writes in a style reminiscent of the great eighteenth-century French essayists. His strategy is similar to Jonathan Swift's in "A Modest Proposal," in which Swift appears to advocate cannibalism to make sensible use of the corpses of starved Irish children, while covertly expressing his profound moral objections to the ruling class's callous exploitation of the Irish peasantry. Raël proposes we create a slave race of biological robots to perform the unpleasant routine tasks of daily existence so that we real humans might be free to "create, meditate, pursue sports, or art" (Raël 2001a, 78)—or simply indulge in pleasure. These robots can be designed to resemble beautiful humans, but three things render them distinct from us: their lack of "conscience," their lack of "auto-programmability" or free will, and their inability to reproduce. Foreseeing ethical objections to his plan, Raël points out that we don't mind relying on our computers or washing machines as "slaves," and the only difference is that the robot machines, instead of being made of metal, will be made of "100% biological" material (105).

In answer to the predictable response—"But we're talking about flesh and blood here!"—Raël rejoins: "But what about the millions of animals on earth who are our slaves—the draught horse, the donkeys, not to mention our 'gastronomic slaves' like ducks, sheep, cows, pigs?" Assuming his audience will reply, "Well, those are just animals!" Raël administers the coup de grace: "What about the millions of people that toil as veritable slaves, earning barely enough at minimum wage to feed themselves?" (107).

Assuming he's won the debate, Raël concludes on a sanctimonious note: If we can accept biological robots, he argues, we fight against the slavery of human beings, "which is, as we all agree, totally unacceptable!" (108).

But do we? Since biological robots are to be fashioned through cloning and we "real humans" will extend our lives by cloning replacement body parts or by total regeneration, and even our children will be cloned à la carte, we are left with the uneasy impression that in Raël's utopia the line between human and machine is wearing very thin.

The media uproar over Baby Eve has distracted reflection over the deeper meaning of the Raelians' attempt to clone a human. C. G. Jung observed in 1958 that flying saucers were religious symbols, appearing as advanced technological artifacts from utopian societies that have overcome famine, war, death. They represent humanity's desire to dominate nature by means of technology. UFOs are simultaneously a warning of, and a solution to, the threat posed by our mastery of technology. In Raelian culture, the UFO is a sublation of the nuclear threat, for its pilot alights and hands Claude Vorilhon the key to understanding and overcoming our self-destructive inclination to abuse scientific knowledge. The Raelian worldview accommodates, exaggerates, our unquestioning acceptance of global development, our anthropocentric urge to control and obliterate nature, our daily accumulation of fresh data via the media and the Web, our dizzying production of ever-new technologies. These all confirm the universal, if unconscious, reign of the scientific zeitgeist.[7] Such utopian aspirations are ubiquitous in popular culture. They demonstrate that, despite the looming threat of nuclear war and of environmental problems leading to an ecological holocaust, we still proclaim our faith in science to solve the world's problems.

Raël's religion probes and exacerbates this covert unconscious faith in what David Noble calls "the religion of technology." Why else would a small, unconventional "flying-saucer cult" whose messianic founder receives telepathic messages from aliens through his topknot gain such global attention? Why would news that a "UFO sect" had just won the race to clone evoke such vehement expressions of disbelief, smug mockery, and outrage? It could only be because Raël's proddings—however "spaced out"—have aroused both our deepest defensive awareness of our abuse of science and our latent, inarticulate beliefs.

Appendix

Angels Interview Schedule

1. What kind of angel are you? Pink ____ White ____
2. Social background
   Age
   Country/province of origin
   Profession/work
   Level of education
3. Year of baptism as Raelian
4. Sexual status and lifestyle/domestic arrangement
5. Why did you decide to be an angel?
6. How were you selected?
7. How are you being trained?
8. Describe your relationship with Raël.
9. Describe your vision of the Elohim.
10. What is women's role in the Raelian Movement (RM)?
11. How is the relationship between men and women different in the RM than in mainstream society?
12. How has the Order of Raël's Angels affected male-female roles and relations in the movement?
13. When do you expect the Elohim to arrive?
14. How has becoming an angel affected your relations with men/women in the RM?
15. How has it affected your relationship with Raël?
16. What do you most like/dislike about being an angel?
17. What did you have to give up to be an angel?
18. What is your relationship like with the other angels?

Questionnaire pour les membres du Mouvement Raelien (Questionnaire for the members of the Raelian Movement)

Le 16 Février 2003 au Théâtre Gésu

Fait par Andréa Birchenough-La France et Susan Palmer, distribué par les étudiants de Concordia University et Dawson College

1. Sexe M F
2. Age ____
3. Est-ce que vos parents sont Quebecois?
   Si non, de quelle nationalité sont-ils?
4. À quelle église êtes-vous baptisé?

5. Est-ce que vos parents sont religieux? Oui ____ Non ____
6. Pendant votre enfance, êtes-vous allé à l'eglise?
   Jamais ____
   Quelques fois par année ____
   Chaque Dimanche (ou presque) ____
   Chaque jour ____
7. Quel est (était) le métier de:
   Votre père ________
   Votre mère ________
   Vous ________
8. Quel est votre niveau d'éducation?
   École secondaire Arts Sciences Autres (expliquez)
   CÉGEP
   Programme professionnel
   Université (bacalauriat)
   Maîtrise
   Doctorat
9. Est-ce qu'il y a d'autres Raeliens dans votre famille?
   Père ____
   Mère ____
   Soeur ____
   Frère ____
   Fils ____
   Fille ____
10. Vous êtes à quel niveau dans le mouvement?
    Raelien simple
    Niveau 1
    2
    3
    4
    5
11. En quelle année êtes vous devenu membre? ____
12. Quel est votre premier contact avec le mouvement?
    Emission de television ____
    Les journaux ____
    Un ami ____
    Les livres de Raël ____
    Autre ____
13. Est-ce qu'il y a des traditions catholique (ou semblable?) qui se retrouve dans le mouvement raelien?
    Non ____
    Oui ____ (donnez un example) ________________________________
14. Votre plan affectif
    Hetero Homosexuals Bisexuals Autre (expliquer)
    Celibataire Un ou quelques amants Beaucoup d'amants
    Vous habitez en couple Raelien ____ non-Raelien ____
15. Que'est-ce qui/que vous a attrait au mouvement
    La philosophie ____
    Raël ____

La vie sociale des Raeliens ____
Autre ____

16. Est-ce que vous avez lit des livres de science fiction/ufologie, ou regardé des films/programmes de science fiction ou Star Trek? Oui ____ Non ____
17. Pourquoi avez-vous quitté votre religion d'enfance?
18. Aviez-vous deja été membre d'une autre nouvelle religion avant le MR?
    Si oui, quel mouvement?
19. Dans votre opinion, est-ce que la science peux resoudre tous les problèmes de l'humanité?
20. Quels aspects positifs avez-vous trouvé dans le Mouvement Raelien que vous n'avez pas trouvé dans votre ancienne religion?

Notes

Chapter 1. Contactee Prophets in the History of Ufology

1. Translations are my own, unless otherwise noted. Hereafter, Terrusse and Richard 1994 is cited in the text as *20 ans*.

Chapter 2. The Last and Fastest Prophet

1. I am relying on the IRM's official statistics for this number, since I have no way to verify their claim independently. Raelian membership figures are based on the number of people who pay membership fees and undergo the transmission of the cellular plan (see chapter 3). It is well known that mainstream churches inflate their membership statistics and ignore defections, and it is quite possible the IRM follows suit.

2. Raël's ex-wife was referred to as "Christine" in a recent article (Chantepie 2003), so I will adopt this fictitious name to respect her wish to preserve her anonymity.

3. Jean Gary, Raelian bishop, interview by the author, Dawson College cafeteria, Montreal, 1999.

4. In his second book, *Les extra-terrestres m'ont emmené sur leur planète* (1977), Raël describes his visit to the planet of the Elohim, located in our galaxy but not in our solar system. He did not reveal his celestial origins until his fourth book, *Accueillir les extra-terrestres,* published in France in 1979, since his biological father, Yahweh, "asked me not to reveal to mankind this parental tie until three years have passed" (see Raël 1987a, 105).

5. See *Apocalypse* 2, 101 (1996): 6.

6. See "Sa Saintete le Dalai Lama souhaite rencontrer Sa Saintete Raël" (His Holiness the Dalai Lama wishes to meet His Holiness Raël), *Contact,* no. 201, August 7, 2003.

7. *Contact,* no. 138, December 17, 2001.

Chapter 3. How to Construct a New Religion

1. See "Transmission of the Cellular Code" in *An Embassy for the Extraterrestrials* (Geneva, Switz.: IRM, n.d.), 12.

2. Nicole Bertrand, Raelian bishop, interview by the author, Dawson College, Montreal, September 1995.

3. This point was also made by Nicholas Fauteux in "Ma visite chez les Raelians" (*Dernière Heure,* January 21, 1995, 24–28). It was confirmed in an informal survey of the membership by Dawson College students in 1991: Less than one-third of respondents tithed. According to Michel Beluet, former director of UFOland, the only pressure the IRM exerts on members is to attend the summer seminars; through spending time with Raël, their enthusiasm for his mission is renewed and they voluntarily tithe.

4. Elizabeth Bronstein, "Raelians Open Theme Park," *Montreal Gazette,* September 30, 1997.

5. See "Une eglise est née," *La Tribune* (Sherbrooke, Quebec), July 20, 1995.

6. The response of the Canadian Tax Department was as follows: "It is evident that the [Raelian] Church believes in the existence of Elohim. However, . . . the Elohim are not gods. . . . They cannot be identified as the type of superior being recognized by jurisprudence; . . . they do not correspond to jurispridence" (my translation) (Canadian Customs and Revenue Agency, November 21, 2000. Objet: Eglise raelien. File No. 3006418).

7. See Yves Casgrain, "Le condom raelien: Initiative prophylactique anti-democratique," *Le Devoir,* December 4, 1992.

8. "Raël et la masturbation: Les psychologies enquêteront sur la participation d'un des leurs à une conférence" (Raël and masturbation: Psychologists investigate the participation of one of their own at a conference), *La Presse,* July 9, 1993.

9. Eric Thibault. "Raël n'a sêduit que ses fidèles" (Raël seduces no one but his followers), *Le Journal de Québec,* January 24, 1996. See also Michel Rochon, "Débat controversé sur l'évolution: Est-ce pertinent de confronter Raël à la science?" (The controversial debate on evolution: Does it make sense to confront Raël on science?), *L'Exemplaire,* February 1995, 6.

10. Michèle Ouimet, "Un testament que divise: Alphonse Belzile conteste le legs de 200,000 $ de sa soeur, Madeleine aux raeliens" (A divisive will: Alphonse Belzile contests his sister Madeleine's $200,000 bequest to the Raelians), *La Presse,* February 5, 1994.

11. Ciel Mon Mardi, translated literally, means, "Heavens, my Tuesday!" but it refers to a cliché in the theater when the irate husband comes home to find his wife cheating on him and she exclaims, "Ciel! Mon Mari!" (Heavens! My husband!).

12. The Jean Parraga story was explained to me by a Raelian bishop who was living with Parraga's ex-wife in France during the custody dispute, and the basic facts were corroborated in French news reports. Raël also described Parraga's behavior in his 1992 book.

13. Decision Dossier 95-05-23, Roland, Mouvement raelien Canadien et Raël contre Baillargeon et *Le Devoir,* Conseil de presse du Quebec.

14. This is my translation of the passage in *La géniocratie* (1977b, 115), which reads: "Il leur faut avoir une vie intime durant au moins quatre ans [dix-huit ans] les adolescents devraient d'avoir le droit d'avoir une vie sexuelle, politique, et religeuse indépendente de leurs parents."

15. This is my translation of the passage in Daniel Chabot, "Mot du Guide national: Ensemble on va changer le monde!" a speech reprinted in a 1992 flyer.

16. "Engagement face aux reglements sur le camping" (Contract for camp regulations), flyer handed out at the summer seminars.

17. See *Journal Vedettes* 9 (November/December 1993): 1.

18. I interviewed Boisselier at the Valcourt summer seminars in July 1998 and thought wistfully at the time what a great news story this would make. Sure enough, the media evinced a strong interest in the director of Clonaid between 2000 and 2003.

19. Jean-Paul Soulié, "Infosecte n'a pas sa place dans une societé democratique, disent raeliens et scientologists" (Info-cult has no place in a democratic society, say the Raelians and Scientologists), *La Presse* (Quebec), April 14, 1993.

Chapter 4. Mutating the Millennium

1. I am indebted to Bryan Sentes for this charming phrase (see Sentes and Palmer 2000).

2. Raelian Information Pack, handed out at the February 1997 meeting, Montreal.

3. Ibid.

4. Ibid.

5. Michel Beluet, director of UFOland, interview by the author, 1992.

6. David Johnston, "Raelians' Use of Swastika and Conversion Bids Offend Jews," *Montreal Gazette,* July 22, 1991.

7. See "Tracts anti-prêtres catholiques" at http://www.kath.ch/infoseketendocu ments16.htm=20.

8. Harvey Shepherd, "Raelians Abandon Cross Burning," *Montreal Gazette,* October 7, 2002.

9. Daniel Sanger, "Cult of Freedom," *National Post,* February 28, 2003.

10. I began to doubt my memory, and to wonder if the date had indeed always been 2035, so I checked my old notebooks for when the guides first spoke to my class at Dawson College in 1988, and I found the date 2025 written down. In August 2003 I had a conversation with a religious-studies professor at University of Laval, Alain Bouchard (1989), who has published important research on the Raelian Movement in its early stages in Quebec. He told me he had a tape of a speech that Victor Legendre (Raël's first national guide in Canada) had given in Quebec City in the late seventies, in which Legendre clearly set 2025 as the due date for the Elohim. Moreover, as recently as 1993, one of my students interviewed a Raelian who told her that "the Elohim is [*sic*] going to come down to tell all of us the truth in 2025 in Jerusalem" (Krautgasser 1993).

11. This observation was confirmed by my interview with Lear, a guide who is empowered to perform transmissions.

Chapter 5. A Visit to the Court of Raël

1. I was present at this meeting with a group of my students and noticed that Lear had closed his eyes but continued to move around the room and to speak, as if he were in a trance. His audience obeyed him perfectly. I was lying on the floor breathing deeply, coping with the noxious fumes of carpet cleaner, so I missed Raël's entrance.

2. Grossman 1993. I thank Max Grossman for allowing me to include his vivid, well-written report here.

Chapter 6. Sexy Angels for Amorous Aliens

1. See S.C.I.U.R.E. (Synthèse Cohérente d'Informations Utiles sur le Raelisme et des Elohims), at Frank Muhletaler's Web site, www.prevensectes.com/sciure.

2. "The First Encounter: A Never-Ending Story," undated Summum tract.

3. When I went to visit Summum in June 2002 in Salt Lake City, I had a chat with Amon Ray ("Corky"), standing in the courtyard outside the golden pyramid. On discovering that I was Canadian, he said, "Wait!" entered his house, and returned with a net bag heavy with Canadian quarters. "People keep putting these in our [gumball] machines," he said. "We've been to every bank. They all refuse to change Canadian quarters."

CHAPTER 7. "ENEMIES WITHIN!"

1. At the risk of sounding defensive, I do speak French, at least well enough to understand Raël's lectures or conduct an interview. During my 2001 research in France, I was frequently complimented on my French; only in Quebec is my French often criticized. Actually I found it useful to go along with the assumption that I was a dumb Anglophone, because I could pick up information not intended for my ears.

2. See "La crise 1992–2000 dans le mouvement raëlien par Les Apôtres des derniers temps" (The 1992–2000 crisis in the Raelian Movement by the Apostles of the last days), *Les Apôtres des derniers temps,* September 2000.

3. I have used a fictitious name to refer to this ex-member at his request, although his story and real name appeared in the media. (See Michele Ouimet, "Un ex-raelian revele le vrai visage de Raël" (An ex-Raelian reveals the true face of Raël), *La Presse,* September 23, 1995).

4. "Un ex-membre dit tout sur les raeliens" (An ex-member tells all about the Raelians), *Derniere Heure,* October 14, 1995, 14–16.

5. See *Apocalypse* 116, 1 (1999): 17.

CHAPTER 8. CLONING AROUND—HOAX OR HERESY?

1. I am indebted to two of my Dawson College students, Thalia Vaillancourt and Jasmine Noël, for attending the September 21, 2000, "Cloning Mothers" press conference and submitting excellent field reports.

2. In the end, the cloning mothers' services were not needed, except for those of one alleged Japanese Raelian. Clonaid's clients (an infertile Israeli couple, Dutch lesbians, etc.) preferred to give birth to their own clones. It was never made clear why Mark Hunt's wife did not want to bear the clone of her first son—or simply have another baby.

3. Dan Kapelovitz, "Holy Clones: Cloning—Sacred or Sacrilege?" *MEAN Magazine,* March 2001.

4. Giordano Bruno was a sixteenth-century Italian astronomer burned at the stake for heresy—and also for insisting that ours was not the only planet with intelligent life.

5. Joe Lauria, "Cloning Attempt," *Montreal Gazette,* August 11, 2001.

6. Ibid.

7. "Group Says It Has Begun Cloning Humans," *National Post,* April 12, 2002.

8. "Human Clones in Gestation," *AFF* (American Family Foundation), October 4, 2002.

9. Ibid.

10. Jacques Goddard, "Alien Worshippers Deliver Gospel at Holiday Inn," *Toronto Globe and Mail,* December 28, 2002.

11. Gavin Taylor, "Cloning Sensation," *Montreal Gazette,* December 29, 2002.

12. Tu Thanh Ha, "Cult's Cloning Claim in Doubt as DNA Test Is Called Off," *Toronto Globe and Mail,* January 7, 2003.

13. Malcolm Ritter, "Cloning DNA Test Shelved," *Montreal Gazette,* January 7, 2003.

14. "Maisonneuve à l'écoute," January 5, 2003, www.radio-canada.ca/rdi/maison neuve.

15. "Is She the Raël Thing?" *Montreal Gazette,* January 3, 2003.

16. "Purported Clone Executive Won't Testify," Associated Press, January 23, 2003.

CHAPTER 9. "SCIENCE IS OUR RELIGION"

1. See Richard N. Ostling, Associated Press, January 9, 2003.

2. "Human Cloning Brings a New Racism, Vatican Warns," www.zenit.org, September 24, 2002. Succeeding quotes from this article are cited in the text in parentheses as zenit.org.

3. Ravel quoted in Ostling, Associated Press.

4. Jaenisch, quoted in ibid.

5. Ravitsky, quoted in ibid.

6. Massimo Introvigne, "Raelians: Science without Limits, and Lots of Press," part 2, www.zenit.org, January 17, 2003.

7. I am indebted to Bryan Sentes for the ideas (as well as the prose style) in these last two paragraphs (see Sentes and Palmer, 2000).

References

Adamski, George. 1955. *Inside the Space Ships.* New York: Abelard-Schumann.

———. 1961. *Flying Saucers Farewell.* New York: Abelard-Schumann.

Aidala, Angela. 1985. "Social Change, Gender Roles, and New Religious Movements." *Sociological Analysis* 46, 3:287–314.

Alford, Alan. 1996. *Gods of the New Millennium.* Walsall, U.K.: Eridu Books.

Andersson, Pia. 2000. "Ancient Astronauts." In *UFOs and Popular Culture: An Encyclopedia of Contemporary Myth,* edited by James R. Lewis, 20–24. Santa Barbara, Calif.: ABC-CLIO.

Auchterlonie, Jane. N.d. "Tony Almost of the Raelians." Student paper, Dawson College, author files.

Balch, Robert W. 1979. "Two Models of Conversion and Commitment in a UFO Cult." Paper presented at the annual meeting of the Pacific Sociological Association, Anaheim, Calif.

———. 1982a. "Bo and Peep: A Case of the Origins of Messianic Leadership." In *Millennialism and Charisma,* edited by Roy Wallis, 13–71. Belfast: Queen's University.

———. 1982b. "Conversion and Charisma in the Cultic Milieu: The Origins of a New Religion." Paper presented at the annual meeting of the Association for the Sociology of Religion, Providence, R.I.

———. 1995. "Waiting for the Ships: Disillusionment and the Revitalization of Faith in Bo and Peep's UFO Cult." In *The Gods Have Landed,* edited by James R. Lewis, 137–166. Albany: SUNY Press.

Barker, Eileen. 1989. *New Religious Movements.* London: HMSO.

Bednarowski, Mary Farrell. 1980. "Outside the Mainstream: Women's Religion and Women Religious Leaders in Nineteenth-Century America." *Journal of the American Academy of Religion* 48:207–241.

Bibby, Reginald W. 1987. *Fragmented Gods: The Poverty and Potential of Religion in Canada.* Richmond Hill, Ontario: Irwin.

Birchenough-La France, Andrea. "The Raelians: Tradition and Reinterpretation within a New Religious Movement." Paper submitted to Professor Vered Amit, Department of Anthropology, Concordia University, February 2003.

Bishin, Lesley. 1999. "Angels Research Project." Student paper, Dawson College, author files. March 23.

Blanchette, Natalie. 2001. "Interview with an Angel." Student paper, Dawson College, author files. March.

Bouchard, Alain. 1989. "Mouvement Raelien." In *Nouvel Age . . . Nouvelles Croyances.* Under the direction of the Centre d'Information sur les Nouvelles Religions. Montreal: Editions Paulines and Mediaspaul.

Bourret, Jean-Claude. 1997. *Ovnis 1999: Le Contact?* Mougerre, France: Michel Lafon.
Bromley, David, ed. 1998. *The Politics of Religious Apostasy.* Westport, Conn.: Praeger.
Bujold, Alain. 1988. "Field Report of Raelian Meeting." Student paper, Dawson College, author files. December 13.
Bullard, Thomas E. 2000. "Foreword: UFOs-Folklore of the Space Age." In *UFOs and Popular Culture: An Encyclopedia of Contemporary Myth,* edited by James R. Lewis, ix–xxv. Santa Barbara, Calif.: ABC-CLIO.
Campbell, Colin. 1972. "The Cult, the Cultic Milieu, and Secularization." In *A Sociological Yearbook of Religion in Britain,* 126–130. London: SCM Press.
Camplese, Daniele. 1992. "Interview with an Ex-Raelian." Student paper, Dawson College, author files. November.
Chantepie, Emmanuelle. 2003. "Le Passé secret de Raël dévoile par ses proches." *Dernière Heure,* January 18, 10–13.
Clark, Jerome. 1998. *The UFO Book: Encyclopedia of the Extraterrestrial.* 2nd edition. Detroit: Visible Ink Press.
Collins, Chloe. 1992. "Field Report on a Raelian Meeting." Student paper, Dawson College, author files. November.
Cummins, Emily West. 1996. "A Study of the Raelians." Student paper, Dawson College, author files. April 15.
Da Kalki. 1990. *Two Secrets, Yours and Mine.* Clearlake, Calif.: Dawn Horse Press.
Dawson, Lorne L. 2002. "Crises of Charismatic Legitimacy and Violent Behavior in New Religious Movements." In *Cults, Religion, and Violence,* edited by David G. Bromley and J. Gordon Melton, 80–101. New York: Cambridge University Press.
DiMaio, Ananda. 2001. "The Raelian Movement: A Field Report." Student paper, Dawson College, author files. February.
Dover, Cecily. 2003. "Field Report on the Raelians." Student paper, Dawson College, author files. December.
Drolet, Natalie. 1999. "Raelian Angels: A Dawson College Research Report." Student paper, Dawson College, author files. March 21.
Eliade, Mircea. 1950. *Shamanism: An Archaic Technique of Ecstasy.* Princeton, N.J.: Princeton University Press.
Ellwood, Robert S. 1976. *Religious and Spiritual Groups in Modern America.* Englewood Cliffs, N.J.: Prentice Hall.
———. 1993. *Islands of the Dawn: The Story of Alternative Spirituality in New Zealand.* Honolulu: University of Hawaii Press.
"Enemies Within!" *Apocalypse* 4, 49: 4–5
Evangelista, Jerry. 1988. "The Raelian Movement: An In-Depth Interview." Student paper, Dawson College, author files. April.
Festinger, Leon, Henry Reichen, and Stanley Schacter. 1956. *When Prophecy Fails.* Minneapolis: University of Minnesota Press.
Foster, Lawrence. 1981. *Religion and Sexuality: Three American Communal Experiments of the Nineteenth Century.* New York: Oxford University Press.
Fourier, Charles. 1971a. "On the Condition of Women." In *Design for Utopia: Selected Writings of Charles Fourier,* edited by Charles Gide, 76–81. New York: Schoken.
———. 1971b. "The Role of the Passions." In *Design for Utopia: Selected Writings of Charles Fourier,* edited by Charles Gide, 55–67. New York: Schoken.
Friedman, Allison. 1993. "Field Report of a Visit to a Raelian Meeting." Student paper, Dawson College, author files. December 7.

Gagnon, Marie-Anne. 1999a. "Angels: Dawson College Research Project." Student paper, Dawson College, author files. March 21.

———. 1999b. "Field Report of a Raelian Meeting at the Theatre Nationale." Student paper, Dawson College, author files. February 21.

Grossman, Max. 1993. "My Impressions of a Raelian Convention." Student paper, Dawson College, author files. December 7.

Grunschlöb, Andreas. 2003. "Ufological Discourse in Germany." In *UFO Religions,* edited by Christopher Partridge, 179–193. London: Routledge.

Hancock, Graham. 1995. *Fingerprints of the Gods.* New York: Crown.

Helland, Christopher. 2000. "Ashtar Command." In *UFOs and Popular Culture: An Encyclopedia of Contemporary Myth,* edited by James R. Lewis, 27–40. Santa Barbara, Calif.: ABC-CLIO.

Hexham, Irving, and Karla Poewe. 1986. *Understanding Cults and New Religions.* Grand Rapids, Mich.: Eerdmans.

Iasenza, Sonia. 1997. "Field Report on Raelian Meeting." Student paper, Dawson College, author files. November 21.

Introvigne, Massimo. 1995. "The Secular Anti-Cult Movement and the Religious Counter-Cult Movement: Strange Bedfellows or Future Enemies?" In *New Religions and the New Europe,* edited by Robert Towler, 32–54. Aarhus (Den.): Aarhus University Press.

James, William. 1964. *The Varieties of Religious Experience.* New York: Mentor Books.

Joern, Travis. 2002. "Field Report on Raelian Meeting at the Theatre Gesu." Student paper, Dawson College, author files. December.

Jones, Benoit. 1988. "Field Report, Meeting at the Holiday Inn." Student paper, Dawson College, author files. November.

Jung, Carl G. 1978. *Flying Saucers: A Modern Myth of Things Seen in the Skies.* Translated by R.F.C. Hall. Princeton, N.J.: Princeton University Press.

Kanter, Rosabeth Moss. 1972. *Commitment and Community: Communes and Utopias in Sociological Perspective.* Cambridge: Harvard University Press.

Krautgasser, Sonia. 1993. "Interview with a Raelian Member." Student paper, Dawson College, author files. December 7.

Labreque, Claude. 1986. *Les voilers du crespuscule.* Montreal: Editions Paulines.

Lawrence, Bruce. 1989. *The Defenders of God.* San Francisco: Harper.

Lewis, James R. 2000. "Heaven's Gate." In *UFOs and Popular Culture: An Encyclopedia of Contemporary Myth,* edited by James R. Lewis, 146–149. Santa Barbara, Calif.: ABC-CLIO.

———. 2002. *The Encyclopedia of Cults, Sects, and New Religions.* New York: Prometheus Books.

Lindy, Danielle. 1993. "My Conception of a Raelian Meeting and Some Interviewees." Student paper, Dawson College, author files. December 13.

Martin, William. 1982. "Waiting for the End." *Atlantic Monthly,* June, 31–37.

Mayer, Jean-François. 1985. *Sectes nouvelles, un regard neuf.* Paris: Cerf.

McIntyre, Jamal. 1999. "Angels: Dawson College Research Project." Student paper, Dawson College, author files. March 22.

Melton, J. Gordon. 1985. "Spiritualization and Reaffirmation: What Really Happens When Prophecy Fails." *American Studies* 26:17–29.

———. 1995. "The Contactees: A Survey." In *The God Have Landed,* edited by James R. Lewis, 1–13. Albany: SUNY Press.

Mezzagno, Vince. 1999. "'Why I Believe in Raël': Interview with a Raelian." Student paper, Dawson College, author files. November 26.

Millikan, David. 1994. "The Children of God, the Family of Love, the Family." In *Sex, Slander, and Salvation,* edited by James R. Lewis and J. Gordon Melton, 181–252. Stanford, Calif.: Center for Academic Publication.

Montgomery, Ruth. 1985. *Aliens among Us.* New York: Putnam.

Naymark, Pamela. 1998. "Raël's Birthday: A Field Report." Student paper, Dawson College, author files. October.

Nguyen, Thi Phuong Thao, and Tosca Rulli. 1990. "Interview with Raelian Woman Guide." Student paper, Dawson College, author files. May 8.

Noble, David F. 2001. *The Religion of Technology: The Divinity of Man and the Spirit of Invention.* New York: Penguin Books.

Noël, Jasmine. 2000. "Clonaid Press Conference: A Field Report." Student paper, Dawson College, author files. September 21.

Nordhoff, Charles. 1965. *The Communistic Societies of the United States.* New York: Schoken.

Palmer, Susan J. 1992. "Woman as Playmate in the Raelian Movement: Power and Pantagamy in a New Religion." *Syzygy: Journal of Alternative Religion and Culture* 1, 3:227–245.

———. 1994. *Moon Sisters, Krishna Mothers, Rajneesh Lovers: Women's Roles in New Religions.* Syracuse, N.Y.: Syracuse University Press.

———. 1995a. "The Raelian Movement International." In *New Religions in the New Europe,* edited by Robert Towler, 194–210. Aarhus (Den.): Aauhus University Press.

———. 1995b. "Women in the Raelian Movement: New Religious Experiments in Gender and Authority." In *The Gods Have Landed,* edited by James R. Lewis, 105–136. Albany: SUNY Press.

———. 1998. "The Raelians Are Coming: The Future of a UFO Religion." In *Religion in a Changing World,* edited by Madeleine Cousineau, 139–146. Westport, Conn.: Praeger.

———. 2001. "The Raël Deal." *Religion in the News* (newsletter of the Leonard E. Greenberg Center for the Study of Religion in Public Life, Trinity College, Hartford, Conn.) 4 (summer), 2.

———. 2003. "UnRaël!" *Religion in the News* (newsletter of the Leonard E. Greenberg Center for the Study of Religion in Public Life, Trinity College, Hartford, Conn.) 6 (spring), 1: 17–18.

Partridge, Christopher, ed. 2003. *UFO Religions.* London: Routledge.

Pascal, Anna. 1992. "Interview with a Raelian Member." Student paper, Dawson College, author files. December.

Piech, Stefan. 1999. "An Interview with a Pink Angel in the Raelian Movement." Student paper, Dawson College, author files. March 22.

Raël (as Claude Vorilhon). 1974. *Le livre qui dit la vérité: "j'ai rencontre un extra-terrestre"* (The book which tells the truth). Clermont Ferrand: L'Edition du Message.

———. 1977a. *Les extra-terrestres m'ont emmené sur leur planète* (Extraterrestrials took me to their planet). Brantome: L'Edition du Message.

———. 1977b. *La geniocratie: Le génie au pouvoir!* (Geniocracy). La Nègrerie, Brantome: L'Edition du Message.

———. 1978. *Space Aliens Took Me to Their Planet: The Book Which Tells the Truth.* Translated by "a group of Raelians." Liechtenstein: Edition du Message.
———. 1979. *Accueillir les extra-terrestres* (Let's welcome the extraterrestrials). Vaduz: Fondation Raelienne.
———. 1980. *La meditation sensuelle* (Sensual meditation). Vaduz: Fondation Raelienne.
———. 1987a. *Let's Welcome Our Fathers from Space: They Created Humanity in Their Laboratories.* Tokyo: AOM Corporation.
———. 1987b. *Sensual Meditation: Awakening the Mind by Awakening the Body.* Translated by "a group of Raelians." Tokyo: AOM Corporation.
———. 1992. *Le racisme religieux financé par le gouvernement socialiste: Halte à la violation des droits de l'homme en France* (Religious racism financed by the socialist government: Stop the violation of human rights in France). Geneva: Fondation Raelienne.
———. 1995. *Vive le Québec libre: Faire du Quebec la Suisse d'Amerique du Nord* (Hurray for a free Quebec: Let's make Quebec the Switzerland of North America). Laval: Editions A.R.
———. 1998a. *The Final Message.* London: Tagman Press.
———. 1998b. "The Order of Raël's Angels." Dictated by the Elohim, December 13, 1997. July.
———. 2001a. *Oui au clonage humain: La vie éternelle grace à la science* (Yes to human cloning: Eternal life thanks to science). Beauceville, France: Quebecor World L'Eclaireur.
———. 2001b. *Yes to Human Cloning: Immortality Thanks to Science.* London: Tagman Press.
———. 2003. *The True Face of God.* Vaduz: Raelian Foundation.
Read, Benjamin. 1999. "Interview with a White Angel." Student paper, Dawson College, author files. March 21.
Reuther, Rosemary Radford. 1983. *Sexism and God-Talk.* Boston: Beacon Press.
Roberts, Allister T. 2001. "Field Report on Raelian Meeting at Salle Gesu." Student paper, Dawson College, author files. April.
Robillard, Lissa. 1999. "Interview with an Angel." Student paper, Dawson College, author files. March 24.
Rochette, Jean. 1983. *Qui croire? Essai sur les nouvelles religions.* Saint-Georges-de-Beauce, B.C., Can.: Editions Jean Rochette.
Rothstein, Mikhail. 2000. "The New Age." In *UFOs and Popular Culture: An Encyclopedia of Contemporary Myth,* edited by James R. Lewis. Santa Barbara, Calif.: ABC-CLIO.
———. 2001. "The Myth of the UFO in Global Perspective: A Cognitive Approach." In *New Religions and Globalization,* edited by Mikhail Rothstein, 133–149. Renner Studies on New Religions, vol. 5. Aarhus (Den.): Aarhus University Press.
———. 2003. "UFO Belief as Syncretistic Component." In *UFO Religions,* edited by Christopher Partridge, 256–273. London: Routledge.
Roulston, Lynn. 1994. "Interview with a Raelian Guide." Student paper, Dawson College, author files. November 20.
Saliba, John. 1995a. "Religious Dimensions of the UFO Phenomenon." In *The Gods Have Landed,* edited by James R. Lewis, 15–64. Albany: SUNY Press.

———. 1995b. "UFO Contactee Phenomena from a Sociopsychological Perspective: A Review." In *The Gods Have Landed,* edited by James R. Lewis, 207–250. Albany: SUNY Press.

Schutz, Michael. 1980. "Sociological Aspects of UFOs." In *Encyclopedia of UFOs,* edited by Ronald Story, 340–341. New York: New English Library.

Sendy, Jean. 1968. *La lune: Clé de la Bible.* Paris: Editions René Julliard.

———. 1972. *Those Gods Who Made Heaven and Earth: The Novel of the Bible.* New York: Berkeley.

Sentes, Bryan, and Susan Palmer. 2000. "Presumed Immanent: The Raelians, UFO Religions, and the Postmodern Condition." *Nova Religio: The Journal of Alternative and Emergent Religions* 4, 1 (October): 36–105.

Sitchin, Zecharia. 1976. *The Twelfth Planet.* New York: Avon Books.

Stark, Rodney. 1987. "How New Religions Succeed: A Theoretical Model." In *The Future of New Religious Movements,* edited by David G. Bromley and Philip E. Hammond, 11–29. Macon, Ga.: Mercer University Press.

———. 1996. "Why Religious Movements Succeed or Fail: A Revised General Model." *Journal of Contemporary Religion* 11, 2 (May): 133–146.

Stark, Rodney, and William Sims Bainbridge. 1983. "Concepts for a Theory of Religious Movements." In *Alternatives to American Mainline Churches,* edited by Joseph Fichter, 3–25. New York: Rose of Sharon Press.

Sunnenback, Chloe. 1995. "Interview with a Fringe Raelian." Student paper, Dawson College, author files. October 17.

Szabo, Andrea. 2003. "The Raelians." Student paper, Dawson College, author files. April 29.

Tannenbaum, Lesley. 2003. "The Raelian Movement: A Field Report." Student paper, Dawson College, author files. April.

Terrusse, Marcel, and Michèle Richard. 1994. *20 ans: La génération des pionniers* (Twenty years: The generation of pioneers). Nimes Cedex, France: Mouvement Raelien.

Tumminia, Diana. 1998. "How Prophecy Never Fails: Interpretive Reason in a Flying Saucer Group." *Sociology of Religion* 59: 57–70.

Tumminia, Diana, and R. George Kirkpatrick. 1995. "Unarius: Emergent Aspects of an American Flying Saucer Group." In *The Gods Have Landed,* edited by James R. Lewis, 85–104. Albany: SUNY Press.

Unger, Robert. 1990. "Interview with a Raelian Guide." Student paper, Dawson College, author files. April.

Vaillancourt, Thalia. 2000. "Report on Raelian Press Conference: Presentation of the Cloning Mothers." Student paper, Dawson College, author files. September 21.

Vallée, Jacques. 1965. *Anatomy of a Phenomenon: Unidentified Objects in Space—A Scientific Appraisal.* Lincolnwood, Ill.: NTC/Contemporary Publishing.

———. 1969. *Passport to Magonia.* Chicago: Henry Regnery.

———. 1979. *Messengers of Deception: UFO Contacts and Cults.* Berkeley: And/Or Press.

———. 1991. *Revelations: Alien Contact and Human Deception.* New York: Ballantine Books.

Vendramin, Linda. 1988. "Interview with a Raelian Ex-Jesuit Priest." Student paper, Dawson College, author files. December 8.

von Däniken, Erich. 1970. *Chariots of the Gods? Unsolved Mysteries of the Past.* Translated by Michael Heron. New York: Putnam.

Wallis, Roy. 1976. *The Road to Total Freedom: A Sociological Analysis of Scientology.* London: Heinemann.

———. 1984. *The Elementary Forms of the New Religious Life.* London: Routledge and Kegan Paul.

Weber, Max. 1947. *The Theory of Social and Economic Organization.* New York: Oxford University Press.

Wessinger, Catherine. 2000. *How the Millennium Comes Violently: From Jonestown to Heaven's Gate.* New York: Seven Bridges Press.

Worsley, Peter. 1968. *The Trumpet Shall Sound: A Study of "Cargo" Cults in Melanesia.* 2nd edition. London: MacGibbon and Kee.

York, Dr. Malachi Z. 1995. *Are There UFOs in Our Midst?* Eatonton, Ga.: Holy Tabernacle Ministries.

Index

About the Author

SUSAN J. PALMER is a researcher and ethnographer in the field of new religious movements. She is a tenured teacher in religious studies at Dawson College and adjunct professor and lecturer at Concordia University in Montreal, Quebec, and has authored or edited eight books, notably, *Moon Sisters, Krishna Mothers, Rajneesh Mothers; Children in New Religions* (with Charlotte Hardman); *Millennium Messiahs and Mayhem* (with Tom Robbins); and *The Rajneesh Papers* (with Arvind Sharma). Palmer has written many articles for scholarly journals, as well as for the mass media: for *Esquire* magazine (UK), *The Times Higher Educational Supplement, Religion in the News,* and the *Montreal Gazette.* She has worked in documentary films on alternative religions, such as *Au Nom des tous les dieux* and *The Love Prophet.*